251

Women and the First World War

D0308586

SEMINAR STUDIES IN HISTORY

Women and the First World War

SUSAN R. GRAYZEL

An imprint of Pearson Education

London · New York · Toronto · Sydney · Tokyo · Singapore · Hong Kong · Cape Town
New Delhi · Madrid · Paris · Amsterdam · Munich · Milan · Stockholm

PEARSON EDUCATION LIMITED

Head Office:
Edinburgh Gate
Harlow
Essex CM20 2JE
Tel: +44 (0)1279 623623
Fax +44 (0)1279 431059

London Office:
128 Long Acre
London WC2E 9AN
Tel: +44 (0)20 7447 2000
Fax: +44 (0)20 7240 5771
Website: www.history-minds.com

The Sheffield College
Peaks - Learning Resource Centre
(0114) 260 2462

Acc. WITHDRAWN
5 0 0 1 0 0 7 2 9 3

Class
940.3 GRA

Loan Category
ORT

First published in Great Britain in 2002

© Pearson Education Limited 2002

The right of Susan R. Grayzel to be identified as author
of this work has been asserted by her in accordance
with the Copyright, Designs and Patents Act 1988.

ISBN 0 582 41876 3

British Library Cataloguing in Publication Data
A CIP catalogue record for this book can be obtained from the British Library

Library of Congress Cataloging in Publication Data
A CIP catalog record for this book can be obtained from the Library of Congress

All rights reserved; no part of this publication may be reproduced, stored
in a retrieval system, or transmitted in any form or by any means, electronic,
mechanical, photocopying, recording, or otherwise without either the prior
written permission of the Publishers or a licence permitting restricted copying
in the United Kingdom issued by the Copyright Licensing Agency Ltd.,
90 Tottenham Court Road, London, W1P 0LP. This book may not be lent,
resold, hired out or otherwise disposed of by way of trade in any form
of binding or cover other than that in which it is published, without the
prior consent of the Publishers.

10 9 8 7 6 5 4 3 2 1

Typeset by 7 in 10/12 Sabon Roman
Produced by Pearson Education Asia Pte Ltd.
Printed in Malaysia, LSP

The Publishers' policy is to use paper manufactured from sustainable forests.

This book is for my daughters: Sarah, Rebecca and Miranda.
May they help to promote peace and justice in
our war-torn world.

CONTENTS

INTRODUCTION TO THE SERIES

Such is the pace of historical enquiry in the modern world that there is an ever-widening gap between the specialist article or monograph, incorporating the results of current research, and general surveys, which inevitably become out of date. *Seminar Studies in History* is designed to bridge this gap. The series was founded by Patrick Richardson in 1966 and his aim was to cover major themes in British, European and World history. Between 1980 and 1996 Roger Lockyer continued his work, before handing the editorship over to Clive Emsley and Gordon Martel. Clive Emsley is Professor of History at the Open University, while Gordon Martel is Professor of International History at the University of Northern British Columbia, Canada, and Senior Research Fellow at De Montfort University.

All the books are written by experts in their field who are not only familiar with the latest research but have often contributed to it. They are frequently revised, in order to take account of new information and interpretations. They provide a selection of documents to illustrate major themes and provoke discussion, and also a guide to further reading. The aim of *Seminar Studies in History* is to clarify complex issues without over-simplifying them, and to stimulate readers into deepening their knowledge and understanding of major themes and topics.

AUTHOR'S ACKNOWLEDGEMENTS

The research and writing of this book was aided by a Faculty Small Research Grant and a Liberal Arts Summer Research Grant from the University of Mississippi. As my book is a work of synthesis as well as analysis, I am indebted to many scholars, too numerous to acknowledge here, whose work may be found in the bibliography. Among those whose direct assistance has been most valuable, I would like to thank Gordon Martel; the staff of the Interlibrary Loan Office of the J.D. Williams Library, University of Mississippi; staff at the Imperial War Museum, London; Fara Shook, Debbie Townsend, and Rachael Pailet for the extraordinary care they have given my children; Deborah Cohen for her invaluable comments; and Joe Ward for making its writing and my life better.

PUBLISHER'S ACKNOWLEDGEMENTS

We are grateful to the following for permission to reproduce copyright material:

The literary executors of Vera Brittain for her poem 'The Superfluous Woman' published in *Verses of a VAD*; Coopers Square Press for extracts from *With the Armies of the Tsar: A Nurse at the Russian Front in War and Revolution 1914–1918* by Florence Farmborough; HMSO for the table on 'Wartime birth rates for Great Britain' published in the *Annual Report of the Registrar General for England and Wales, for Scotland, for Ireland and for Northern Ireland* © Crown Copyright; and Presses Universitaires de France for the table on wartime birth rates in France published in *La Population de la France Pendant la Guerre* by Michel Huber © Presses Universitaires de France.

In some cases we have been unable to trace the owners of copyright material and we would appreciate any information that would enable us to do so.

CHRONOLOGY

This chronology of the First World War highlights events of special significance to women.

1914

28 June	Assassination of Archduke Ferdinand and his wife, Sophia, in Sarajevo by Serb nationalist Gavrilo Princip.
5 July	5,000 French women demonstrate in Paris for women's suffrage.
28 July	Austria-Hungary declares war on Serbia.
31 July	French Socialist leader Jean Jaurès is assassinated.
1 August	Germany declares war on Russia.
3 August	Germany declares war on France, and sends troops through Belgium. Italy declares its neutrality.
4 August	Britain declares war on Germany. Millicent Fawcett, leader of the NUWSS, and others address a women's peace meeting in London.
5 August	Clara Zetkin, a German socialist feminist, calls for proletarian women to resist war.
6 August	Austria-Hungary declares war on Russia. Serbia declares war on Germany.
8 August	Britain passes the Defence of the Realm Act (DORA), which is revised throughout the war, and initiates censorship.
10 August	Britain and France declare war on Austria-Hungary. Suffragettes imprisoned in Britain are offered an amnesty.
11 August	Austria-Hungary invades Serbia.
30 August	First bombing of Paris by German aeroplanes.
5–12 September	First Battle of the Marne ends the German advance and starts trench warfare.
Late September	Women's Volunteer Reserve and Women's Defence Relief Corps are set up in Britain.
30 October	International Women for Peace mass meeting in New York.
1 November	Russia declares war on the Ottoman Empire.
5 November	Other Allies declare war on the Ottoman Empire.
21 December	German air raid on Dover, Britain.

1915

7 January	First official reports of German violations of human rights in occupied France are published. They launch a debate over 'the children of rape' in France (which lasts until May).
10 January	Founding of the American Women's Peace Party.
19 January	First German Zeppelin raid on Britain.
1 February	Endell Street Military Hospital (first to be staffed entirely by women) opens in London.
2 February	British naval blockade of Germany begins.
4 February	Germany announces its own blockade of Britain and initiates submarine warfare to ensure this.
18 February	Imprisonment of Rosa Luxemburg for anti-war actions.
Late February	Protests in London and Berlin over the rising cost of living and food shortages respectively.
17 March	War Service Register for British women opens, after the government and unions reach an agreement to employ women in munitions factories.
25–27 March	Clara Zetkin organises an anti-war conference of socialist women in Berne, Switzerland.
22 April	Gas is used for the first time by Germany on the Western Front.
24 April	Genocidal attacks on the Ottoman Empire's Armenian population begin.
25 April	British and Australian forces land at Gallipoli.
28 April–1 May	The Women's International Peace Conference meets at The Hague, with no French women attending – the largest French women's organisations instead issue their own address to women of neutral nations. The Hague Conference does create an International Women's Committee for a Permanent Peace which later becomes the Women's International League for Peace and Freedom.
May	Bryce Report, an investigation into alleged German atrocities in Belgium, is issued in Great Britain.
7 May	*Lusitania*, a British ocean liner, is sunk by German submarines.
19 May	British Coalition government is formed.
23 May	Italy declares war on Austria-Hungary.
Late May	More demonstrations by women in Berlin and Trieste.
10 June	French minimum wage law now applies to women in the clothing trade working at home.
17 July	Women's 'Right to Serve' march takes place in London.
29 July	Clara Zetkin is arrested for treason for distributing a manifesto emerging from the Berne Conference.
4–6 August	More Zeppelin raids on British towns.

August	Military Service Law in Germany requires all men and women between the ages of 15 and 25 to register for war service.
August	National Register for men and women between the ages of 16 and 65 is set up in Great Britain.
5–8 September	Socialist Conference in Zimmerwald is divided between support for peace and advocacy of class warfare.
2 October	Louise Saumoneau, French socialist feminist, is arrested.
12 October	Germany executes British nurse Edith Cavell for aiding the escape of Allied soldiers from Belgium.
14 October	Bulgaria enters the war.
23 October	More demonstrations by German women protesting against high prices.

1916

27 January	Conscription is introduced in Britain (except for Ireland) with the First Military Service Bill.
29–31 January	German Zeppelins raid Paris and parts of England.
21 February	Battle of Verdun begins (very heavy French and German casualties, lasts until December).
March	Women's National Land Service Corps is created in Britain.
22 April	Deportations of young women in occupied France for forced labour begins.
24 April–1 May	Easter Rising in Ireland.
29 June	First strike by French women munitions workers.
1 July	Start of the Battle of the Somme (produces very high casualties and lasts until November).
27 August	Romania enters the war on the Allied side.
15 September	Introduction of tank warfare by Britain on the Western Front.
3 October	Deportations of Belgians for forced labour begin.
2 November	Women's anti-war demonstration in Dresden.
27 November	Greece declares war on Germany.
1 December	Women's Army Auxiliary Corps is created in Britain.
5 December	Auxiliary Service Law is enacted in Germany and compels war work of all German men aged between 17 and 60.
7 December	British Prime Minister Asquith is replaced by Lloyd George.

1917

8 January	Strikes by women workers in Paris and Leeds.
10 January	US Women's Suffrage advocates picket the White House.

23 January	Coal rationing begins in France; there are demonstrations in Paris over coal shortages.
31 January	Germany declares no restrictions on its submarine warfare.
February	Demonstrations continue in Germany over the cost of, and access to, food. Loi Violette authorises French women to serve as guardians.
4 February	Strikes in Petrograd on the anniversary of 1905 Bloody Sunday.
March	Wave of strikes hits France.
3 March	Women's Army Auxiliary Corps enrolls its first members.
8 March	The 'February' Revolution begins in Russia after women strike and participate in food riots in conjunction with mutinying soldiers.
16 March	Tsar Nicholas II abdicates.
April	More demonstrations against the war and its costs in Germany.
1 April	Women demonstrate in Petrograd for the right to vote.
6 April	The United States of America enters the war.
16 April	Start of French offensive along the Chemin des Dames, and of the resulting mutinies.
12 May	Start of more strikes in France, especially of women workers; also mutinies in the French army continue until June.
21 May	Maria Botchkareva launches the first Russian Women's Battalion of Death.
13 June	Daylight air raids in London do extensive damage.
25 June	First American Expeditionary Forces reach France.
31 June	Start of the Battle of Passchendaele.
August	Riots by women in Turin, Italy.
2 August	Russian Provisional Government passes universal adult suffrage.
14 September	Canada passes legislation enfranchising women who are close relatives of men serving in the military.
20 September	Canadian women performing war service are enfranchised.
15 October	Mata Hari, alleged German spy, is executed in France.
24 October	Battle of Caporetto.
7 November	Second phase of the Russian Revolution leads to the Bolshevik takeover of government with the 'October Revolution'.
16 November	Clemenceau assumes the position of Prime Minister of France.
18 November	Arrest of Hélène Brion for treason.
29 November	Women's Royal Naval Service is created in Britain.
15 December	Armistice between Russia and Germany takes Russia out of the war.

1918

January	Strikes by German workers protesting about food shortages halt the munitions industry; similar strikes occur this month in Vienna and Budapest.
6 February	Representation of the People Act passes through the British Parliament, enfranchising most women over the age of 30.
25 February	In Britain, rationing of meat and fats begins.
3 March	Treaty of Brest-Litovsk recognises independent states and cedes Russian imperial territory to Germany.
21 March	German offensive on the Somme begins.
23 March	Long-range German cannons bombard Paris.
29 March	Trial of Hélène Brion concludes with a guilty verdict of 'treason' and a suspended sentence.
1 April	Women's Royal Air Force is created in Britain.
2 April	First US troops engage in battle on the Western Front.
9 April	Britain's Women's Army Auxiliary Corps is renamed Queen Mary's Army Auxiliary Corps.
29 April	American women arrive in France to serve in the US Signal Corps.
May	More strikes in France protesting against the war.
1 May	Bombing of the British hospital at Etaples.
19 May	Bombing of the Canadian hospital at Etaples kills nurses.
29–30 May	Bombing of hospitals at Abbeville and Etaples – WAACs and nurses are among the dead.
27 June	Hospital ship is sunk and life boats are attacked – the dead include 14 Canadian nurses.
15 July	Second Battle of the Marne.
27 July	A Women's Signal Corps is created in Germany.
8 August	Passage of Maternity and Child Welfare Act in Britain.
29 September	Bulgaria signs an armistice with the Allies.
29 October	German naval mutiny begins at Kiel.
30 October	Ottoman Empire signs an armistice with the Allies.
November	French women workers are 'demobilised'.
3 November	Austria-Hungary signs an armistice with the Allies.
8 November	Insurrection in Munich — workers declare a Republic.
9 November	Abdication of Kaiser Wilhelm II; Social Democrats assume control of the government amid strikes and unrest.
11 November	Germany signs an armistice with the Allies.
December	Demobilisation of the British army begins.

1919

15 January	Rosa Luxemburg and Karl Liebknecht are murdered.
18 January	Paris Peace Conference begins.
10 February	Conference of Allied Women convenes for the duration of the Peace Conference.
February–May	Debates over the vote for women begin in France. It will be passed by the lower house but is delayed and then voted down in the Senate in November 1922.
12–20 May	Women's International Peace Congress in Zurich.
28 June	Treaty of Versailles is signed.
12 July	Blockade of Germany is shut down.
28 November	Nancy Astor becomes the first woman Member of Parliament.
23 December	British Sex Disqualification Removal Act allows women to enter trades and professions.

1920

31 July	Enactment of a law to repress abortion and outlaw advertising for contraception in France.
11 November	Unveiling of the Tomb of the Unknown Warrior in London and of the Unknown Soldier in France.

PART ONE BACKDROP

CHAPTER ONE

INTRODUCTION

On Saturday 1 August 1914, a young middle-class Englishwoman named Vera Brittain started her diary entry by recording first that 'the last hope of peace is about to be abandoned', and then that she 'went up to the tennis club' (Brittain, 1981: 83). When the First World War began a few days later, her journal alternated between descriptions of a world caught up in the excitement and confusion of international events and their effects on friends, acquaintances and family. Although Brittain's later fame as both writer and activist make her an exceptional figure, her reaction to the war's arrival was fairly typical of many European women. Within a week of its outbreak, she found herself 'knitting' as 'the only work it seems possible as yet for women to do' (Brittain, 1981: 89). By the time the fighting officially came to a halt on 11 November 1918, there was almost no work that women in the belligerent nations had not done to aid the war effort.

This book offers an introduction to the experiences and contributions of women during what may be accurately labelled the first modern, total war, one requiring the mobilisation of both civilians and combatants. Particularly in Europe, the main theatre of the conflict, this war demanded the active participation of both men and women. It even gave rise to the expression 'home front' to characterise the presumably new contributions that those at 'home' made to the war effort. Yet, as the use of this new term might suggest, those residing at home, primarily women, were defined as having a distinct relationship to the war and to their war-torn nations.

This book will explore the many ways in which women experienced the war in a variety of nations and contexts, including Europe and its colonies, the United States and other participants such as Canada, Australia and New Zealand. It will attempt to show the global dimensions of the war by looking at such things as its effect on women in places as far removed as Japan or India, or on the female family members of colonial soldiers mobilised from Africa. While showing the vast reach of the war's impact, it will focus on Europe as the central site of the conflict, in part because of the enormous amount of information available to convey and analyse. One consequence is that there will inevitably be gaps. Indeed, several volumes could cover the experience of women in Britain alone. As a result, this book seeks to highlight the points of commonality in the experience of women across national borders and, in particular, the heated public debates about women's social, cultural and political roles that the war inspired in participant nations. In addition to showing how specific wartime developments shaped women's status and actions, it will also cover some issues that dominated the immediate postwar years – the question of women's waged work, the origins of the welfare state, and the granting of women's suffrage – in order to examine some of the war's more long-term effects.

In addition, this work will touch on several significant events associated with the war, events which it would be impossible to imagine without the impetus of the war but which have much more deep-seated roots. These include the Ottoman Empire's genocidal attack on its Armenian population in 1915, the Easter Rising of 1916 in Ireland, and the Russian Revolution of 1917. Once again, each of these examples merits a study of its own and each had long-lasting consequences that are not entirely the direct legacies of the First World War. However, they are important in the context of looking at the war as they shaped the overall experiences and perceptions of those living in each of these belligerent nations, including women.

Recently, much attention has been paid to women's writing on and of the war, with several new anthologies published to highlight these. Rather than have a separate section on women's cultural productions or the representation of women in war literature generally, this book will integrate wartime cultural productions into discussions of specific aspects of the war and how they affected women. The bibliography will also suggest further reading in women's war literature, whether written in or translated into English. Undeniably, the art, literature and other cultural artifacts produced by women during the war helped to determine the effects of the war upon women and of women upon the war, and readers are wholeheartedly encouraged to explore these fascinating works.

One obvious question emerging from a study such as this is why study women separately? Why not just consider them as part of the overall history of the war? Why indeed. Some noted historians of war, such as John Keegan, have insisted that 'warfare is ... the one human activity from which women, with the most insignificant exceptions, have always and everywhere stood apart' (Keegan, 1994: 75). This suggests that the study of war easily excludes women since any participation by them is 'insignificant'. I hope that the following book will demonstrate convincingly that this is not so.

We must study women and war together. First, because in order to comprehend war's political, social and cultural effects, we must understand the experience of the entire population of the nations involved. One could argue that wars are decided on battlefields, but in the case of total war on the massive scale of the First World War, the battles are not enough. For instance, an essential part of Allied war strategy was the blockade of Germany. Historian Niall Ferguson has argued that this economic blockade did not matter since the resulting 'maldistribution of income and scarce food' in Germany only affected groups that 'were relatively unimportant' such as 'women' (Ferguson, 1999: 455). Recently, however, historian Belinda Davis, by examining the conditions of women and men in First World War Berlin in great detail, has revealed the significance of such changes, because they radicalised women and directly contributed to the revolutions that tore Germany apart in 1918 (Davis, 2000). Putting the experiences of the so-called home front and of women into the history of the First World War illuminates what made the various efforts succeed or fail.

Nor were battle zones devoid of women, as invading armies inevitably encountered civilians and as women themselves, albeit in tiny numbers, did serve as soldiers. Furthermore, with the advent of new technology, homes literally became battle zones under aerial bombardment which made the distinction between home front and war front obsolete. It is also of significance to those trying to understand the transformation of society and culture in the twentieth century to look at the war and women. For the war provided women with a range of new opportunities, however short-lived, and the effects of these are well worth exploring. In the long, gradual march towards recognising the equality of men and women, the First World War looms as a historical conundrum. On the one hand, women in many participant nations (the United States, Germany and Great Britain, for instance) gained basic voting rights in its immediate aftermath that they had never possessed before. On the other hand, their overall economic and social status showed few, if any, notable transformations. Such a puzzle merits our concerted and continued attention.

Many of the early studies of women and the First World War – and these date back to the war years themselves – fell into a pattern of listing and praising the variety of war work that women performed. Some also noted sadly that the war had caused women to lose some of the things deemed to be most important to them, in addition to their actual loved ones; their war work might have made them reject motherhood and domesticity. From early on, the war has been seen as either being 'good' or 'bad' for women. What follows will argue that it is far more complex than this. Not only do invidual experiences of women vary so widely as to render such generalisations misleading, but also the war could and did produce multiple and contradictory effects: simultaneously granting suffrage and depriving women of loved ones or offering access to professions without access to equal wages.

While several new general histories of the war now pay some attention to women's roles, they often fail, for lack of space, to demonstrate the complexity and diversity of women's experiences and their interaction with those of men. In contrast, this book will show the significance that the war had for women during this time period in a number of contexts, including the ways in which differences among women based on class, race, ethnicity and national origin shaped individual experiences. The careful reader will also discern how debates conducted during the war about such things as women in combat, women's relationships to nationalism and pacifism, and women's responsibilities at home and in public, political life still resonate in contemporary society.

PART TWO   EXPERIENCES OF WAR

CHAPTER TWO

THE WAR BEGINS: PROPAGANDA, RECRUITMENT AND STATE SUPPORT OF FAMILIES

Vera Brittain, like other young women of her class and age, may have felt initially that little could be done to aid the war effort, and that there was little that the nation needed women to do. However, governments as well as other organisations quickly seized upon certain images of women to help translate the complicated political and diplomatic crises that had led to the outbreak of war into much simpler terms. The defence of women and children, of family and honour, became one important way to define the reasons for the war on the Allied side. Such concepts were translated visually through posters and eventually cinema, and also became a staple element of wartime media.

One consequence of this emphasis was that governments wanted to be seen as supporting the women and children of their own nations. Thus, many military leaders believed that offering state support to the dependents of military men would strengthen troop morale and help ensure success. It would do no good, supporters of such familial aid reasoned, to send men to fight a war in defence of a mythical 'home land' and 'home life' if the well-being of those in their individual homes were threatened. Government agencies, often in conjunction with private charities, therefore instituted measures such as 'separation allowances' or pensions in an attempt to ensure that servicemen's families would not suffer as a result of the men going to war. Most importantly, funds were meant to enable them to afford food and shelter.

In August 1914, photographs across Europe depicted cheering crowds of men, women and children sending off the troops. Some accounts recall singing and some the tears shed by women who still attempted to smile, but most emphasise confidence, resolution and seemingly unquestioned support for the war effort (Sweeney, 2001). That this support had to be manu-factured, in some cases, and sustained throughout the war is evident in the efforts to mobilise and remobilise popular support as well as man and woman power (Horne, 1997). Wartime can obscure social differences as states and their populations rally to defend the nation, yet the messages sent to women in the early months of the war reflect a presumption of their special role in sustaining the war. As Britain's *Evening Standard* proclaimed on 26 August 1914: 'If the men of our country offer in many cases not only themselves, but their future prospects and their careers, it is not too much to expect that the women who have bid God-speed to those they love with a cheery word and a smile should take the fortunes of war with an equally serene and calm confidence'.

Women were told they had a duty to be virtuous as well as cheerful. *The Vigilance Record*, the newspaper of the British National Vigilance Association, an organisation devoted to promoting social purity, reminded young female readers in November 1914 that the man 'fighting for us women and our homes' needed to take away as his 'last remembrance of the women and girls of England' all that was 'pure and gentle and straight and true' (Grayzel, 1999: 129). On 25 August 1914, Julie Siegfried and Ghenia Avril de Sainte Croix, two leaders of the influential Conseil National des Femmes Françaises (National Council of French Women), wrote to their members to implore them to do 'their duty and more than their duty' in the midst of the nation's trauma. 'We will go to work like our soldiers to the fire, without reproach and without fear', they continued, 'we will be proud to be women of our time, those who have finally become the true companions of man' (Letter, 25 August 1914, DOS 396 CON Bibliothèque Marguerite Durand, Paris). In August 1914, the German Patriotic Women's Associations launched this appeal: 'The Fatherland expects of Germany's girls and women the same devotion, the same readiness to sacrifice as of its sons' (Schulte, 1997: 126).

Thus, from the very start, wartime media in a variety of nations – whether produced by men or women – called upon women specifically. They urged them to service and sacrifice, to 'appropriate' action and emphasised their importance for the war's success or failure. This could be manifest in a variety of actions, starting with emotional support and ranging from recruiting men to working to aiding the wounded and the bereaved. That women were seen as vital to the war can be found in one of the First World War's innovations: propaganda produced by governments specifically to shape public opinion.

FEMININE IMAGES IN PROPAGANDA

Britain, which began the war with a volunteer army and thus had rapidly to recruit men, provides a particularly potent example of the process of using images of women and home in order to motivate men. The message that the essence of the war was the defence of home – and thus principally of women and children – from an amoral and brutal enemy almost immediately found its way into the posters of the Parliamentary Recruiting

Plate 1 British recruiting poster, Imperial War Museum, London, Q 80367
PR 680–0554

Committee, which used images of women to encourage men to enlist. In several well-known posters, women of all ages appeal to their men: a young mother proclaims that 'Women of Britain say Go!', a young girl sitting on her father's lap asks 'What did you do in the Great War Daddy?', and an elderly grandmother points the way to a younger man, 'Go! It's Your Duty!'. In the more tense atmosphere of Ireland, the government issued a poster entitled 'For the Glory of Ireland', where a woman holds a rifle and gestures to burning Belgium behind her, while asking 'Will you go or must I?' (Imperial War Museum [hereafter IWM]) (see plate 1, page 11).

The enemy's direct attacks on civilians, including women and children, also became powerful emblems. After German cruisers shelled Scarborough, killing and injuring civilians including women and children, a recruiting poster demanded if the 'Men of Britain' would 'stand' that '78 Women & Children were killed and 228 Women & Children were wounded by German Raiders' (IWM). It couched its demands in visual as well as verbal terms by dramatically picturing a small girl holding a baby in front of a destroyed home.

Governments and individual artists also made use of allegorical and archetypal images of women as the nation, as Britannia (Britain) or Marianne (France) urged their 'sons' to do battle. Such images often showed defiant and powerful women, as in the image of Marianne, the incarnation of Republican France, with one breast bared, holding both a sword and a tattered flag in a poster for the French war loan of 1917. An equally powerful Columbia, with an American eagle and flag as a breastplate, holds up the sword of justice in a 1917 United States' Naval recruiting poster. An Italian poster for its 1917 war loan shows a feminine Italy literally in the act of stabbing an attacking barbaric Goth (Paret et al., 1992: 31, 54, 73).

In addition to representing the nation, feminised allegories of Liberty, Victory and Justice all aimed to connect these attributes with the rightness of the nation's cause. As the war continued, such images became prevalent on posters for war loans as well as those designed simply to promote the war. In Russia, for example, allegories could link not only ideal qualities but nations together as in an image of 'Accord' showing Russia as 'Faith', standing between 'Love' (a French woman) and 'Hope' (an English one), while all are fighting the barbarism of Germany, which is represented by hovering zeppelins and explosions in the background (Jahn, 1995: 24–6). Other visual examples stress the depravity of the enemy by depicting it as a corrupt or sinful woman; such is the fate of Germany in several Russian wartime posters (Petrone, 1998: 106).

Eventually women themselves became the targets of such messages as they were urged to 'do their bit' by saving food, supporting their menfolk, and participating in specific activities ranging from making munitions to joining some of the new women's armed forces' auxiliaries that were created in Britain. In these posters, women were urged to do everything from conserving foodstuffs ('the kitchen is the key to victory') to helping 'pick fruit for the fighting forces' (IWM) (see plate 2, page 14). Similar themes can be found in American war posters that stress conservation of the food supply, that 'food is ammunition – don't waste it', and the need for food production in victory gardens ('the seeds of victory insure the fruits of peace') (Paret et al., 1992: 86–7).

The images of women that also appeared on such posters reinforce the sense that the home, their presumed domain, was also essential to the war effort. A halo virtually surrounds the woman in a poster Howard Chandler Christy designed for the United States Food Administration in 1918 that told its viewers: 'in her wheatless kitchen she is doing her part to help win the war' (Rawls, 1988: 118). Even more explicitly, another American poster showed the female 'house manager' with her basket of food proudly marching in formation with armed troops (Rawls, 1988: 150).

As women's work was deemed more instrumental to victory, the range of their work expanded, and so government posters tried to recruit them to a variety of tasks. In Britain, women could join the military's auxiliary corps and be 'the woman behind the man behind the gun' (IWM). Other appeals reminded both women and men of the linkage between wartime production and military success. They were told that women munitions workers were 'doing their bit' as the soldier marching away was counter-balanced by a woman donning a munitions worker's garb or, as another poster depicting a female munitions worker put it, 'on her their lives depend' (IWM; Woollacott, 1993). Posters informed them that aeroplanes were needed and asked 'women come and HELP!'. Most explicitly, one poster, addressed to the 'women of Britain', stated clearly that 'every woman employed releases a man for the firing line' (IWM).

Similar messages can be found in posters recruiting women for munitions work in both Russia and Germany. A 1916 Russian image of a woman standing calmly in a factory urged 'everything for the war', while a much more grim image of a German woman performing industrial work stood above the words 'German women, work for victory' in a 1918 poster (Paret et al., 1992: 63). The active recruitment of German women was something that intensified in the latter years of the war, as we will see in Chapter 3 below. Other visual propaganda in Russia revealed women working even more directly in support of the military effort, as in a poster showing peasant women capturing the crew of a downed Austrian plane with nothing more than their farming tools (Petrone, 1998: 106).

Propaganda also reminded women that work on the land was as essential as any other form of national support. This was especially true in Britain, given the difficulty of importing foodstuffs during the war. A British poster for the Women's Land Service Corps showed a departing soldier

Plate 2   British propaganda for those at home, Imperial War Museum, London, PC 711 Cat. No. Imperial War Museum, London PST/4907

holding out his hand to be grasped by a woman, beside whom stands a wheel barrow and a small boy, with the message 'I leave the land to YOU'. A robust woman patting a small calf stands in the foreground of another poster while an equally cheerful woman in the background takes to the fields as viewers were told that 'for food production, forage & timber the help of British Women is urgent and indispensable' (IWM). Once America entered the war, its role as a provider of resources, particularly food, to war-torn Europe became a feature of appeals to women. One American poster vividly demonstrated this by placing a woman in overalls in the foreground, while a soldier with bayonet drawn stands shadowed behind her, asking the viewer to 'get behind the Girl he left behind him: Join the land army' (Rawls, 1988: 122).

Later in the war, civilians, especially women, began to appear on posters advertising war loans. In 1917, a French poster by Georges Redon showed a mother putting her child to bed beneath the picture of her soldier husband. The words beneath asked readers to subscribe to the war loan so that 'your children will no longer know the horrors of war' (Gervereau and Prochasson, 1987: 20). French posters for loans throughout the war used the iconic image of mother and child or children sending their soldier father on his way to remind viewers that their support at home would hasten the war's end and father's return. This can be seen in images that depict rural France in 1915 and Algeria in 1917. In the poster directed at Algerians, an Algerian mother and child in traditional costume bid the soldier father farewell in a pose reminiscent of those employed in posters in mainland France. This suggests their incorporation into the national family, and that regardless of any religious, ethnic or gender differences, all of France was united (Paillard, 1986: 50, 136). Another war loan poster from 1918 combined both the allegorical heroine Marianne and the heroine of the harvest. It showed an evocative rural scene of mother and child in the foreground of a field; the mother holds her tool in one hand and her small child in the other, while above them Marianne, in a faint outline, points the way forward for a group of soldiers (Grayzel, 1999: 107).

A 1915 Austrian war loan poster makes the appeal seem to be from, rather than to, women by showing a knight in armour protecting a mother and child (Paret et al., 1992: 73). Other posters appealed to more intimate sacrifices by women. As the blockade caused increasing shortages in Germany, women were asked to contribute their long hair to substitute for hemp or leather in drive belts and insulation. Such sacrifices were part of a wider effort by German women to sustain the nation through charitable endeavours. A poster from 1918 acknowledges the pain of doing this particular act by depicting a pale woman shrouded in the black hair she offers up against the backdrop of a red cross (Paret et al., 1992: 83).

THE 'RAPE OF BELGIUM', THE BRYCE REPORT AND ATROCITY PROPAGANDA

Perhaps the most vivid, and arguably the most effective, sources of propaganda on the Allied side emphasised the extreme brutality of the German army. As a way to justify Britain's participation in the war, the invasion of neutral Belgium soon became known as the 'rape of Belgium' and was quite literally and vividly depicted as such. As the German army's push into France from Belgium produced a stream of refugees, they in turn carried tales of atrocities committed against innocent civilians, most drastically against women and children.

In an effort to substantiate the swirling rumours of mutilated children and violated women, official commissions in both France and Britain mounted investigations into the treatment of civilians by the invading and occupying forces. Presented as a series of eye-witness accounts, both what became known in Britain as the Bryce Report and the French Official Investigation stated unequivocally that the Germans had, among other crimes of war, raped and mutilated women. The French report was issued in January 1915 and the Bryce Report in April of the same year, a moment when the war had revealed itself, especially on the Western Front, as far different from the quick and easy conflict that both sides had predicted in 1914. So the timing of the reports was crucial as they apparently substantiated for the civilian populations of these two Allies that the enemy they were battling against was bloodthirsty, ruthless and devoid of morality. In short, this propaganda completed the transformation of Germans into 'Huns'.

The French reports, publicised and excerpted in major newspapers under such headlines as 'the crimes of the German army' or 'the German atrocities', recounted the experience of civilians during the German invasion (Grayzel, 1999: 256). The presentation of such attacks was straightforward – the deposition of a witness, with the name, age, location, date and brief summation of each abuse provided. Each account was also signed by the complaining witness. In cases of sexual assault, the witness remained anonymous. Among the litany of abuses, women told of rapes by German soldiers. The Bryce Report, a bestseller in Britain when it was issued, similarly detailed brutal sexual attacks on women [*Docs 2 and 3*].

In addition to both the official reports of German abuses and the visual propaganda depicting them, the British Parliamentary Recruiting Office issued a series of pamphlets directed at women that called upon images of German atrocities. Its leaflet No. 23, *Women and the War*, spoke to women who had deliberately held back their men. While acknowledging that '[i]t is natural that mothers and wives and sweethearts' should be reluctant to send their men, they were putting themselves in danger of their 'homes being ruined and laid waste'. Women were urged to 'think of what has happened in Belgium. Towns and villages have been destroyed by fire and sword, women and children outraged and killed, mothers separated from their children, and wives from their husbands, not knowing whether they are dead or alive.' Explicitly asking British women if they wished 'to share the unhappy fate of Belgian women', this propaganda played upon the previously circulated images of German cruelty, reminding them that the saying 'Your country needs You' meant not that the King or Government needed them but that 'British cottage homes, British women and children, peaceful fields and villages' needed men to defend them (*Women and the War*, 1915).

In addition to these emotive appeals using the brutalised, naked bodies of women that appeared in this new form of Allied propaganda, the sinking of the *Lusitania* in May 1915 further suggested that the Germans were violating fundamental assumptions, embraced by all 'civilised' societies, about the need to protect women and children. The attack on the *Lusitania* provided ample fodder for propaganda images aimed at an American audience and designed to persuade them to support the United States' entry into the war. Images of a drowning, helpless mother and child underscored the brutality of the German 'Hun' in a 1915 poster designed by Fred Spear that set only the word 'enlist' in blood-red letters against this backdrop (Rawls, 1988: 68) (see plate 3, page 18). The bestial 'Hun', with simian features, was further seen devouring the world with bloody hands or carrying off a hapless female while a poster's bold letters asked American viewers to help 'destroy this mad brute' or risk a war 'fought to a finish ... on the soil of the United States' (Rawls, 1988: 66).

Another 1915 incident that seemed to set the Germans apart in their brutality towards women was the German army's execution of British nurse Edith Cavell for aiding Allied soldiers in escaping from Belgium. While no one questioned that Cavell's behaviour not only made her far different from an 'ordinary' nurse, but also crossed the line against which women could be considered uninvolved in dangerous, military action, Britain made much of the fact that Germany would execute a 'heroic' and 'virtuous' woman. Visual as well as verbal propaganda underscored her femininity and victimhood to suggest the outrageousness of Germany's action, as a recruiting poster featuring her photo under the heading 'Murdered by the Huns' reveals (Wheelwright, 1992: 122).

The war was thus increasingly constructed as a battle between 'Civilisation' and '*Kultur*' – a Germanic culture that was militaristic, violent, and 'barbaric'. One vivid marker of this was the behaviour and treatment of women – a fact not lost on women's organisations in the Allied nations themselves. Accompanying the visual images and official reports of the appalling behaviour of Germany came novels and stories that translated

Plate 3   American atrocity propaganda, Imperial War Museum, London, PC 704
Cat. No. Imperial War Museum PST/3284

the official language into more 'popular' melodramas. Such atrocity literature provided readers with innocent women victims with whom they could empathise, especially as they illustrated that the rape of women had broader consequences for their families and their nations. Both French and British tales – and the British ones typically found an American audience as well – highlighted the brutality of the German army and the vulnerability of women (Grayzel, 1999).

A novel such as Mary Floran's 1916 *L'Ennemi* [*The Enemy*] stressed the intrinsic, 'racial' difference between Germans and all others by using an atrocity that led to the victim's death as a pivotal event. Floran's main plot involves the courtship of a young Frenchwoman 'Odile' and a German officer, Otto, in prewar 1914, a relationship broken off by the outbreak of war. As a result, Otto, the officer, helps lead the invading army as Odile first flees and, once safe, then turns to nursing. Yet Floran's aim is to reveal the true colours of the enemy, to show that to be 'Prussian' is to be evil incarnate. Floran vividly demonstrates this by having Otto's forces arrive at the home Odile has been forced to abandon. While there, a young woman is taken off as a 'contribution to the war' and raped by soldiers under his command. When this woman's mother comes looking for her daughter, Otto coldly executes them both. He subsequently orders that the entire village, including its church, be burnt to the ground (Floran, 1916: 231–3). His very calmness, in contrast to the young woman's 'terror and madness', implicitly caused by the rape, demonstrated for Floran's readers how much the veneer of civility belied the criminal instincts within this German. They also suggest a greater danger because this evil was initially disguised. At the end of the novel, Otto finds himself wounded and under the care of Odile the nurse. Here, Odile finally learns the truth, as she eavesdrops on the wounded German officers, including Otto, who boast to one another of their crimes. Thus, Floran attacks the possibility for *rapprochement* between France and Germany and the idea of there being pan-European politics and culture, given the treatment of women by the 'subhuman' German enemy.

Nor were German women spared from such evocations. One of the most startling propaganda images of any woman appears in a British poster entitled 'Red Cross or Iron Cross?'. As a wounded British soldier reaches out his hand for a glass of water, the German nurse 'pours it on the ground before his eyes. There is no woman in Britain who would do it. There is no woman in Britain who will forget it' (Paret et al., 1992: 22). As if all of this were not enough to motivate support for the war, governments tried not only to persuade women to support the war effort at home but also to make use of them as active recruiters of men.

BEYOND IMAGES: WHITE FEATHERS AND THE RECRUITING
OF MEN

Propaganda representing battered and abused women in efforts to enlist
male sympathy and action served its purpose in Britain of helping to recruit
a volunteer army. The first phase of the war witnessed a wave of voluntary
recruiting by women in Britain that could well have taken its cues from the
messages of officially-sanctioned propaganda but went further. The
questions posed by recruiting posters included one which asked 'the young
women of London' to consider that if their 'best boy does not think that
you and your country are worth fighting for – do you think he is
WORTHY of you?' (IWM).

In this way, propaganda sought to use women's powers of persuasion
to recruit men, and one of the most controversial and vivid results of this
was the white feather campaign. By handing white feathers – a symbol of
cowardice – to men out of uniform, women tried to shame them into
joining up. This practice met with mixed responses. While posters had
urged women to consider that the man who neglected his country might
easily neglect his best girl, the aim of much of this sort of propaganda was
to promote acts of private persuasion. Mothers were urged to send their
sons and sweethearts to send their beloveds to the army, but these messages
had a dual aim of convincing both men and women to act privately within
their homes and families. The vividly-remembered, if limited, white feather
campaign instead relied on public display and visible shaming, and this
proved to be controversial because some men out of uniform, for instance,
were wounded soldiers. The women who handed out white feathers to such
men were eventually themselves made to feel ashamed of acting so
unwomanly as to challenge men in public. That they both felt empowered
to do so and yet became objects of criticism for acting so aggressively shows
how much and how little had changed regarding women's public activities,
especially those involving men and the military (Gullace, 1997b).

While the givers of white feathers might include mothers, the promise
of an exchange of sexual favours for men's willingness to join up shifted the
focus on to single women. Women then assumed responsibility for securing
the cooperation of their men. This notion permeated other forms of popular
culture, posters and popular fiction, and even public entertainment. Song
lyrics had the desirable woman proclaiming that 'on Saturday I'm willing, if
you'll only take the shilling/To make a man of any one of you' (Wilson,
1986: 706).

If women began to 'recruit' in England itself, it should hardly be
surprising that they also assumed this role in the British Empire and
Commonwealth. Australian women formed organisations such as the
Women's Compulsory Service League that tried to shame unwilling men

into enlisting. This had the added impetus of demonstrating that women in places like Queensland, who had recently received the vote, were 'worthy' of it and could act like 'loyal' citizens (Shute, 1995: 25–7). The importance of the role of women in recruiting men reached a peak in referenda on conscription, where both sides tried to appeal to women voters (Scates and Frances, 1997).

In other parts of the world, recruitment was even more complicated. In India, some nationalists urged support for the war and those advocating Home Rule, such as Annie Besant, argued that it would demonstrate that Indians deserved it (Pati, 1996). In Ireland, efforts to introduce conscription met with fierce resistance. In contrast to the propaganda aimed at ensuring that women would persuade men to fight for them, many Irish women organised themselves against conscription and circulated 'A Solemn Pledge for the Women of Ireland'. Those signing it were asked not only to oppose conscription but also to refuse to 'fill the places of men deprived of their work through refusing enforced military service' (IWM). Resistance to recruitment was widespread in parts of Africa controlled by warring Europeans, and in the case of Malawi, if men fled, their wives were captured and held hostage until they returned. In other parts of colonial Africa, both men and women were recruited for forced labour during the war (Page, 2000: 46, 54).

Living in a neutral nation at the start of the war, women in the United States came surprisingly quickly to play a role in promoting the war. Government propaganda was aimed at them to encourage their support, and they appeared in a series of famous images, particularly as 'Christy' girls, created by artist and illustrator Howard Chandler Christy. These ethereal women, dressed in military uniform but still feminine and enticing as their curls peek out beneath their hats, visually dominated posters, trying to seduce men into the armed services with such phrases as 'Gee!! I wish I were a Man – I'd join the Navy' or offering a new connotation of the phrase 'I want you for the Navy' (Rawls, 1988: 78, 80). Christy also painted allegorical women in posters for war loans, where a woman in a low-cut and often transparent white gown wields the flag or wraps herself in it (Rawls, 1988: 209, 223). Such images both ignored the real-life service of women in the navy and elsewhere and played up the idea of women serving as rewards, particularly sexual rewards, for male valour.

Propaganda could take many forms and actively involved women, either as the means of delivering the message or as the targets of wartime messages themselves. This sometimes backfired, as in the case of the white feather. However, other images became part of the war myths, such as the 'rape of Belgium'. Propaganda's ability to persuade people to support the war effort aimed to sway them emotionally; yet governments also decided that this might not be enough. Thus the First World War also called forth extensive material and financial support for those most likely to be hurt by mass mobilisation: the families and dependents of fighting men.

SEPARATION ALLOWANCES AND WIDOWS' PENSIONS

As the mass mobilisation of fighting troops proceeded in the late summer and autumn of 1914, it deprived many households across Europe of their main source of income, even in working-class families where both spouses worked. Once it became apparent that a quick and easy victory was no-where in sight, the question of how to care for military men's dependents arose as a central concern. How would states ensure that neither military morale nor family members would suffer from domestic hardships? The solution lay in the implementation of 'separation allowances', government monies paid directly to the dependents of soldiers. Every participant nation created some version of such policies, although the amounts of the allowances and means of payment varied. Some countries took into account the number of children who needed to be supported and others considered the mother's wage as well, but recipients all gained control over the money in a way not possible prior to the war (Bock, 1994).

In Germany, financial support for so-called 'warrior families' from local and state authorities started with the outbreak of war. Support was paid out at the local level, some of which would be reimbursed by the national government, and was meant to support those in need. Some estimates suggest that by the end of 1915 about four million families received such aid (Daniel, 1988: 283).

The government presumed, in places like Germany, that not only would such allowances help soldiers feel better about leaving their loved ones, but that the general population would regard this kind of financial support as only fair. Those who fit the definition of dependent included not only wives and children, but also siblings and elderly parents. Yet some ordinary citizens in the capital city of Berlin felt a great deal of hostility towards 'soldiers' wives', a category of women whom they saw as benefiting from the war rather than performing a special service (or sacrifice) in support of its objectives. Such critics believed that only the soldier was truly serving the state and thus deserved support. They therefore viewed separation allowances as unjust and the recipients as spoiled and undeserving. Instead, they called for the state to support and feed all of its inhabitants equally. This feeling became more widespread after 1916 as conditions deteriorated and the need was much greater. One concrete change, despite military officials' fears that this might hurt morale, was the means testing of allowances and the assumption that the state would care for the population overall (Davis, 2000).

French policy on allowances paid to soldiers' dependents provoked rather less heated responses. This may well have been due to the fact that French allowances were means tested. Children under the age of 13 automatically qualified but all adults had to demonstrate both prewar dependency on the absent male's wages and current need. Furthermore, men as well as women could claim allowances under these terms. Thus the criticism of German soldiers' wives for receiving allowances was absent in France, in part because material conditions for most families in Germany became so much worse, especially after 1916.

In contrast to either France or Germany, the existence of a volunteer, rather than a conscript, army in Britain had a significant impact upon the perception and kind of separation allowances granted. The British government viewed separation allowances as an aid in recruiting; with generous allowances, men could join up and feel confident that their families would not suffer any financial or material harm due to their absence. The living standards of soldiers' and sailors' families would be maintained, at first, by a combination of private and public sources that granted payments to all wives, and through them, children, regardless of need. The link between separation allowances and recruitment can be clearly seen in the fact that the government issued propaganda posters designed to publicise the monies available to families through separation allowances (IWM; Pedersen, 1993).

The combination of the need to recruit men and the power of trade unions meant that a consensus emerged in Britain that allowances had to be universal, fairly administered by the state and substantial enough to counter hardship. The rates of separation allowances increased periodically throughout the war, and women continued to receive them even if they found or had other sources of income. However, because this allowance was paid to soldiers' wives (and *de facto* wives) and was granted as a right based on a soldier's labour for the nation, women could and would be disqualified if they failed to fulfil their duty as 'wives'. In other words, the state saw part of its role as being obliged to scrutinise women, and infidelity and misbehaviour became grounds for the denial of this benefit (Pedersen, 1993).

Although women could stop receiving allowances because of certain types of behaviour, the benefit itself had some important, positive effects. Separation allowances came to women through their husbands, but they were paid directly to women. This gave them complete control over how to spend these monies. In response, some charity workers or journalists initially claimed that this meant women would waste their payments on drink and frivolous luxury items while their men suffered on the battlefield. The specific fears about drunken soldiers' wives also reflected concern with their role as mothers, that an alcohol-abusing mother meant neglected children. However, soldiers' wives also had defenders. And for many women and their families, direct control over the allowance meant that they had a more reliable source of income that only served to enhance family well-being (Pedersen, 1993) [*Doc. 4*].

Separation allowances could also be used to meet other societal needs. In Austria, for example, wives of conscripts who did not have young children to care for found their allowances cut off when the government wanted to encourage married women to enter the wartime waged workforce (Sieder, 1988: 119). It is worth noting that similar efforts in Germany failed, in part because ambivalence about women in the waged workforce meant that few financial incentives existed to shift them into factories. If family allowances offered little beyond subsistence support, women's low wages did not offer much more and provided little motivation to get women mobilised into the wartime workforce (Daniel, 1988: 267–8).

Elsewhere in Europe, Italy, once it joined the Allied war effort in 1915, had to determine how to provide for soldiers' dependents in a society where the state had only regulated the private sector prior to the war, rather than providing funds itself. As early as May 1915, the government began to subsidise the families of military men who were in need. Even those not legally connected to servicemen could obtain this benefit. In other words, unmarried women were eligible as long as the fighting man's intentions to provide for them had been made obvious (Lagorio, 1995).

In Canada, the government was forced to concede that the mobilisation of the Canadian Expeditionary Force would create hardship for many families, particularly those of the working class. It thus promised to take care of families and saw that this could be a persuasive recruiting tool. Instead of separation allowances, however, the government created a policy known as 'compulsory assigned pay', which proved to be inadequate to support an entire family, and was therefore supplemented by family allowances paid out by the Canadian Patriotic Fund. Such monies went to unmarried mothers and their children for as long as they could demonstrate that they needed assistance. Since money was allotted for each child, the system ended up better supporting women as mothers rather than solely as dependents. In general, soldiers' wives fared better than soldiers' mothers because wives with children to care for received more funding. The administration of allowances equated men's service to the nation with the nation's obligation then to maintain their familial dependents but put a premium on women's active mothering of future citizens (Christie, 2000).

In addition to separation allowances, Australia also put a War Pension scheme into action, designed to compensate female relatives. Under this plan, soldiers' dependents received funds to preserve the family, and a combination of state and charitable support helped to sustain wives and children, and sometimes soldiers' mothers. Widows without children were presumed able to help themselves. Funding in all of these cases often proved inadequate, and the behaviour of recipients was tightly monitored (Damousi, 1999; Scates and Frances, 1997).

Despite its short-lived involvement in the war, the United States ended up passing among the most progressive legislation in support of soldiers' dependents. In October 1917, the War Risk Insurance Act instituted a system of allotments and allowances to be paid to soldiers' dependents. All enlisted men and non-commissioned officers allotted $15 of their monthly pay (approximately half) to dependents, which was then supplemented by a government allowance of $15 for a wife, $10 for a first child, $7.50 for the next and $5.00 for each one thereafter up to $50.00. Thus with monthly benefits of $30 for wives and up to $65 for wives and children, these payments exceeded the income of many families before the war, particularly in rural areas. What made the allotment and allowance system so progressive, in addition to the size of the payments, was that these monies were need-blind, went directly to women, and were identical for black and white Americans. Married servicemen were required to make allotments for wives and children, but parents, siblings and grandchildren were also eligible for support if their financial dependence on the soldier could be proved. Soldiers and sailors could also file for exemption on the grounds of misbehaviour by their wives; thus in America too, support for servicemen put the government in the position of watchdog over women's behaviour, although women received the benefit of doubt (Hickel, 2001).

The payment of state support to the dependents of soldiers provoked dissent in the United States in a very specific context. By offering a steady source of income to African American southerners, for example, the payments disrupted prewar hierarchical patterns of labour; it got these women out of the fields and out of domestic service. This led to overt attempts to force black women back into these roles, by local laws requiring all adults to work for the war effort (but selectively enforced against African Americans) and by violence. Thus one of the side-effects of this wartime legislation was that wartime support to the African American dependents of soldiers gave them enough 'material security' to enable them to shift employment (Hickel, 2001).

State support for service men's families became incorporated into the wartime policies of almost every belligerent state. These had widespread implications for both the wartime and postwar status of women. Women secured this financial support through demonstrating their connection to men and so the state stepped into the role of the absent male breadwinner. This made the women objects of scrutiny and in some cases surveillance to ensure that government funds (and their private components) were being spent appropriately and not for 'immoral' purposes. Moreover, there was opposition, in places such as Berlin, to the idea that these women and their families were entitled to anything more than the government provided to all its citizens, all of whom were deemed necessary to the war effort.

As the war continued, philanthropic, feminist and sometimes government objectives seem to have coalesced around the idea of supporting women as mothers. This can be seen in things like the creation of Britain's National Baby Week in 1917. Wartime propaganda, in contrast, deployed a variety of images of women from maternal icons to sexual temptations. It too made the significance of women's support and the need to preserve traditional notions of femininity an essential part of the war effort. Making motherhood compatible with other wartime activities raised certain obvious contradictions when almost all belligerent nations also began to mobilise a female labour force. It was within that workforce that some of the most vivid evidence appears of the potential for the war to bring changes in women's lives.

CHAPTER THREE

WOMEN'S WAR WORK: REMUNERATIVE, VOLUNTARY AND FAMILIAL

RECRUITMENT, MOBILISATION AND EXPERIENCE

One of the more visible changes in women's lives during the war came with their entrance into a wide range of occupations, some of which had never before included women. What quickly became clear was that given the mass mobilisation required by total warfare, the entirety of the nation needed to contribute. As male waged labourers were lost to the armed services, women filled their ranks, finding employment on a scale neither seen before the war nor sustained afterwards. Women entered not only wartime factories, but also banks and places of business and government as clerks, typists and secretaries. They were found running trams and buses, delivering milk, and even joining newly-created armed forces' auxiliaries and becoming police officers. With a bit of regional variation, women worked on the land and sustained agriculture. Not all women who were employed during the war were new to the world of waged work and few indeed were new to unwaged work. Thus while the war caused some women to shift jobs, it enabled others to join the paid workforce for the first time. However, this chapter will examine the totality of women's work, from waged labour to family maintenance.

Already within the first year of the war, women's paid employment increased by 400,000 in Britain, and this was before a mass demonstration in July 1915 where women, organised by feminist leaders such as Emmeline Pankhurst of the suffragette Women's Social and Political Union (WSPU), with the encouragement of politicians like David Lloyd George, demanded the 'right to serve' (De Groot, 1996: 69). From the outset, some women were motivated by patriotism and others by necessity and some by both. For instance, certain groups of women entered the workforce directly as 'replacements' for absent husbands or for dead ones. Of the nearly 14,000 women employed as street-car workers in Germany in late 1915, 20 per cent were married to workers in that occupation who had been mobilised into the army (Daniel, 1997: 55). Across Europe, other women took over small family businesses or ran farms. Contemporary published accounts of women and the war emphasised women's atypical occupations, and they also expressed concern that such new roles or new incomes did not change their 'essential' nature and that women would still place family, and in particular child-rearing, first.

As the war continued, both Britain and Germany saw campaigns to conscript women's labour. In December 1916, Germany enacted the 'Auxiliary Service for the Fatherland' law in order to shift workers from civil to military industries and to mobilise more of the population by requiring all adult males between the ages of 17 and 60 to perform 'war work' (Daniel, 1997). The leaders of the German women's movement urged that women also be included, even if not on the identical terms as men, as did some members of the German High Command [*Doc. 5*]. However, the final legislation was a compromise between trade unions, employers and the government, and ultimately excluded women, for fear they would displace male workers and also because they had a more important task as wives and mothers (Daniel, 1997). This made the decision of women to participate in the workforce voluntary, and Germany never saw the same rates of participation as other belligerent states, in part because of trade union opposition (Daniel, 1997; Frevert, 1989). In Britain, the decision to institute conscription in 1916 followed the creation of a National Register in August 1915, recording the age, sex and occupation of all men and women between the ages of 16 and 65 (Wilson, 1986). Prominent leaders of the women's movement urged that women be included in the Register and hoped that when conscription occurred, they would be included again. Instead, despite public comments advocating 'compulsory service' for women, this was deliberately not enacted (Grayzel, 1999). Thus while overt compulsion was not a factor in any wartime state and some states made it easier for women to work outside the home than others, many women through various means thus sustained their nations at war.

WAGED WAR WORK IN FACTORIES

A common vision appeared across belligerent Europe during the war of the feminine and heroic munitions worker: costumed in workmanlike clothes, pulling a lever, carrying an artillery shell, an integral part of the nation's arsenal. The women who went into the factories, quite literally providing the hands that armed the men of the war zones, became important figures in wartime propaganda. They also played an essential part in supporting the war effort, even if they generated controversy [*Doc. 6*].

Did women's factory work, particularly in the vital and rapidly growing munitions industry, represent a break from the past? After all, women factory workers were not anomalies in any European nation prior to 1914. Despite the importance of the stories of upper-class or middle-class wives who found solace in the production of weapons to preserve or avenge their husbands' lives, very few of those employed by wartime factories came from these sections of society. What the First World War provided were opportunities for working-class women to shift the nature of their employment, for greater employment of married women with children, and for short-lived changes in the kinds of industrial work that women were permitted to perform. The strength of predominantly male unions, however, helped ensure that women's work did not threaten male wages or, ultimately, their access to jobs.

Although the exact number of women who worked in the munitions industry during the war is unknown, it provided employment for more working-class women than other types of war work. Some moved from previous employment in textile factories and most worked primarily for financial rather than patriotic reasons. Many married working-class women sought factory work because the separation allowances paid by the state to maintain their families while the male breadwinner served in the armed forces proved insufficient. Overwhelmingly, however, women gladly left domestic service for the better pay and greater personal freedom afforded by factory work. Munitions workers might put in long hours and have difficult working conditions, but servants often worked longer hours and laundresses' working conditions were often worse. Moreover, the wages paid to women for munitions work, while not always the equal of male counterparts, were certainly higher than most women had previously received (Braybon, 1981; Griffiths, 1991; Pyecroft, 1994; Watson, 1997; Woollacott, 1994b).

What did these women do? The munitions industry in wartime Britain encompassed a wide range of activities controlled by the Ministry of Munitions. These included, in addition to producing weapons and ammunition, the manufacture of everything the army needed from textiles to food. Within factories, women performed a full range of tasks, from running machines to welding. The work was often risky, because producing ammunition put women in contact with dangerous and even deadly chemicals, and industrial accidents were not uncommon. Exposure to materials such as TNT caused jaundice, and so-called 'canary girls' were easily identified by their yellow skin. Moreover, poisoning, whether by TNT or other chemicals, injured or killed some female workers and so too did explosions in munitions factories (Thom, 1998; Woollacott, 1994b).

Like the army, wartime factories brought together people from a wide variety of backgrounds. A mixture of ages, ethnicities, regions, as well as classes, to a certain extent, and nations, as women from Australia, Belgium, Canada, South Africa and the West Indies, to cite just a few examples, found work in British factories (Woollacott, 1994b). In general, these women took the place of both unskilled men (as 'substitutes') and skilled workers (as 'dilutees').

In either case, the question of pay became a heated one; if women earned less than men for the same job, they undercut male employment. On the other hand, paying men and women equally seemed far too radical and, some argued, unfair since male workers were undoubtedly superior. As a compromise, women and men were paid the same for piece work, but not for time rates (Thom, 1998). Women war workers also met with hostility from male workers, and it required government intervention to allow for the full use of their labour. And it was labour that became accepted largely because it was ultimately cheaper and easily exploitable, especially under wartime conditions (Thom, 1998).

As was the case with Irish men serving in the British army, the situation of Irish women workers in the munitions factories of Britain was more complicated than that of other British subjects. Wages for women were higher in English factories than for those in Northern Ireland or Dublin, and single Irish women were made aware of this by advertising campaigns that tried to recruit them. While such a financial incentive may have been persuasive, nationalist organisations like Sinn Féin produced their own wartime propaganda against helping the British war effort, which must have exerted its own kind of pressure on women workers. Certainly, the presence of Irish women in wartime factories cannot necessarily be attributed to the same motivations as English women. In some cases, outright conflict broke out between Irish and English women munitions workers over the former's 'anti-patriotic' behaviour. After one 1917 incident at a shell-filling factory in Hereford, an escalation of conflicts between Irish workers who sang Sinn Féin songs and insulted soldiers and English ones who objected to this, the Irish workers found themselves sent back home (Culleton, 1999; Woollacott, 1994b: 43).

France saw women entering new fields and in greater numbers, but it did not witness the same seemingly explosive growth of women into wartime factories as did Britain. In part, this occurred because France already had one of the highest rates of female participation in its labour force (Robert, 1988: 253). The serious recruitment of women, the workforce of last resort, into new war industries began in 1915, and yet by late 1917 the number of women working in commerce and industry combined was only 20 per cent higher than before the war. By 1918, only 25 per cent of the munitions factories' workforce was female (Dubesset et al., 1992: 185–6).

As was the case in Britain, female workers came from a wide range of backgrounds. Despite popular images of such workers being young girls, many were older and married. Few had any previous experience in such fields as metalworking but most had previously worked outside the home. Such war work, as was the case in Britain, carried certain risks and involved harsh conditions. First, there was the extraordinary pace of work with work periods of thirteen days before a day off, enforced overtime without an increase in wages, and strict discipline imposed by supervisors (Downs, 1995: 50–5). In addition, many male workers, especially union officials, were hostile to the introduction of women in their factories, fearing that they would drag down wages and dilute the strength of unions because, in France, as elsewhere, women's wages were kept below those of men (Dubesset et al., 1992).

Despite the continuing wage differential between men and women, French women still sought wartime factory jobs out of financial necessity. Money, not patriotism, was the major incentive for working. With male heads of households' wages gone and replaced by an inadequate allowance for the family, which also did little to keep up with inflation, women worked to meet their families' material needs. That the better earnings now available to them increased their social status was not insignificant either (Downs, 1995). Furthermore, as the war continued, women's earnings rose dramatically compared to their state before the war (Robert, 1988: 257–8). Despite the increased money available to women factory workers, the end of the war saw a marked decrease in women's industrial labour in France, particularly among married women. The reasons for this were both voluntary – some women chose work that was less difficult and a few chose not to perform waged work at all – and involuntary, as men replaced the women who had replaced them. The demobilisation of women in France, as elsewhere, was often abrupt and left many women in dire economic straits, with neither jobs nor unemployment benefits (Dubesset et al., 1992: 208). Even women who continued to work in the metalworking trades experienced the sexual division of labour anew, and were restricted to low-skilled, usually repetitive and lower-waged jobs.

Of all participant nations, Germany saw among the lowest number of women participating in its wartime factory work. This reflected prewar patterns of female labour participation and that, in part because of pressure from trade unions, women's compensation proved insufficient compared with state welfare to recruit them in large numbers. Here, as elsewhere, those who entered the war factories were not strangers to waged work for most had shifted from other trades to wartime industries and most women factory workers were classified as 'unskilled' (Daniel, 1988; Dobson, 2001). In Germany, the system of family allowances also meant that women could choose not to enter factories, and furthermore, employers did little to encourage their participation (Feldman, 1966: 302). Thus, there is no obvious pattern suggesting that the war brought women into the factories, despite serious government efforts in the second half of the war to mobilise them in the face of a labour shortage (Daniel, 1997: 277).

Some German women, particularly those with dependent children, were unlikely to enter 'skilled' munitions work because they assumed such jobs would not last beyond the end of the war. The amount of labour needed to sustain families in the economic conditions of blockaded Germany also dissuaded these women from pursuing waged labour in addition to their other labour (Daniel, 1997: 277–8). Others found state support which did not keep up with inflation so inadequate that even without the threat of having welfare suspended if a woman refused to work, they entered the workforce. Still the female wartime factory worker generally came from the ranks of those already employed as domestic servants and agricultural and textile workers. Once participating in the wartime workforce, women found themselves performing tasks that had previously been characterised as 'male' in metalworking or chemical industries (Daniel, 1997). Moreover, the public impression remained that women's work had changed radically as women now took on such previously male-defined tasks as delivering mail or using pneumatic drills (Frevert, 1989). Women's union participation was far below their rate of participation in the workforce, which left them even more vulnerable as unions looked out for the interests of male workers first (Dobson, 2001: 141). All of their new opportunities were limited, and this becomes clear when considering that after the December 1916 Auxiliary Services Law, making war work mandatory for German men, was passed, and industrialists obtained the 'skilled' workers they wanted, they fired women workers (Feldman, 1966: 302). This pattern repeated itself after demobilisation, when many jobs held by women during the war were given to men (Bessel, 1993).

Russian women, like their German counterparts, experienced harsh living conditions due to the scarcity and cost of basic necessities, and responded to this crisis by seeking waged work in urban areas. As was the case elsewhere, jobs vacated by men called up into the army awaited them. Some educated women were able to move into office jobs previously held exclusively by men, but more striking changes came in the factories. Between 1914 and 1917 the percentage of women in Russian industry grew to 43 per cent from 26 per cent, and more dramatic developments occurred in fields like metalworking and chemical production (Clements, 1994: 29). It was also the case that women left seasonal work and more traditional female occupations in search of better wages in larger wartime factories (McDermid and Hillyar, 1999). One thing that distinguished Russian women from those in other nations was that they essentially worked a 'double shift', spending almost as much time searching and standing in line for food and fuel as they did in working for pay. They also worked long hours with unpaid overtime for minimal wages (McDermid and Hillyar, 1999).

Italian women, whose country had joined the war in 1915, also quickly became part of the mobilised industrial workforce. At the war's conclusion, there were approximately 200,000 such workers, comprising about 22 per cent of this workforce (Tomassini, 1996: 579). Despite measures taken to 'protect' these women by providing dormitories and canteens, this brought many of them into public activities in new ways (Adamson, 1999: 327; Tomassini, 1996). Traditional family structures and work cycles also impinged on the recruitment of women workers from the countryside. For instance, most married women would not do night work without their husbands' permission (which usually was not forthcoming) and many insisted on returning to agricultural labour in the spring. In addition, once male workers could be punished for workplace protests by being sent off to fight or to prison, while women were not, women became much more active in unions (Tomassini, 1996: 580). This did not mean that women were completely free since they were still prevented from leaving one job for another at will. Nor did it mean that the Italian government did not have to confront public opinion concerned about the potential exploitation of women and children in wartime factories. Given these new roles, women not only formed a core component of the workforce, but they also became far more active participants in strikes, especially in 1917, than they had been before the war (Tomassini, 1991: 72).

As was the case elsewhere, the situation of Austrian women demonstrates that once initial unemployment for factory workers disappeared, women were in demand because mass mobilisation soon produced a labour shortage (Sieder, 1988). In Austria, estimates suggest that nearly one million women entered the waged workforce during the war. One dramatic result was that in greater Vienna, after 1915, almost half of all metalworkers were women (Sieder, 1988). Women even performed jobs that had previously been the sole province of men, such as welding or using lathes. Unsurprisingly, women's earnings were often only one-third of those paid to men. This in part reflects women's lack of participation in unions until the very end of the war. With the war's conclusion, moreover, many women were pressured into leaving wartime factory work so that jobs might be available to returning veterans, presumed to be heads of families. This did not meet with widespread resistance, even though here, as elsewhere across Europe, some of the women being thrown out of the factories did not have a male breadwinner to turn to, and the plight of widows was particularly acute (Sieder, 1988).

Even in the United States, where wartime conditions only existed for a few years (1917–19), similar patterns of changing jobs within what had been women's waged work and of allowing women to take 'non-traditional' jobs emerge. One key difference to consider, in contrast with the European states just discussed, lies in the divergent work patterns and opportunities available to white and African American women. Overall, the number of African American women employed in such occupations as servants and cleaners decreased between 1910 and 1920, while the number employed in fields ranging from office work to semi-skilled manufacturing workers increased markedly. Despite this, the overall increase in numbers of women in the workforce was minimal (Greenwald, 1980: 13) [*Doc. 9*].

One reason for these changes, even prior to the United States' entry into the war, came from the labour shortages produced by the marked decrease in immigrants from Europe after 1914. This prompted the consideration of two new sources of labour: white working women and rural black men and women. Within wartime industries themselves, white women occupied an extensive range of manufacturing positions; often the jobs that these women left in domestic, industrial and clerical spheres fell to black women (Greenwald, 1980). Whenever possible, women chose to avoid domestic service, and some African American women were quick to explain that even the less desirable factory work now available to them was preferable to the restrictions imposed on them as well as the lower wages they had had as servants (Greenwald, 1980). Beyond material rewards (and monetary ones were crucial for most women) came the sense that their war-related work was also worth something more, it was respected and vital for the nation – a message repeated in a variety of wartime media (Greenwald, 1980).

Women in a nation like Australia, far removed from the combat zones and yet deeply involved in the war in Europe, also entered into new venues for waged labour. Here, about 15 per cent of the male labour force left to participate militarily in the war, which created some opportunities for women workers (Crew, 1989: 28). These remained limited as even during the war Australian industry was not dominated by it. Thus the war did relatively little to alter women's wages for factory work as, for example, war bonuses, meant to counteract the effects of the rising cost of living, remained higher for men than for women (Crew, 1989).

As we have now seen, wartime women entered new types of employment within factories and some entered the factories themselves for the first time. This was certainly the case in all belligerent nations as mass mobilisation and the war's duration ultimately produced labour shortages. Examining women's wartime factory work across a wide comparative perspective reveals marked similarities in terms of new opportunities for waged and skilled work that was previously restricted to men, shifts from domestic to factory, and from rural to urban work. It also yields some interesting contrasts in the number of women employed, the type of women employed, and the 'success' of the entire enterprise. There are some intriguing interpretations of the varying degrees of success that governments had in mobilising women. Is it merely a coincidence that the countries that lost the war, Germany and Austria-Hungary, had the greatest difficulty in getting women out of homes and into wartime factories? Is it unremarkable that Britain and France succeeded because they not only mobilised all available labour but also suppressed and/or avoided strikes and turmoil (unlike Russia)? Obviously, this factor is not solely responsible for the war's outcome. Nonetheless, if we think of wartime conditions as a whole, the capacity of nations like Britain to mobilise a female workforce by gaining the support of trade union leadership, in contrast to Germany where such leadership opposed it, helped the war effort both in terms of supplying material support and bolstering morale. This suggests that military strength alone may not have been enough to secure victory.

SOCIAL WELFARE AND POLICE WORK

By bringing so many women into wartime factories, the war also brought to the surface anxiety about this 'new' female workforce. This can be seen in efforts to assure their correct moral behaviour as well as their health. Of primary concern was that women should not jeopardise their reproductive capabilities. As a result, in places like Britain, France and Germany, the war also opened opportunities for a new kind of middle-class employment, that of the workplace welfare supervisor, and of social workers more generally (Downs, 1992; Hong, 1996; Woollacott, 1994b).

In France, voluntary efforts to provide canteens for women workers began with the entrance of women into factories in increased numbers. Then, in May 1917, feminist leader Cécile Brunschvicg organised an association to train women to become welfare supervisors. This formal step was meant to elevate a charitable task into a profession, and the association started a school, which by the war's end had trained and placed 50 such women in factories. Welfare supervisors reported directly to employers, not to the state, and were meant to link management and its female workforce. Their dual task was to ensure that production flourished (so they had the ability to discipline workers) and that the well-being of women, especially as real or potential mothers, was maintained so that the family and, by extension, the nation would not suffer (Downs, 1992).

In Britain, two types of women worker looked out for women engaged in wartime factory work: factory inspectors and welfare supervisors. The former, empowered by law since the end of the nineteenth century to monitor the working conditions of women in factories, were responsible for such things as safe and clean facilities and the treatment of workers in terms of work and compensation. The newer role of welfare supervisors arose under the auspices of the Ministry of Munitions, which in 1915 created a Welfare Department. Its primary role was to ensure adequate production through an efficient and healthy labour force and, as a result, women welfare supervisors under its direction took charge of canteens, first aid and rest rooms.

They also assumed a role as 'moral guardians', designed to manage petty disputes, pilfering and immoral behaviour in part by offering appropriate social and recreational activities. These included showing films, organising dances and exercise. Given the class divide between middle-class supervisors and the working-class women they supervised, it is not surprising that tensions emerged, especially as some supervisors had the capacity to hire and fire as well as to punish violations of the rules. As in France, much depended on the individuals: some were viewed as strictly working for management; others were viewed as being as concerned with the genuine welfare of women workers (Woollacott, 1994b).

In Germany, middle-class women came to function as a bridge between the state and working women. A leading government official believed that only with the assistance of women overseeing welfare agencies would the necessary female labour force be mobilised. The numbers of women welfare assistants in factories greatly expanded, from twenty before the war to 900 by October 1918. In addition, women's organisations played a crucial role in organising voluntary welfare services for women workers (Frevert, 1989: 160; Hong, 1996).

If welfare supervisors and inspectors could be seen as extending women's appropriately 'nurturing' role into a new sphere, one of the war's most striking changes for many observers came in the employment of women in roles previously closed to them. British contemporaries were particularly struck by women in uniform, which sometimes required masculine attire. Observers now found women employed as conductors on trams and buses, and acting as cleaners, porters, guards and ticket collectors on trains. Women also took on visible roles as road sweepers, window cleaners and postal workers (Braybon, 1981).

In addition, one of the more discernible challenges to gender roles came in the form of women police, as new organisations emerged to provide a female force to monitor the behaviour of women during the war. Among these, two stood out: the Voluntary Women Patrols, sponsored by the National Union of Women Workers, and the more uppercrust (and suffragette) Women Police Service (WPS). In contrast to the women patrols, the WPS saw itself as an independent body that could coerce appropriate social (and sexual) behaviour from men and particularly women, and root out the ills of the male police force as well. Women employed in both organisations performed the basic task of policing – the street patrol – taking on the job of, among other things, separating couples found in public parks and thoroughfares. In general, the type of women who became policewomen differed from those taking on other more traditionally masculine trades. They were more likely to be older, married, and from the upper-middle and elite classes. Their authority rested on a combination, then, of class privilege and official sanction (Bland, 1985; Douglas, 1999; Levine, 1994; Woodeson, 1993).

THE MEDICAL PROFESSIONS

Employment for women within medicine grew during the war both because of the expansion and professionalisation of nursing services and of new opportunities for medical training and for women doctors. Given the difficulty of securing medical education for women prior to the war, few women were in position, at first, to offer their services as doctors, and their efforts to participate were not always welcomed. This differed from the reception that greeted women who wanted to nurse. The opportunity to serve as a wartime nurse was presented to women as offering them a way of directly helping the military and, by extension, the nation. It kept women subservient to male doctors and it drew on their allegedly natural capacities for caring and nurturing. In short, it did not offer a direct challenge to conventional gender roles. However, nursing exposed many relatively sheltered young women to some of the war's most visceral horrors, and in so doing, changed their lives.

At first, women doctors who offered their services to the military or government directly were rejected. Thus, those who went had to organise themselves, find their own way to where they were needed, and set up shop. The exact numbers of American women doctors, for instance, are hard to come by as some freelanced while others served with the Red Cross or in the American Women's Hospitals, which they created in order to find work for themselves (Gavin, 1997; Schneider and Schneider, 1991). Those American women who did serve overseas, including at least two African American women, found that their lack of official military status could prove a real obstacle in dealing with fellow doctors and sometimes with patients (Jensen, 1998). In Russia, some women doctors worked beside men in field hospitals, although here, too, in small numbers (McDermid and Hillyar, 1999).

The war also opened the doors for women's medical education in Britain, if temporarily. Many of these women took over the functions of male doctors who joined the Royal Army Medical Corps (RAMC), and Dr Jane Walker, for example, became an adviser to both the Ministry of Food and Ministry of Munitions. Yet female physicians also insisted on serving in areas where they could care for wounded soldiers, and the War Office, reluctantly at first but then with greater acceptance, allowed them to do so (Leneman, 1994b: 161).

In 1915, the War Office gave Drs Louisa Garrett Anderson and Flora Murray, co-founders of the Women's Hospital Corps, permission to establish a military hospital in London. Opened in May 1915, the Endell Street Hospital grew in size throughout the war, serving some 26,000 patients until it closed in 1919. In many ways, it was easier for women to serve the military in Britain as several officials actively discouraged the idea of British women doctors treating soldiers near the firing line. However, by mid-1916, the need for physicians on the Western Front had grown so much that women doctors were actively recruited for hospitals in Malta. By the war's end, some of these women had been transferred to Salonika, Egypt, India, East Africa and Palestine (Leneman, 1994b: 170–1).

The largest British medical endeavour completely run by women was that of the Scottish Women's Hospitals (SWH) founded by Dr Elsie Inglis, a leading Scottish suffragist. This organisation began by launching an appeal through the *Common Cause*, the newspaper of the National Union of Women Suffrage Societies (NUWSS), in September 1914 to raise money for medical services that would be offered by women. By the end of October, sufficient funds had been raised to allow the SWH to create its first hospital in France and later to found several others there and also in Serbia and Russia. Eventually more than a thousand women from all parts of the United Kingdom and its dominions served as doctors, orderlies, nurses, ambulance drivers and other support staff under SWH auspices. These hospitals allowed women to perform medical and surgical work unimaginable in Britain, and the grateful governments of France and Serbia awarded some of these doctors their highest medals (Leneman 1994a).

A far more visible emblem of the war – heavy with symbolic value as well as actual usefulness – was the war nurse (Darrow, 1996). Along with the professional ranks, whose origins in places like Britain were linked with wartime service, other agencies, such as the Red Cross, operating in individual nations also recruited many young and often inexperienced women. Nursing gave women an opportunity to get close to the battlefields and to provide vital aid while still enabling them to be seen as fulfilling a caregiving and therefore feminine role.

Military nursing offered women of every nation the chance to perform obvious and necessary service. From Russia, where it enhanced the visibility of professional women, to Britain, where tensions arose between regular trained nurses and newly-formed Voluntary Aid Detachments (VADs), nursing became one widespread way that women were seen as directly contributing to the war effort. Nurses' own experiences indelibly shaped them as they came into first-hand contact with the full effects of modern war, such as the aftermath of gas attacks.

In Russia, nurses were not supposed to be close to the firing line and were to remain in mobile field hospitals. During the course of the war, they ended up gathering wounded bodies and experiencing notable casualties under direct fire (Meyer, 1991). Keeping nurses away from the battlefields proved futile throughout the war's geographic scope. While the initial regulations of the French Medical Service excluded women from the battlefield, this not only turned out to be impossible to enforce but also counter to need. By 1918 the rules had changed, and French nurses staffed dressing stations as well as hospitals. As with Russian nurses, they were killed in the line of duty, which helped them inspire one of the dominant images of women's wartime heroism (Darrow, 2000; Thébaud, 1986).

As was the case throughout Europe, the early phases of the war surprised all those in authority with their savageness and human costs. Medical services raced to catch up. The French Red Cross, for example, greatly simplified its training to allow more women to learn the fundamentals of basic nursing as quickly as possible. However, because it relied exclusively on volunteers, it eliminated those who could not afford to work without pay. Not until 1916, when facing a nursing shortage that would continue throughout the war, did the army create the position of Temporary Military Nurse and pay women for nursing. Approximately 30,000 such women were hired, along with over 60,000 Red Cross nurses at the height of their activity (Darrow, 2000: 140–1).

Over the course of the war, the German Imperial Commissar and Military Inspector for Voluntary Nursing employed some 92,000 nurses and aides. Many of them came from the Red Cross, others from religious orders. It is likely that many of these women had upper-class and middle-class backgrounds and saw nursing as fulfilling a socially useful and still feminine role (Schulte, 1997: 124–5). As important, it allowed them to answer the call to service and to feel that they participated in a direct way in the war effort. Here too, nurses were meant to staff military hospitals not field outposts, but in reality they did both (Schulte, 1997).

The experience of German nurses also exposed them to two very different sectors of the war, the Western Front and the Eastern one. First-hand accounts emphasise that the East, especially its cold and darkness, made nursing there much worse than in the West. More seriously, nurses working in the East were more likely than those in the West to be exposed to malaria and typhus. More nurses in this area, suffering from overwork and exhaustion, fell ill and died. Those who survived both of these battle zones often felt displaced in postwar society (Schulte, 1997).

British military nursing had powerful antecedents in the myth (and work) of Florence Nightingale, which provided British women with a convenient role model for a nation at war well before 1914 (Summers, 1987). When the war came, trained women enrolled as nurses and the unskilled joined the Voluntary Aid Detachments. In Ireland alone, around 4,500 women became VADs and served either there or abroad (Jeffery, 2000). By November 1918, the Queen Alexandra's Imperial Military Nursing Service and Territorial Force Nursing Services together employed 12,769 trained nurses and 10,816 partially trained or untrained ones. This does not include the 2,396 British nurses and 1,685 VADs working for the Royal Army Medical Corps in August 1918 or those smaller numbers employed by the British Red Cross Society, St John Ambulance Brigade Hospital, Friends' Ambulance Unit, and First Aid Nursing Yeomanry Corps

(Marwick, 1977: 167–8). As first-hand accounts of wartime nursing reveal, tensions often arose between nurses and VADs as there were significant class and other differences between the two. Professional nurses, by and large, saw themselves as doing vital national work as part of a career; the VADs who nursed, many of whom came from a higher socio-economic status than nurses, saw themselves primarily as performing a war service.

Nursing also provided a way for substantial numbers of women who lived miles from the battleground to experience the devastating effects of war. Even before their nation's official entry into the war, American women served in the Red Cross in locations as far away as Russia. Others joined either the Army or Navy Nurse Corps as adjuncts to the military. The range of tasks performed by these nurses overseas was impressively wide. Some served as anesthetists, others participated in mobile (flying) surgical units or in American mobile hospitals that could be set up in a day (Schneider and Schneider, 1991). The military recognised that nurses were an essential component of its work and gave army nurses a status above enlisted men, but it balked at giving them military rank. As a result, these women could not exercise authority or receive full credit for their work, and the army excluded women from retirement benefits (Zeiger, 1999).

Despite America's late entry into the war, American army nurses arrived in France when the Allies were experiencing both a nursing shortage and some of the most intense fighting seen since the early days of the war. Many describe nursing through the fighting of July 1918 as especially harrowing, and the experience of being so intimately connected with the costs of the war could have a profound effect. As one nurse put it, 'You see I am where I am seeing something of the *business* of war. There is no glamour whatsoever about it' (Zeiger, 1999: 134).

Women of the British Commonwealth also joined up as nurses. Despite the government's initial reluctance to send women overseas, approximately 650 New Zealand nurses went abroad. The majority worked directly with the New Zealand forces but others nursed for the French or British Red Cross (Pugsley et al., 1996). Some 2,500 Australians served as nurses overseas, many of whom ended up in France but some spent the war taking care of the sick rather than the wounded in Egypt or Salonika. What motivated them was akin to what motivated others: a sense of duty, a close connection to a loved one (brothers or sweethearts) also serving overseas or simply a desire to have an adventure. What many of them encountered as their first engagement was the aftermath of the disastrous landings at Gallipoli in 1915. Stationed on hospital ships off-shore, they were ill-equipped to handle the massive casualties that resulted. Subsequent nursing, if less traumatic, was no less difficult (Scates and Frances, 1997).

As was true elsewhere, relationships between soldiers and nurses were constrained by a number of factors. Since only single women were supposed to be sent abroad as nurses, they were assumed to be 'innocent' and in need of protection. In an effort to safeguard both the men and the women, Australian nurses were regarded as honorary 'officers' and thus forbidden to fraternise with other ranks, which included most of the men for whom they cared. That this regulation was often violated mattered little, it helped create a climate which made the interaction between soldiers and nurses suspect. Nurses could negotiate this tension in a variety of ways, most often by acting as pure-minded, friendly sisters or mothers, and denying the possibility of any sexual overtones in their behaviour (Holmes, 1995).

Like Australians, Canadian nurses had to meet certain requirements. In addition to having graduated from a recognised nursing school, this included being single and between the ages of 21 and 38. Despite these restrictions, there were more applicants than places for military nurses. In addition to serving directly under the military, Canada also established eight university-based hospitals that employed nurses. As with nurses from all of the belligerent nations, many of these women had close family and friends serving in the military, which lent both renewed purpose and an emotional edge to their work (Mann, 2000) [*Doc. 7*].

The nursing experience of women during the war left a complex legacy. As we saw in Chapter 2, they were often used in propaganda to represent the most self-sacrificing of women, and heroic nurses became a staple of wartime popular media, whether in real-life examples such as that of Edith Cavell, or in fiction such as in *L'Ennemi*. On the other hand, because most participant nations ended up actively recruiting women from the educated, middle and upper classes, these women found themselves performing previously unthinkable tasks, including having intimate contact with male bodies. This had the effect of making the societies to which they returned sometimes suspicious of their morals and behaviour. When Vera Brittain returned to university after her war service, she recounts being treated as liable to harm the other women students around her because 'tales of immorality among VADs ... had been consumed with voracious horror by readers at home; who knew in what cesspools of iniquity I had not wallowed? Who could calculate the awful extent to which I might corrupt the morals of my innocent juniors?' (Brittain, 1978: 476–7). The wartime world required this service from women, but the postwar world was not always sure what to do with the women who had performed it.

ON THE LAND

As has already been shown, the labour of women sustained Europe's war-torn nations. As the war continued, sustenance itself – the maintenance of an adequate food supply – also became part of their contribution. Women agricultural workers proved even more essential in places like France, as men from rural areas were swallowed up by the war, and Britain, an island nation where the importation of food became difficult. Yet there was mixed success in the efforts to persuade urban women to work on the land.

In Germany, where the food supply was deeply affected by a blockade, urban women responded to the return of a 'quasi-subsistence economy' by growing vegetables in urban allotments and keeping small livestock in their homes (Daniel, 1997: 190–1). With almost 60 per cent of male agricultural workers called up to serve in the army, the government tried to convince urban women to relocate to rural areas to replace this labour force. The War Office appealed directly to women, claiming that agricultural work would both aid their health and the nation (Bessel, 1997: 219). This effort not only proved unsuccessful in mobilising women to leave the cities for the land and convincing farmers to accept their aid, but also led to further food shortages. It eventually collapsed altogether (Jackson, 1996: 570–1).

Whether or not Germany felt desperate, by 1916 it had begun to remove civilians from regions that the German army held under occupation and to require these same civilians to perform forced labour (Jackson, 1996). This further fed into indignation and became yet another piece of evidence in the Allies' propaganda attacks on Germany: its brutal treatment of foreign women. France widely advertised the German army's Easter-week deportations of young women from Lille, for instance, as serving a more nefarious purpose than agricultural work. Did such treatment of 'enemy' women reassure German women at home that they were not being expected to suffer the pains of the food shortages alone? As will be discussed further in Chapter 4, this was not how the French viewed it (Grayzel, 1999; McPhail, 1999).

In comparison with Germany, Britain more successfully mobilised women both in rural communities and from urban areas to help maintain the food supply. Its Women's Land Army evolved from earlier volunteer organisations like the Women's Legion and the Women's Defence Relief Corps, which aimed to solve the food problem by using women's labour. From the outset, these groups sought specifically and often explicitly to attract single women of the educated middle classes. Starting with bringing women together to do seasonal land work, it soon tried to gather sufficient women to replace absent men.

The Women's Land Army, administered under the Board of Agriculture, was always one of several options for women interested in working for overwhelmingly *patriotic* reasons. Officials recognised that agricultural employment involving difficult physical work and often meagre accommodations lacked the glamour of other forms of war service. Thus, they had to persuade women of its extreme usefulness as well as its desirability. In the uniform of smocks, breeches and puttees, 'Land Girls' performed a variety of essential tasks from taking care of livestock to planting crops. A subsection, the Women's Foresty Corps, supplemented the care of livestock and crops by felling and harvesting wood. If the numbers of women who worked the land were never extensive, they greatly assisted with the last two harvests of the war and even came to serve as symbols of a revitalised English countryside (Grayzel, 1999).

French, Italian, American and Russian women continued to work the land in much the same way as they traditionally had, but the amount of work they needed to do increased. As noted above, Italian authorities bemoaned their difficulties in keeping 'peasant women' in the factories when they felt the pull of agricultural labour in the spring (Tomassini, 1996: 580). French women not only took on the work of their absent men, but also of field animals requisitioned by the army (Thébaud, 1986). American women and their families were urged to supplement the food supply by growing 'victory gardens'. Once again, enormous variation in the use of women in agriculture existed in combatant nations; in every case, this labour was deemed essential for the war.

FEMALE SPIES AND THE QUESTION OF WARTIME TREASON

There was yet another type of warfare waged during the First World War: a war of information and espionage. In the early days of the war, Britain seethed with rumours about spies, and fears of what German women – serving as governesses or domestic servants – might be up to contributed to a climate that led to the eventual internment of many aliens. Germany's popular magazines early in the war similarly depicted spies as women too ignorant to know the value of national loyalty (Davis, 2000: 40). In France, rumours of a mysterious 'lady in a hat' abounded, fuelled by prewar spy literature (Darrow, 2000). There were in fact women in many countries who aided their own war efforts by gathering and passing along information.

This situation was intensified in areas under hostile occupation such as Belgium and northern France. Here networks developed to try to aid and enable Allied soldiers to escape to safety. As was discussed earlier in Chapter 2, in 1915 the Germans executed British nurse Edith Cavell for aiding and abetting the enemy as she had been active in one such network. Other women in Lille and the surrounding countryside, in particular Louise Thuliez, hid soldiers and led them to Cavell's clinic in Brussels and from there to safety, often through the Netherlands (McPhail, 1999). When the network was discovered, Cavell was arrested and condemned to death along with Thuliez and the Comtesse de Belleville, who with Princess Marie de Croÿ had offered her home as a refuge along the way. Cavell chose not to appeal, and was executed along with Philippe Baucq; Thuliez's sentence, together with several other supporters, was commuted to life imprisonment with hard labour. While Cavell's execution roused international indignation, even British espionage agents found her conviction by the Germans well-founded, although they disagreed about the appropriateness of executing a woman (Wheelwright, 1992). The image circulated in propaganda ignored what Cavell had done and instead stressed her role as nurse to patients of all nations, thus above suspicion and 'innocent'.

Frenchwoman Louise de Bettignies serves as another example of a woman who manipulated the border between war and free zones. She not only helped Allied soldiers to escape capture but also collected and passed on vital material from informants in occupied France, including troop movements and locations. She worked directly with British intelligence, and was caught, along with her main aide, Marie-Léonie Vanhoutte, in October 1915. Given the outrage provoked by Cavell's execution, the two women's lives were spared, but de Bettignies died of illness in a German prison in September 1918. After the war, her body was returned for reburial in France. She received several posthumous honours from the British and French governments, and a statue was erected to her memory in the centre of Lille (Darrow, 2000; McPhail, 1999). Other women served as spies in even more complicated and potentially risky ways. Marthe Richer, also known as Marthe Richard, a French aviator, worked as a double-agent based largely in Spain, and passed along secrets obtained from her liaison with a German officer (Darrow, 2000; Thébaud, 1986; Wheelwright, 1992).

However, from the moment of her execution in France in 1917, Mata Hari (Margaretha Zelle MacLeod) has come to personify the archetypal female spy, not only of the First World War but also of the modern era, one who seduces men into betraying their country's secrets and then passes them on to the enemy. Mata Hari's prewar career consisted of performing allegedly sacred dances from what was deemed 'the Orient' which involved removing most of her clothing. A Dutchwoman married to a British officer in the colonial army who lived for a time in Indonesia, she reinvented herself as the daughter of a Malay princess and a European father. Her brief fame as an exotic dancer led to a life as a prototypical courtesan, where she lived off various male lovers. At the outbreak of the war, however, her career in both senses was on a downturn; she had ended an engagement in Germany and had gone back to Holland, where she had little to do. So in 1916, already labelled suspect in British intelligence reports, she returned to Paris, where the head of French intelligence, Georges Ladoux, recruited her to spy for France. The original plan was for her to use her powers of seduction on the Crown Prince of Germany and thereby obtain information. She demanded a million francs in order to do this, as she was badly in debt. She then tried to head back to the Netherlands via Spain. Stopped by British authorities who refused to allow her to continue her journey, she returned to Spain. Here she credibly believed herself to be aiding the French by initiating a relationship with a ranking German official in order to get military 'secrets' to pass along, which she dutifully did. However, after receiving no response from Ladoux, who was convinced she was truly spying for Germany, she decided to return to France, hoping to be rewarded for what she had been able to accomplish.

In the context of the Russian Revolution and the waves of strikes and mutinies that beset France in 1917, this was not a wise move. Her arrest in February and subsequent imprisonment in St Lazarre, her trial in July of that year and execution in October appear hardly surprising. Mata Hari was an unlikely double-agent, and there is no evidence that she ever acted solely as a German spy. However, her trial was closed, and the conclusion predetermined. Looking back, the bulk of evidence in the Mata Hari case now reveals her main 'crimes' to have been promiscuity and arrogance. Her reputation and previous career as a famed exotic dancer, an emblem of a decadent prewar life, then contributed to the desire to find her guilty of treason (Darrow, 2000; Thébaud, 1986; Wheelwright, 1992).

Examining Mata Hari in light of the treatment of Edith Cavell reveals the convoluted nature of women in First World War espionage (Wheelwright, 1992). On the one hand stands Mata Hari, known by her stage name, emblematic of unbridled sexuality, claiming to have slept with Germans to obtain information for France and expecting to be well compensated for it. On the other hand, the unmarried, 'asexual' nurse Edith Cavell actively helped Allied soldiers to escape from occupied Belgium. Her actions took her beyond the realm of caring for the wounded and into the realm of political resistance and defiance of the German army. The purity of Edith Cavell's selfless motives contrasts vividly with the aura of corruption and decadence surrounding Mata Hari. Questions of actual guilt or innocence aside, women who defied wartime conventions as broadly as did Mata Hari could be subjected to the most extreme punishment. Women thus gained a place in espionage, but unless they were as 'pure' as Edith Cavell, it was one that would place them in a precarious position, even within their own nations.

WOMEN'S UNPAID WORK

With the mass mobilisation of 1914 came the interconnected social problem of how to alleviate the hardships experienced by family members left behind and how to make use of the largest group of adults not called up or actively recruited for armed service. One response to both of these problems occurred largely outside governmental initiatives in the form of voluntary services established to provide for those fighting and those suffering behind the lines. This included vast numbers of organisations created, headed and staffed by women; immediate relief of servicemen's families came from private charitable institutions in both Germany and Britain. Some of the women's groups saw themselves as fulfilling a particular feminine responsibility during wartime to care for others. Some (often but not exclusively those with a more feminist slant) devoted themselves to alleviating the condition of women hurt by the mobilisation of male breadwinners and other disruptions to economic and familial life.

As we have already seen in Chapter 2, certain categories of women such as widows received direct state support. However, this left others, including women thrown out of work by immediate wartime economic dislocation, in dire straits. Feminist publications thus urged female consumers to continue to buy clothes in order to keep women in the clothing industry employed, and feminist leaders urged that their organisations' members relieve women in distress (Holton, 1986; Thébaud, 1986). Ultimately, many of these women workers would find employment doing war work, but at the war's outset, the charitable work of other women helped them survive.

Another one of the war's most visible problems was the wave of refugees, mainly women and children, that it produced. The care of these refugees, be they Belgians in England, inhabitants of the invaded territories in the rest of France, Galicians fleeing to other parts of Austria-Hungary, or the masses on the move in the Russian empire, became primarily the concern of women. While some welfare workers also cared for women, much of the aid given to wartime refugees came from women's voluntary organisations, and this aid was extensive. The Red Cross in almost every nation, in addition to its work for soldiers, also supplied comfort and supplies to refugees in need.

In Austria – including Vienna, Bohemia and Moravia – Jewish women devoted particular energy to caring for Jewish refugees from Galicia. These refugees began to appear as early as September 1914 and many were unable to return for the war's duration. As a result, despite some government aid, many refugees, especially Jews (approximately 40 per cent of the more than 385,000 refugees fleeing Galicia and Bukovina in 1915 were Jewish) needed more support in terms of housing, food and clothing. The response of the Austrian Jewish community to the refugees' plight allowed them to demonstrate both their service to the nation overall and to their community in particular. They provided money, as well as created soup kitchens, schools and clinics. In addition to local support in areas that received refugees, Jewish women's organisations throughout the country gathered basic necessities for them (Rozenblit, 1995: 200, 205–6).

Given the flood of refugees produced by the war in Russia, many middle-class women took on another role in caring for them. They insisted that their assistance was necessary because so many of the refugees were women with children. As women, they felt they could make a difference in terms of the well-being of the refugees, both physical and moral. Recognising how vulnerable they were, women welfare workers thus tried to protect the refugee women from becoming prostitutes or succumbing to other vices. They also established practical charities to feed and clothe them (Gatrell, 1999).

In Germany, women's local associations devoted themselves to volunteer efforts for their communities, particularly for refugees, children and female war workers. They established soup kitchens and crèches, and gathered supplies such as clothing and footwear. Primarily, middle-class women often working with the main German women's organisation, the Bund Deutscher Frauenvereine (BDF), pursued charitable works as a means of national service. Given some of the inadequacies of state support, these women's networks proved essential in meeting the basic needs of the nation's families (Domansky, 1996; Frevert, 1989; Hong, 1996).

Along with helping other women, many women's groups across war-torn Europe also organised themselves so as to best help soldiers. This first took the form of providing material comforts, including knitted items such as socks and parcels filled with cigarettes, food, writing paper, treats and 'morally uplifting' literature. In Ireland, for instance, 6,000 women volunteered to manufacture equipment for the Irish War Hospital Supply Depot, while in Red Cross Workrooms in Dublin, 300 women knitted 20,000 pairs of socks and 10,000 scarves for servicemen (Jeffery, 2000: 33). Approximately 10,000 women's patriotic clubs, societies and sewing circles emerged in Australia, where, in addition to knitting socks, they packed these along with cakes, tobacco, magazines and an inspiring letter into 'comfort' bags to be sent to soldiers in the field (Scates and Frances, 1997: 45–6). In New Zealand, so many patriotic groups emerged to provide comforts for soldiers, among other things, that they had to be regulated under the War Funds Act of 1915, establishing a Federation of New Zealand War Relief Societies (Pugsley et al., 1996). Meantime, in Austria, Jewish women as well as others organised themselves to help the war effort, and the former deliberately sought to aid Jewish soldiers by sending gift packages for Chanukah and Purim and kosher food for Passover (Rozenblit, 1995: 203).

Soon women's organisations established outposts at train stations, canteens for military personnel and even for female munitions workers themselves. One purpose of the 'Foyers du Soldat' (Soldiers' hearths), as they were called in France, was to provide an alternative to the café or public house where men might be led astray by alcohol and prostitution. The many women who flocked to the aid of soldiers envisioned themselves as entertaining the troops in an appropriate, patriotic fashion. Organisations such as the YMCA (Young Men's Christian Association) and the Salvation Army provided entertainment huts, where women served 'doughnuts to doughboys' (Gavin, 1997; Marwick, 1977; Thébaud, 1986; Zeiger, 1999).

One effort to create more personal and, presumably, sustaining ties between individual soldiers and civilian women can be seen in the creation of the *marraines de guerre* in France. Each *marraine* (godmother) adopted a *filleul* (godson) in the trenches, and sent him packages and letters. While these ties were designed to elevate the morale of each participant, they also evoked suspicion as popular culture began to sexualise these relationships (Grayzel, 1997a).

Despite America's late entry to the war, American women quickly organised themselves to help soldiers. As was the case with women war workers, however, race became a complicating factor. Despite the efforts of women such as Addie Hunton and Kathryn Johnson, who were among a handful of women able to go to France to provide support to these troops, efforts to provide recreation and sustenance to African American soldiers fell far short of those provided for white troops (Hunton and Johnson, 1920). The segregated United States army at first had no recreational activities or YMCA clubs, deemed so vital for morale, set up for any African American troops at its training camps or abroad. Facilities for white soldiers were put off limits to non-whites. Despite this, African American women strove to support their soldiers as best they could, as the testimony of those African American women volunteers who made it to France attests (Bristow, 1996; Hunton and Johnson, 1920) [*Doc. 8*].

The time required of such services meant that the bulk of those performing voluntary, charitable work came from the middle and upper classes, although women of the entire nation could contribute pennies to war loans and send comforts to soldiers. All such work appealed to women as patriots, as vital constituents of their nations at war, but much of this charitable work did not challenge any preconceived ideas about gender roles or actions. There were some notable exceptions, as some of the most difficult tasks associated with the war, such as ambulance driving done by British women, were unpaid. In these instances, women of means – some from as far away as New Zealand – paid their way to France or Britain, provided their own uniforms and received little material support of any kind (Marcus, 1989; Pugsley et al., 1996). The compensation for all members of the Voluntary Aid Detachments was so minimal that almost all VADs came from the middle class, and were motivated by many factors including the desire to be of service and to test their own capacities (Donner, 1997).

Given the abundance of organisations created by women during the war, a collective portrait of women emerges. It reveals that those who participated saw voluntary work as a means of serving the nation. Women who took up the tasks of providing comforts and aid to soldiers saw this as a way, however small, of contributing to the war effort and thus to their own men and nation at risk.

'THE KITCHEN IS THE KEY TO VICTORY': WORK IN THE HOME

No matter what type of organised volunteer activity or paid employment women performed during the war, their wartime nations also assumed that they had a vital second role: managing their homes. This task only became more difficult as the length of the war began to affect the supply of basic necessities and food. Germany, for instance, had not prepared for a lengthy war and its inhabitants were deeply affected by the shortage of foodstuffs. Britain also had to worry about its reliance on imported foods, and both of these nations, as we saw earlier, made serious efforts to encourage women to produce more agricultural goods. In addition to trying to raise food production, these governments and others also began to control consumption. They launched campaigns that focused on women, urging them to avoid wasting food, to substitute other foods for those that were in short supply, and to learn how to navigate a new system of rationing. We have already seen visual evidence of this in the discussion of propaganda in Chapter 2. In many ways, this was easier to do in the countryside than in the urban areas where much of the European population lived.

The management of food resources was especially vital and fraught among the participant nations Austria-Hungary and Germany, although not restricted to them. Belgium may provide the best example of wartime food deprivation as not only was it subject to the Allied blockade as an occupied territory but, in addition, its own resources were raided by Germany. As we will see in Chapter 6, food shortages led to prolonged and often violent street action by women in the capital cities of Germany and Austria-Hungary, and contributed to the revolutionary climate of wartime Russia, especially in the major cities of Petrograd and Moscow.

MUNITIONS VERSUS MOTHERHOOD: ATTITUDES TO WAR AND WORK

It is hardly surprising that the many outward changes in women's appearances and in their working lives provoked strong reactions. In particular, they initiated debates about the national dangers of women's work. Factory and industrial work in particular was contrasted with women's allegedly more natural and equally important task of reproduction – literally ensuring a human supply of citizen soldiers for the nation [*Doc. 10*].

The British and French governments, for instance, were concerned with regulating the behaviour of the many women who were called into war-related work, especially in factories. However, by focusing on women's health and their children's health, they reveal a deeper concern with the nation's future need for healthy citizens (Grayzel, 1999). One concrete result already mentioned was the creation of welfare supervisors for female factory workers – a paternalistic safeguard.

Better working conditions, higher wages and fewer hours might have helped all women, including mothers, but this contradicted the wartime need for increased production at reduced costs. Instead, the French government, for example, after lengthy discussion managed to pass one substantive piece of new legislation: a law supporting breast-feeding women in wartime factories by giving them time off to nurse and creating rooms in which they could do so.

Concern with the declining birthrate in France predated the war, and concern about demographic shortcomings would pervade postwar Europe. Some concrete changes recognised women's new responsibilities, enabling them to be official guardians of their children, for instance. As we will see in Chapter 7, several pieces of legislation at the war's end and in its aftermath also sought to do more than recognise women. Reform measures that are among the basis of a welfare state emerged to compensate women financially for rearing children (Pedersen, 1993).

Women in combatant nations faced many similar challenges – anxiety about men and children, economic difficulties and social upheavals. However, the opportunities provided for their participation in the war effort, in waged war work, varied from state to state and, within states, by class, ethnicity or region. Urban, middle- and upper-class women enjoyed a wider range of options than poorer and rural women. Despite these divergences, the home and the care as well as production of its inhabitants was thus construed as a vital part of the women's war effort. New technologies would mean that homes would also literally become a target. In addition to the changes wrought in many women's lives by wartime work, waged and voluntary, willing and unwilling, specific wartime circumstances brought women into the line of fire. Experiences such as living under occupation or becoming victims of air raids far from the battlefields had dramatic effects on women's lives and livelihoods.

CHAPTER FOUR

WOMEN IN THE LINE OF FIRE

Perhaps the most vivid example of how the First World War affected women's lives can be found not in their wartime mobilisation but in their wartime experience of both traditional and new kinds of warfare. The First World War began typically enough with the mobilisation of national military forces to attack those of the enemy, and this would have a profound effect on the civilian populations that stood in their way. Invading armies like Germany's not only subjected civilian women in the territories that they overran to oversight by the military, but they also produced waves of refugees. In some instances, people fled internationally; such was the case with Belgians who sought refuge in France and in Britain. In other circumstances, the exodus of refugees was internal; this was the case in France, parts of Austria-Hungary, and most dramatically in Russia. Yet, what made this war different, in addition to its scale, was that it threatened women far beyond the battle zone.

Before detailing the conditions for European women, it is worth putting these in a wider context, for one could certainly argue that the entire experience of indigenous women in the European colonies of those powers involved in the war was of living 'under occupation' as well. In Africa, as tensions mounted among German, French and British colonisers, for instance, African men were subject to forcible conscription and women were not immune from being used as forced labour. Efforts to compel men to serve led some European 'recruiters' to hold wives hostage until their men appeared. These endeavours, as well as the compulsory labour of women, for instance in internment camps for German subjects and in order to transport war supplies, increased hostility between Africans and European colonisers. Actual combat was restricted to parts of East Africa, Cameroon, South West Africa and initially Togoland, but these areas of the continent were not alone in feeling the economic and thus social consequences (Page, 1987, 2000). There are, of course, vast differences between the experiences of African and European women, yet both could be subject to forced labour and other abuses, and they could be viewed as especially vulnerable because of their gender.

LIFE UNDER OCCUPATION IN EUROPE

When the German armies pushed into Belgium and then northern France in 1914, they became an occupying force that would stay for much of the duration of the war. International agreements, specifically the Hague conventions, had dictated rules for occupation of enemy lands. Despite these, many actions by occupying troops ignored both the letter and spirit of the law. Although now overshadowed by the more brutal occupations of the Second World War, the experience of women under occupation in this war produced its own set of unique and complicated experiences. Many Frenchwomen found themselves separated from their male heads of households, and most suffered economic deprivations that were more severe than those felt in the rest of the country. Moreover, the connotations for France, in particular, of having its women subjected to the authority of the German army were far-reaching. If propaganda generated by the Allies vividly depicted the 'fiends' from Germany butchering unarmed civilians, mutilating children and sexually abusing women, the actual situation of those in occupied Belgium and France, if less dramatic, was often grim.

Recent historical work has documented that wartime abuses of civilians did occur, including the rape of women (Audoin-Rouzeau, 1995; Harris, 1993; Horne and Kramer, 1994). In France, the fear of what rape might produce, namely enforced pregnancies and 'half-barbarian' children, most captured public attention and indignation. In all of these official and published debates, no reference was made to French women who consented to sexual relationships with German soldiers. That these also occurred is confirmed in private writings and censored documents (Becker, 1996: 639–40; Grayzel, 1999).

As with the atrocity propaganda discussed earlier, depictions of rape helped create an image of a subhuman, uncivilised enemy. Certainly the stories had enough credence after the issuing of the French government's report in January 1915 that a member of the legislature proposed altering the laws on abortion to make this a viable option for the victims of the invading and occupying army. Such a move launched a heated public debate over the 'child of the enemy': should women be allowed to terminate such pregnancies or should they instead be persuaded to raise these children, in the hope that French maternal blood would render them good citizens despite their 'horrific' paternity? Doctors, writers, feminists and politicians all participated in this overwrought and rather prominent argument and no clear consensus emerged. In the end, the law was not altered and the numbers of such infants remained both hidden and rather less than expected. However, the controversy over these 'children of rape' lasted well beyond 1915, for the trial of a young woman named Josephine Barthélemy for infanticide in 1917 evoked these issues when she claimed that she killed her child because it 'was born of a Boche' (Audoin-Rouzeau, 1995; Grayzel, 1999).

After the stories of abuse that were initially circulated in the first two years of the war, the German army gave fodder to further denunciation by deporting and imposing forced labour upon civilians, particularly young girls during Easter week 1916. At first, the occupiers had recruited women for a variety of domestic work, such as washing, cleaning and cooking. However, by 1915, village women had to work in the fields as well, and anyone who refused was punished. Exceptions were made for girls under the age 14 and women over 60 as well as the mothers of small children (McPhail, 1999). What changed in 1916 was the rounding up, almost indiscriminately, of young girls in the urban areas of Lille, Roubaix and Tourcoing. Depictions of this use of women and girls, emphasising the mixing of respectable middle-class ones with those of the lower classes, including prostitutes, confirmed Germany's depravity for the French public (Becker, 1996; Grayzel, 1999; McPhail, 1999) [*Doc. 11*].

Less controversially and dramatically, like other inhabitants of the occupied zones, women suffered from shortages of food. They further experienced the deprivations of material items that were requisitioned by German forces. Inhabitants lost their clothes, leather, copper, wood and wool among other items seized by the Germans. Living conditions worsened, with food and fuel shortages (Becker, 1996). Given the deprivations suffered by women in Germany, the justification for mistreatment of civilians in occupied territory stemmed in part from a desire to alleviate conditions at home lest women's agitation disrupt the German war effort.

France and Belgium were not the only nations occupied by the German army. The much less well-known case of Romania, a nation that only entered the war in 1916 and whose southern part was occupied by foreign troops, shows that similar economic hardships ensued for a civilian population that was predominantly female. Lack of food and fuel produced dismal conditions and even provoked protest by women (Bucur, 2000: 39). Ultimately, there was little French, and for that matter Belgian or Romanian, women living under occupation could do to ameliorate their living conditions. Yet, they could and did resist their occupying forces in actions ranging from the creation of networks to disseminate information, described earlier in Chapter 3, to feeding prisoners of war, to refusing to cooperate with German authorities.

IN THE ARMY: WOMEN'S MILITARY SERVICES

One reaction to the outbreak of war among those who felt themselves temperamentally unsuited for anything less than direct action was a desire to participate in as military a fashion as possible. In Britain, members of organisations such as the Women's Emergency Corps and Women's Voluntary Reserve began to wear khaki uniforms and practice drilling and parading, expressing their desire to defend the nation in case of invasion (Roberts, 1997). By 1915, such activities – greeted with a range of public responses from support to indignation – led to newspapers falsely reporting that a battalion of 'Amazon' suffragettes had landed in France, ready to help the Allied cause (*Le Figaro*, 25 February 1915; *Daily Mail*, 26 February 1915). Even in far-off Australia, a group of women who wanted to serve in the military created the Australian Women's Service Corps, which by January 1917 had 700 members who practised marching and drilling (Scates and Frances, 1997).

No regiment of British or Commonwealth women was established at this juncture, but a few individual British women nonetheless managed to serve in the armed forces. Dorothy Lawrence, an aspiring journalist, disguised herself as Private Denis Smith. She was able to spend ten days on the Western Front with the tunnelling company of the British Expeditionary Force before she confessed her true status to her superior officer. Treated as a possible spy while the British authorities decided what to do with her, she was eventually sent back to England where she published a postwar memoir of her activities. Especially in the early, more disorganised stages of the war, other women, such as Australian Louise Mack, were able to visit the trenches in male guise.

More visible and active military heroines emerged in the Eastern Front. Flora Sandes stands out as one of the more exceptional women to act as a combatant. Although she went off to Serbia at the age of 38 to serve as a nurse, she transformed herself into a full-fledged member of the Serbian army. As she already possessed the basic skills of being able to ride and shoot, as well as being a visible symbol of British support for Serbia, Serbian soldiers welcomed her into their ranks. With close-cropped hair and wearing the same uniform as the men, she became 'one of the boys'. She was wounded in 1916 and received a military medal for non-commissioned officers; by the time she was demobilised, she had reached the rank of captain (Wheelwright, 1989).

Another solitary female hero also emerged in the war's Eastern sector. Ecaterina Teodoroiu started the war by nursing the wounded in Romania, but after the deaths of her two soldier brothers, she herself volunteered for the army. She not only escaped after being taken prisoner, but died while taking part in an attack in September 1917. Unique in being the only woman allowed to fight alongside men in the Romanian army, Teodoroiu was commemorated after the war as a 'virgin heroine', compared to Joan of Arc, and raised up as a mythic, national figure (Bucur, 2000).

The most celebrated example of women soldiers during the First World War are the Russian Women's Battalions of Death. This official summoning of women soldiers was something that could probably only have existed in the chaos of the Russian war zone and in the aftermath of the February Revolution. Nevertheless, at the urging of Alexander Kerensky and with the support of the Provisional Government in 1917, Maria Bochkareva formed a battalion by calling upon women to protect Russia with their lives; this was one of several battalions that would emerge in the summer of 1917 but only one, consisting of about 300 women and led by Bochkareva, actually participated in the war. Others would form in Moscow and Petrograd; a report by Bernard Pares to the British War Office at the time suggests that these were meant to replace male conscript units whose troops were too demoralised to fight on (Abraham, 1992: 131).

The most famous of these battalions was that of Bochkareva, who like a few other exceptional Russian women, such as Marina Yurlova, had already fought in the war with a male unit. British nurse Florence Farmborough noted in her memoirs that she had treated several women soldiers in the regular Russian army (Abraham, 1992: 133). Now, however, in the confusion of a Russia transformed by revolutionary upheaval, Bochkareva personally felt that a women's battalion could not only serve the nation but also serve as an example to her countrymen (Bochkareva, 1919). Certainly, the battalion and Bochkareva herself attracted a good deal of mostly positive public attention outside Russia. When British feminist leader Emmeline Pankhurst visited Russia in June 1917, she insisted on meeting her and inspecting the troops (Abraham, 1992; Wheelwright, 1989). For outsiders such as American and British journalists who spent weeks observing the battalion, it offered potential evidence that women could fight and bridge this final gap between the sexes (Higonnet, 1999: 143–4, 156) [*Doc. 12*].

Bochkareva recruited women between the ages of 18 and 35, although the youngest established age was 17, and about 2,000 women responded to the initial call in late May. However, disagreements about military discipline and Bochkareva's style of command in particular greatly reduced this number. There were somewhere between 200–300 women in Bochkareva's battalion when it departed for the war zone in late June, presumably the same number who saw action in July near Smorgon. In this encounter, the battalion successfully helped to capture some German troops along the south-west front. Several accounts mention the bravery of the women involved. Yet the treatment of this group of women within Russia both during the war and in its aftermath suggests the ongoing ambiguity towards female combatants. The actions of Bochkareva and her battalions failed to inspire male soldiers, and in fact her regiment met with direct hostility and even assaults (Abraham, 1992).

At the time of the October Revolution, members of the battalion dispersed, in part because of threats to their lives. As will be discussed in

Chapter 6, members of the Petrograd battalion were among those making a last stand to defend the government at the Winter Palace during the final Bolshevik assault. Bochkareva herself fled to the United States and published her memoirs (Abraham, 1992).

The Russian Women's Battalion of Death and the exceptional circumstances of a woman such as Flora Sandes aside, many more women came to participate militarily in the war by doing everything short of serving as combatants. Only in Britain, however, did this labour receive the very public acknowledgment of its importance when, in 1917, the government created the Women's Army Auxiliary Corps (later Queen Mary's Army Auxiliary Corps), followed by the Women's Royal Naval Service and Women's Royal Air Force Service. These official organisations channelled the desire of women to participate directly in what they saw as the heart of the war effort by also offering competitive wages. All of these services, of course, had the explicit purpose of freeing men in auxiliary roles – such as clerks, cooks, drivers – for active combatant roles (Grayzel, 1999).

This formal British recognition was very important since it did not set a precedent for other countries, which continued to exclude women from the military. In France, the military was willing to employ some women in similar support roles. However, it explicitly defined these workers as 'civilians'. Such women filled positions ranging from cooks and typists to a tiny percentage of drivers. Still, the military remained hostile to their presence and terminated the services of women at the war's end (Darrow, 2000). Unlike the British case, where women had been successfully integrated into the armed forces, or the Russian case, which saw women mobilised as combatants, the French case was more typical in refusing to treat women's service to the army as being 'military' service.

The other women engaged in service under fire, discussed in Chapter 3 above, included ambulance drivers and others involved in treating the injured, such as nurses and doctors. Women ambulance drivers engaged in an activity that was closely related to the military service of men in that it, too, constantly exposed them to bombardments as well as air raids. Americans were among the many nationalities of women who joined motor corps and drove ambulances whose routes were often under direct fire. One such woman recalled driving a load of wounded men as 'shrapnel whizzed past my head and there was a tremendous crash close beside' (Schneider and Schneider, 1991: 101).

Among the great successes of postwar novels depicting women's experience in the battle zone is the story of a corps of British women serving as ambulance drivers. Published shortly after the appearance of Erich Maria Remarque's *All Quiet on the Western Front* (1930), *Not So Quiet: Stepdaughters of War* recounts the disillusioning horrors experienced by a group of British volunteer ambulance drivers. Based on the diaries of

Winifred Young, Evadne Price constructed a narrative that lays bare the noisy, filthy, disturbing nature of a war that did not keep women safe and sheltered. Over the course of the novel, the narrator recounts her increasing disillusionment and cynicism with all who continue to support the war from a safe distance, ignorant of what she has seen, heard, smelled and felt. What emerges clearly in this and other accounts is how little concern about protecting women and removing them from danger mattered, for these women were effectively militarised (Marcus, 1989) [*Doc. 13*].

THE EXPERIENCE OF BATTLE AT HOME

Women might find themselves under attack by entering war zones voluntarily or inadvertently or by living in territory attacked and seized by enemy troops. However, civilian populations, including large groups of women, found themselves under fire in their very homes. This transpired through terrifying older forms of aggression, seen in the rounding up and killing of huge numbers of Armenians living in the Ottoman Empire, and through some of the war's innovations, such as aerial bombardments targeting places far removed from the so-called front line. In all of these circumstances, women fully experienced what can only be understood as 'combat' at home.

Sometimes overshadowed by the carnage of the First World War itself, the war witnessed the twentieth century's first genocide, and its victims included women and children. The attacks against Armenians within the Ottoman Empire were not the first hostile actions these people had suffered. However, the Young Turk leaders of the wartime state seized the opportunity provided by the war to label its large Armenian population as now even more dangerous, an enemy within that had to be cleared from its territory or else 'turkified'. Between April and November 1915, the government systematically began to massacre its Armenian population. The atrocities here rival anything reported by Allied propagandists about those occurring in Belgium (Miller and Miller, 1993; Sarafian, 1998).

As was the case with attacks against civilians in Belgium and France, an effort was made to establish the veracity of the reports, resulting in publications in both Britain and France (Higonnet, 1999: 167–71; Sarafian, 1998). One striking feature of accounts of the Ottoman attacks on its Armenian minority is that they exhibit the same sexual overtones as those found in the 'rape of Belgium'. The events were seen as emasculating Armenian men, who could not defend their women and children and who were themselves slaughtered. Defenceless women and girls experienced rape, abuse, servitude – including enforced prostitution – and, in many cases, death (Melman, 1998).

First-hand accounts by survivors reveal women's efforts to resist and, in many cases, their inability to do so. Testimony speaks of the murder of children, of rape and other attacks on women. Most men had already been removed from their communities and absorbed into the army, where they were systematically segregated into special non-combatant units and killed before the wholesale destruction of civilian communities. In late April 1915, male community, intellectual and religious leaders were summarily executed; women and children thus comprised the bulk of those deported from their homes.

These deportations subjected women and their families to horrific conditions, under which many of them died – through assaults, starvation and illness, abandonment, and even suicide. In testimony delivered after the war and in oral histories recorded with survivors, women provide accounts that both emphasise their victimisation and reveal some of the most difficult wartime situations faced anywhere. Several mothers describe watching their children die or being forced to abandon them. Others recount the abduction of daughters, not all of whom returned and some of whom returned having been raped. Still others tell of women making conscious choices to take poison or drown themselves in the Euphrates River rather than continue the long deportation marches (Higonnet, 1999: 167–71, 280–1; Miller and Miller, 1993). Unquestionably, these conditions mark an erasure of many rules of engagement, ignoring not only the protected status of civilians but also the national identity of an ethnic minority.

Women such as Flora Sandes and the members of the Russian Women's Battalions of Death experienced combat first-hand by choice. For them, the distinctions between male combatant and female non-combatant disappeared, and their appearance in military uniform and cropped hair visibly marked their assumption of this ultimate masculine role. Other women found themselves quite literally under fire without losing their non-combatant status, yet at the same time displaying heroism as they and their homes became the targets of old and new instruments of modern war.

First launched by Germany, raids by ships and submarines, and most notably by zeppelins and then aeroplanes upon Britain, forcibly brought the war 'home'. At first, these attacks, such as the naval bombing of coastal Scarborough, were treated as atrocities. Official propaganda emphasised the extent to which such raids made civilians true casualties of war and, as we saw in Chapter 2, the British government's Parliamentary Recruiting Committee lost no time in issuing a poster that defined German brutality – the Germans had shown their true nature 'by murdering defenceless women and children at SCARBOROUGH' (IWM). Visual and verbal propaganda described the child victims of these bombs in much the same lurid way that Belgian women had been portrayed, as desperate and innocent victims. Across the Channel, one young victim of a German bomb, Parisian Denise Cartier, received widespread recognition as a 'heroine' of the war, particularly after the amputation of her limb (Thébaud, 1986: 78).

As the damage caused by aerial warfare increased, propaganda images began to suggest its singular, unnerving nature. Demonstrating how close the 'battle lines' had come and visualising the threat to homes, women and children were designed to encourage enlistment. Most importantly, however, the air raids raised the spectre that no place was safe. If everyone, including women and children, was now endangered, so it was now possible for everyone to display the kind of idealised heroism that was understood to be the domain of soldiers. French women suffering from the occupation were largely portrayed as helpless victims of rapacious Germans. However, in both France and Britain, the air raid was seen as producing a new kind of civic virtue: women could suddenly demonstrate the 'calm heroism' of soldiers under attack. For instance, newspaper accounts of reactions to the air raids of October 1916 in Britain stress that their 'most extraordinary feature' was 'the calm with which they were faced by ... women and children' (Grayzel, 1999: 46). In describing the responses of Parisian women to air raids in February 1918 to the readers of *La Française*, Alice Berthet suggested that they showed themselves 'to be the dignified emulators of "those at the front"' (*La Française*, 9 February 1918) [*Doc. 14*].

Most of the damage in wartime raids was sustained by civilians. In the more frightening cases, attacks hit areas that were seen as immune from the war, such as London. Air warfare, in these instances, directly attacked not only property, in particular the nation's homes, but also the lives of the nation's families. Few inhabitants of London who wrote about the war excluded these often terrifying events. Writing in her diary in October 1915, Vera Brittain notes that there 'was another very bad Zeppelin raid on London & district on Wednesday night. About 50 people were killed' (Brittain, 1981: 288–9).

As German aerial attacks shifted from zeppelins to aeroplanes, they also shifted temporarily in 1917 from night to day. The daylight raids of 1917 on Greater London caused memorable and vivid damage. In one of the worst attacks, on 13 June around noon, bombs dropped from German planes hit the infants' classroom at the North Street School in Poplar, killing 16 and injuring 30. This was one of the most disturbing raids of the war because of the age of the victims, most of whom were under six years and, understandably, it had a profound affect on their families as well. While struggling to figure out how to cope with this new method of warfare, governments had also to encourage the maintenance of civilian morale by urging stoicism. This proved harder to do when the coffins were so small.

The extent to which civilian women as victims of air raids were seen as casualties of war emerges in the related development of something known as 'air raid shock'. The 'new' phenomenon of shell shock documented for men in the battle zone was now applied to civilian women, who suffered the after-effects of raids in nervous exhaustion and disturbing behaviour (Tate, 1998). Air raid shock was used, for instance, to explain an infanticide case in London (Grayzel, 1999). If the creation of air warfare waged against civilian targets changed the nature of warfare itself, it hearkened back in some ways to older notions of war without boundaries yet now with deadly new and wide-ranging technology.

In other places less commonly associated with civilians, air raids hit 'innocent' targets near to the combat zone, contributing to the numbers of women, such as nurses, ambulance drivers, WAACs and others, killed in the line of duty. Numerous memoirs and first-hand accounts by women who served near the battlefields of France contain descriptions of being under attack, watching aeroplanes, and of women support personnel injured or killed as a result of these raids. Australian nurse Hilda Loxton described her hospital being 'levelled by the Hun Machine that came over' in May 1916, leaving in its wake an injured nurse (Scates and Frances, 1997: 26). On the evening of her arrival in Paris, Cordelia Dupuis, a telephone operator with the United States' Army Signal Corps, recorded that the building next door to her hotel was destroyed in an air raid. At first, she noted, 'we didn't know enough to be frightened ... [b]ut we were plenty scared the next day when we saw that huge hole next to our hotel' (Gavin, 1997: 81).

Some of the raids that received the most publicity involving the deaths of servicewomen included the killing of nine WAACs near a hospital in Abbeville and of several nurses in attacks near Etaples in late May 1918. These deaths had an effect on other nurses, as can be seen in the diary of Canadian nurse Clare Gass, who regularly recorded the sighting of aeroplanes or the occurrence of air raids. On 21 May 1918, she noted a 'dreadful air raid at Etaples Sunday night, 1,000 casualties rumoured, 4 of whom are sisters' (Mann, 2000: 196, punctuation added). As *The Times* of London reported of the WAACs, the incident 'makes them one in sympathy and sacrifice with the fighting forces' (*The Times*, quoted in Shaw, 1996: 369). The attack also made these women the first British women in the military to die on active service.

Whether in military uniform or not, substantial numbers of women suffered directly from the war. Attacks on civilian populations – whether by occupying or, in the Armenian case, presumably indigenous troops, or by aerial warfare – decisively altered the lives of those women who experienced them. It killed some of them, wounded others, and forever removed the sense that any place in total war was safe. Perhaps, most substantively, it helped erase the line between 'war front' and 'home front'. It should not then surprise us that women protested vigorously against the war, or that this line was further eroded in the revolutionary upheavals that beset parts of Europe in some respects as a result of this war. Nor is it surprising that the behaviour of women 'at home' was deemed so vital to the successful outcome of the war. The following chapters will show us how the war became a defence of traditional gender arrangements that brought women under increasing scrutiny for a variety of behaviours ranging from 'loose morals' to overt political opposition to the war and to demanding revolutionary change.

CHAPTER FIVE

MORALE, MORALITY AND SEXUALITY

LOOSENING THE DOUBLE STANDARD?: MORALE AND MORALITY AT HOME

As men and, as a consequence, male heads of households enlisted or were called up, a generalised public anxiety swelled about what would become of their homes and families. In part because the war was justified as a defence of women and children, and thus implicitly of traditional gender roles, there was a good deal of concern about how wartime circumstances might alter these. Thus in various nations, debates in public media and even in some legislatures focused on the behaviour of women. Journalists, social reformers and politicians began to wonder aloud how to guarantee that women would not fall to pieces in the absence of their men because of the war's mass mobilisation. As the war dragged on, then, the alleged actions of loose women and dissolute mothers and the social problems, such as an allegedly inevitable increase in illegitimate children, that would follow became heated topics. Other visible changes, such as women entering factories and other public domains, led to surveillance and legislation.

All of this public attention linked moral behaviour with the maintenance of the morale not only of men in the military but also of civilians at home, who had become, in the context of total war, vital to the outcome. Such attention also reflected fears of degeneracy stemming back to the late nineteenth century that re-emerged with the wartime crisis. We can see the significance of this in the portrayal of the Germans as degenerate, bloodthirsty and rapacious Huns. However, the behaviour of the entire population of belligerent nations was scrutinised during the war, because it became part of the war effort to preserve an idealised society that was worth dying for and to maintain the virility and success of the competing armies.

As we saw in Chapter 2, not only was the enemy portrayed as especially degenerate, but women of the nation were called upon to be the embodiment of perfect, traditional morality as they sent their men off to fight. Whether or not the war actually changed women's behaviour, as some seemed to think, or whether some of the changes observed were already well set in motion by the previous activities of the 'new woman', the mobilisation of women in volunteer and waged work served as a catalyst in many places. For instance, it increased the presence of unchaperoned middle-class and upper-class women in more and more public spaces. By the end of the war, commentators could remark upon what they perceived as dramatic changes in women's appearance, such as wearing shorter skirts and shorter hair, and social behaviour, such as drinking alcohol and smoking cigarettes publicly.

At the same time, popular wartime media offered an ambivalent message about women and sex. Sexuality, particularly in the form of alluring women, was also used to 'sell' the war. French postcards depicted women as the rewards for jobs well done; French song lyrics equated valour on the field with valour in the bedroom while those in Britain promised to 'make men' of those who enlisted (Huss, 1988; Sweeney, 2001; Wilson, 1986). As was shown in Chapter 2, some of the imagery in propaganda posters sought to entice men into joining up by portraying barely-clad, extremely feminine and presumably readily available women. While the majority of civic-minded voices might condemn some of this, women such as Britain's Marie Stopes also defended some controversial choices. In Stopes's 1918 play, *The Race*, the heroine seduces her soldier fiancé before he leaves Britain and when he dies before they can marry, she rejoices in her subsequent pregnancy, declaring that by doing so 'my body serves my country' (Grayzel, 1997b: 135).

The image of emboldened women taking up male 'vices' abounds in wartime popular culture – in cartoons, fiction and the news media – and could carry different meanings, from being serious signs of moral decay to simply nothing to worry about. There was no firm consensus that such activities should even be attributed solely to the war. By the end of 1916, articles in Britain's *Daily Express* were asking if 'War Times Loosen Manners and Morals?', referring specifically to the use of 'strong language' by women, while the following year Max Pemberton was addressing the question 'Are Women Losing Men's Respect?' in *Pearson's Weekly* (*Daily Express*, 5 December 1916; *Pearson's Weekly*, 29 September 1917). In these and other accounts by journalists, a palpable transformation had occurred in women's manners, their use of vulgarity, appearance in shorter skirts or male attire or make up, and their adoption of habits like smoking. What varied was whether these changes were entirely due to the war and, if so, whether peacetime would end them.

One additional exchange of views on this subject in Britain may illuminate this further. In August 1917, Dr James Burnet wrote an article on women war workers in which he denounced their moral and sexual behaviour. He noted that women now regularly smoked and drank in public, calling these 'marked signs of deterioration' clearly linked to sexual promiscuity. In response, novelist May Sinclair declared that smoking and drinking were 'flourishing pretty vigorously in pre-war days' (*Medical Press and Circular*, 22 August and 5 September 1917).

At roughly the same time, social commentators elsewhere were noting wartime changes such as the loosening of family ties that helped ensure morality, and the resulting spread of vice. The Humanitarian Society of Milan, in a survey of wartime behaviour, found that '23 per cent of women and 27 per cent of boys took to drinking' and that 'nicotinism' was similarly and perniciously on the rise among the city's youth (Tomassini, 1996: 587). Drinking and smoking were perceived as dangers in themselves but doubly so as they became linked to immorality and sex.

In many nations anecdotal evidence of increased alcohol consumption led to one of the most concrete legislative changes affecting women during the war and can be seen in efforts to control their access to alcohol. This was already evident in the allegations, discussed in Chapter 2, that in Britain soldiers' wives were spending their separation allowances on alcohol and the indignant responses to these. Yet the fear that women would drown their anxieties and sorrows in wine and spirits existed across participant states.

One response to this came in attempts to curtail general access to places where alcohol was served. In Britain, wartime regulations shortened licensing hours, cutting them down to five and a half hours per day and diluting the strength of alcoholic beverages. Yet women were not treated as special cases and, for a variety of reasons, more and more women began to make use of public houses during the war. It soon became clear that these women included more members of the middle class and respectable working class than previously. This did not mean that women drank more or abused alcohol, but that their consumption was more visible, provoking comment (Gutzke, 1994).

The efforts to combat the misuse of alcohol came from women as well. Throughout 1915–18, the pages of the French feminist journals *L'Action Féminine* and *La Française* regularly addressed their wartime 'war against alcohol'. While the primary focus of this 'war' was on men rendered unfit by alcoholism either to serve the nation or to maintain their families, women as mothers also received some attention. The Academy of Medicine warned in 1915 that alcoholism in this case affected not just the individual but 'the race' (*Bulletin de l'Académie de Médecine*, 23 February 1915). The French government seemed more concerned with drunkenness leading to sexual encounters that might infect military men with venereal disease, and in October 1917 promulgated a law barring prostitutes from all establishments where the consumption of alcohol might occur, thereby nationalising what had been a policy only in certain areas (Corbin, 1990: 335).

The problem of women and alcohol might extend across the social and generational spectrum, but commentators in Britain were especially concerned with the behaviour of young women and girls. Unwilling to abide by the rules of conventional morality, such women were seen as suffering from 'khaki fever', because they were aggressively seeking out soldiers and even initiating sexual contact with them (Woollacott, 1994a). This was one reason that the women police, discussed in Chapter 3, were created, so as to safeguard both the soldiers and the women.

Perhaps the most salacious wartime scandal in Britain involved accusations not just of disorderly or aggressive women but also of what contemporaries deemed sexual perversity. The Pemberton Billing scandal coincided with the German campaign of 1918 and began when Member of Parliament Noel Pemberton Billing accused the dancer Maud Allen, who was performing a private staging of Oscar Wilde's *Salomé*, of perversion, implying lesbianism, in print. Allen responded with a libel suit. When the case reached the court, Pemberton Billing reiterated his accusations against Allen and others who were undermining Britain by promoting decadence in the form of homosexuality (Hynes, 1992). He was acquitted, but the entire court case became a widely-publicised scandal, linking sexual deviance to treason. The dynamics of this case not only reveal a new frankness about discussing 'perversity' in public, but also how strongly sexual morality and morale were linked during the war (Haste, 1992).

'WAR BABIES': ILLEGITIMACY AND SEXUALITY

War could thus be seen as overthrowing conventional morals and encouraging women to become more sexually promiscuous. One of the ways in which wartime commentators and sometimes their governments tried to secure the 'home front' was by paying close attention to illegitimacy rates. While the major European participant nations, such as France, Germany and Britain, were deeply interested in population growth, they were also anxious about a presumed increase in illegitimate births as a result of the war, both because of the overtones of illicit sex and because of the higher rates of mortality that did little to repopulate the nation.

A more detailed examination of the statistics concerning illegitimacy reveals a complicated picture. Take Great Britain, for instance, where rates varied considerably. Ireland remained consistent with about 3 per cent of all births occurring out of wedlock throughout the war, although since the overall number of births fell from 1914 to 1918 (as it did throughout Europe), the actual number of illegitimate births in 1918 was about 200 fewer than in 1914. Scotland's number of illegitimate births also remained fairly constant, fluctuating between 7 and 8 per cent and actually declining in 1915. In England and Wales, the total of illegitimate births rose to 8.3 per cent of all births in 1917, at its height, nearly doubling the 1914 rate of 4.2 per cent, but it was back down to 6.3 per cent the following year and soon hovered around the prewar standards of between 4 and 5 per cent of all births. What is striking is that while the number of births went down by nearly 200,000 between 1914 and 1917, the actual number of illegitimate births was higher in 1917 by about 20,000 (Mitchell, 1962: 30–3).

In Britain, this concern about women's sexuality and moral contributions to the war culminated in the crisis of the 'war babies'. 'War babies' were the offspring, suspected to exist in huge numbers, born to unmarried women impregnated by men who had joined the military. This was the consequence, it was felt, of young girls so swept up in patriotic fervour as to offer themselves to any man in uniform. Yet, as was indicated above, the illegitimacy rate remained stable for 1915, only increasing in 1917. Furthermore, illegitimate infants continued to be born into well-established households where the parents, for a variety of reasons, remained unmarried, in essence being common law spouses. But the war baby scandal was not about facts or even about illegitimacy, at least at the outset. It was about how to control women's sexuality in order to preserve the 'home life' that every British soldier or sailor was defending.

One reason for this interest in unwed mothers came from the government decision to grant separation allowances to some women not legally married to servicemen, as long as these women and their children could prove that the man in question had made a home for them. The assumption that these children were the offspring of soldiers meant that they were thus able to make significant and potent demands for charity and for state support. War babies therefore received their protected status through their paternity and their problematic nature through their maternity.

One could simply attribute this to a double-standard that viewed women's sexual behaviour outside marriage more harshly. However, the raised moral stakes induced by the war were also at issue. Wartime commentators both highlighted the vital role of British mothers and warned of the social upheaval and moral decay that could ensue from women's promiscuous interaction with military men (Grayzel, 1997b).

The war baby scandal did not last long past the first year of the war, but debates over the effect of the war on moral standards and sexual behaviour would endure throughout the war, and in almost every participant nation. One way in which France sought to ameliorate its illegitimacy rate in 1915 was by allowing soldiers to marry by proxy, provided they could prove a previous sustained commitment to the mother. Eventually, the government approved legislation that permitted the legitimising of the children of mobilised soldiers even after their death in battle (Grayzel, 1999). Despite this effort, and perhaps unsurprisingly, the number of illegitimate infants recognised by their fathers at birth fell from 15.9 per cent in 1914 to 9.9 per cent in 1915 and 1917 (Huber, 1931: 251) [*Docs. 15 and 16*].

The German birth rate showed similar overall declines, as the general fertility rate fell from 107.5 in 1914 to 53.0 in 1917, with the number of births declining from 1,874,389 to 939,938. Of these, the majority were legitimate, and as a percentage of all births, the number of illegitimate births barely fluctuated during the war (Daniel, 1997: 136). While those illegitimate children of servicemen killed in action were able to receive a pension, this did not mean that attitudes towards sexuality and perceptions of immorality had altered (Sauerteig, 1998: 169).

WOMEN AS 'SUSPECT'

The entire civilian population of states involved in total war was suspect but in Germany as elsewhere women, especially war wives, received special scrutiny. Misbehaviour on their part had the potential not only to spread disease but also to threaten the morale of both soldier and civilian. Authorities were especially appalled by women who had relationships with prisoners of war, as many such men ended up employed in agriculture or industry, thereby coming into contact with civilian women engaged in similar occupations (Daniel, 1997). Any woman viewed as having excessive contact with prisoners could be attacked both through legal measures and public sanction, such as printing her name in the newspaper. As an example, in Leipzig, twenty-five women were fined and jailed for this offence in the first quarter of 1917 (Sauerteig, 1998: 170).

Accusations of immorality against an enemy nation also appeared as another way to promote national honour. In 1916, rumours of alleged German proposals to promote bigamy or polygamy in response to the war's death tolls and that some in France were considering similar ideas provoked a horrified reaction. Editor Jane Misme, writing in the French women's newspaper *La Française* in January, denounced any proposals advocating polygamy as a response to the loss of men because it would indicate 'a singular overthrow of the moral sense' (*La Française*, 23 January 1916).

In the meantime, fears of mixing between men and women in wartime factories led French employers to try to separate women from men in the workplace whenever they could (Downs, 1995: 57). In addition, the mass media's treatment of the female factory worker in both France and Britain ranged from praising her vital contributions to the war effort to denouncing her morals and her frivolity in spending her newly-earned higher pay (Braybon, 1981; Woollacott, 1994b) [*Doc. 6*].

One unique problem for women came from the fact that their nationality changed upon marriage. What then should be done with the wives of men now identified as the 'enemy'? Were German-born women married to French or British men now suspect? In a war-torn world where everyone's contribution suddenly mattered, what could and should be done about this? This dilemma posed a far more difficult problem than that of 'the spying German governess', around whom rumours swelled early in the war. The reaction, in particular, to indigenous women married to foreigners makes most sense if put in the context of fears of women as a threat to morale. Although, in these cases, the relationship between men and women was sanctioned by law, it still represented a personal (and sexual) tie that could potentially threaten the nation at war.

An article in the London *Times* in March 1915 noted the reaction that laws concerning women's nationality in relation to marriage had provoked after the passage of the Aliens Restrictions Act, which among its repercussions included the internment of military-age male Germans and Austrians. It noted that this had proved particularly hard for widows of foreign husbands, still classified as 'aliens', as it had for the wives and families of German men living in Britain. Part of the purpose of the article was to publicise that a British-born widow could 'obtain a certificate of re-admission to British nationality after [her husband's] death' (*The Times*, 26 March 1915). Perhaps it would also serve as a warning to British women contemplating marriage to unnaturalised foreigners. That British-born women married to foreigners were subject to legal action while German and Austrian-born women married to British men were not became an issue for feminists who were upset at the inherent injustice. Such practices merely acknowledged, however, that under British law, husbands were responsible for their wives' actions, which in itself was a source of feminist protest.

The harshest official reaction to the presence of enemy foreigners can be found in the internment of aliens. In Britain, prior to this measure being enacted, all resident aliens had to register with the police. Other measures of the Aliens Restriction Act of 1914 included selectively arresting and imprisoning German and Austrian men and encouraging women, children and men not of military age to leave Britain for their native lands. This situation changed with the sinking of the *Lusitania* in May 1915 and the resulting anti-German sentiment. At this point such alien women and children were subject to repatriation unless they received exemptions (Cesarini, 1992).

In Australia, some 6,000 people of suspect origin (mostly of German descent and Germans of military age) were put in camps for the duration of the war. These included a few women and members of 'German' families evacuated from British colonies in nearby parts of Asia and the Pacific, such as Fiji (Scates and Frances, 1997). Such internments also occurred in New Zealand (Pugsley et al., 1996). Once interned, according to first-hand accounts, these women and their families faced abysmal conditions. Outside camps, women and children of German ancestry or birth found themselves harassed and suffered from financial hardship as a result of their male breadwinners' internment (Scates and Frances, 1997). In New

Zealand, a Women's Anti-German League was founded in 1916 to lobby for strong anti-German measures (Pugsley et al., 1996: 100).

Popular fiction made use of the inherent drama in the conflict facing women either engaged to or married to men of a newly 'dangerous' nationality. Mary Floran's *L'Ennemi*, discussed in Chapter 2 above, shows how German men remain 'brutes' at core, despite a veneer of civilisation.

Perhaps as frightening as women aligned with enemy men were women whose alliances with men of their own countries spread disease. The sexual behaviour of women came under increased surveillance as fears of the spread of venereal diseases and their undermining of military fitness rose.

PROSTITUTION, REGULATION AND 'THE HIDDEN SCOURGE'

In addition to fears of increased illegitimacy and the breakdown of marriage and sexual conventions, wartime prostitution also became an issue of concern across Europe. This occurred in part because of the seemingly new vulnerability of young women deprived of male protection and because of a desire to preserve the strength of the fighting forces by preventing the spread of sexually-transmitted diseases. Overall, the numbers of 'registered' prostitutes – those in official brothels who were known to the police and subject to regular medical examinations – declined across Europe. However, this did not mean an end to illicit sex or the desire to contain it, and intense public debates about prostitution also reflected divergences in strategies to contain it. Governments essentially had developed two main ways to respond to such dangers: regulating prostitution or trying to suppress it altogether.

Countries like France permitted the establishment of 'tolerated houses' or brothels and registered their workers, and the number of such houses increased during the war. The French government also made other serious efforts to prevent the spread of disease by asking the Academy of Medicine to issue a set of guidelines meant to advise military personnel about what they could do to avoid venereal disease. This had mixed results. In some districts of Paris, prostitution seemed to be diminishing. One police report offered the following explanation for this decline: 'It's necessary to admit evidently that it's because the men are absent. But it's also quite necessary to admit that prostitution can no longer recruit among women when work, at a high salary, is assured' (*Report on the Parisian Population*, 9 September 1918, Archives of the Prefecture of Police, Paris). Of course, some women were viewed as victimised by the war, such as those who turned to prostitution to feed their families. Yet, rather than addressing such economic factors for increased or decreased prostitution throughout the war, the government continued to support regulated houses of prostitution. This did little, as public health officials complained, to prevent the spread of diseases by refugees, married women committing adultery while their husbands were away, and other 'unregulated' women, including female factory workers experiencing 'new' freedoms (Grayzel, 1999). Those most directly concerned with the spread of venereal diseases, including physicians who treated them, warned that the most dangerous carriers of disease were not prostitutes but unregulated women.

Each British soldier who joined 'Kitchener's Army' went off to war with an excerpt from their leader's speech in his pay packet envelope warning soldiers abroad that they would find 'temptation in both wine and women', and needed to 'entirely resist both' by 'treating all women with perfect courtesy' and avoiding 'intimacy' (IWM). Soldiers in France were subject to lectures on the dangers 'in a kiss' (Grayzel, 1999: 143). Here, the vulnerability of troops was linked not to the typical weapons of war but to insidious microbes transmitted through casual sexual encounters. Venereal diseases could, governments feared, debilitate the fighting forces and thus had to be prevented.

A variety of responses emerged to this problem. And while soldiers might be warned against loose women and the dangers of 'forgetting' themselves, the main objects of disciplinary action remained the women themselves, typically prostitutes, but also so-called 'amateur girls' (as the phrase went in Britain) who were ready to engage in sexual encounters with any man in uniform. The transmission of disease to soldiers on leave remained an issue. Lectures did little to combat the effects; troops, like those of New Zealand, with one of the highest rates of venereal diseases of British imperial forces, ended up receiving free prophylactics from their government (Pugsley et al., 1996: 140). Other aspects of this 'battle' were waged in the court of public opinion. British, Commonwealth and American journalists reported on the dangerous temptations that illicit women and establishments might pose for their 'innocent' troops and called upon military leaders to ensure that access was restricted.

French 'maisons tolérées' received perhaps even more attention across the Channel, where the idea that British soldiers serving in France might use these official brothels caused substantial concern. The Association for Moral and Social Hygiene (AMSH) spearheaded the attack after debates in Parliament in February 1918 about whether regulated brothels would be placed off-limits to British troops. The existence of brothels near training camps, transportation centres, and capital cities, as well as in the war zone, with the presumption that all soldiers had access to them, was itself a cause for tension among Allied governments.

Colonial, Commonwealth and eventually American leaders demanded that Britain keep their soldiers safe by removing temptations from their innocent men (Buckley, 1977). The Bishop of London launched a 'Cleansing London' campaign in 1916 as part of an effort to 'purge the heart of the

Empire before the boys come back' by eliminating the misbehaviour of women (*Cleansing London*, 1916: 25). Two years later, the problems were once again lamented in newspaper stories that invoked 'the scandal of the streets' (Grayzel, 1999).

The British government tried to appease concerns by using the Defence of the Realm Act, a series of regulations that curbed many civil liberties in order to sustain the war effort and safeguard the fighting forces. It first began in 1916 with Regulation 13A. This measure gave military authorities the power to expel prostitutes from specific areas. However, it failed to consider what all concerned had decided was the greater problem of 'amateur girls'. In response to increasing internal pressure in March 1918, the government took its strongest stand after the failures of earlier measures like Regulations 13A or 35C by issuing yet another Defence of the Realm Regulation, 40D. Regulation 40D forbade women with a venereal disease from soliciting or having sexual relations with soldiers. If charged under this regulation, a woman could be taken into custody for at least a week and be subjected to any medical examination that would determine if she was suffering from venereal disease. Only by vigorously enforcing this and taking equally strong stands against all diseased women would, as a Canadian official put it, 'clean young men who come to give their lives for their country' be safe (Buckley, 1977: 78) [*Doc. 17*].

In practice, women arrested under this measure had to undergo medical examinations and if they were found to have a venereal disease, were subject to imprisonment and fines as well as treatment. By October 1918, there had been 203 prosecutions for violations of Regulation 40D with 101 convictions (Buckley, 1977: 84). Being ignorant of their disease status was no defence for the women in question, nor did it matter if they had been falsely accused. Unsurprisingly, the punitive measures invoked by Regulation 40D and the lack of safeguards provoked a strong feminist reaction (Davidson, 2000; Grayzel, 1999).

Most women's suffrage organisations objected to the discrimination inherent in the wording and enforcement of Regulation 40D; some would not have objected to penalties being enacted for both men and women who spread the diseases. Some took the line that the new regulation mirrored the Contagious Diseases Acts of 1864 that had already been proved a failure and withdrawn. In this instance, social purity activists and feminists made common cause in loud and public protests. These had little immediate impact as the Regulation was not discarded until the war's end.

Concern about the infection of Allied soldiers was not restricted to British officials and extended to the Commonwealth as well. For Australian men mobilised far from home, reports of their interactions with prostitutes in places like Cairo, which helped spread venereal diseases, were widespread. New Zealand soldiers' furloughs in Paris and London undoubtedly included sexual encounters that gave this army among the highest rates of infection with veneral diseases of all those serving the British Empire (Pugsley et al., 1996: 140). By 1916, one Australian government minister was fearful that unless controls were imposed, 'Cairo will do infinitely more harm to Australia than all the Turks will do in Gallipoli' (Scates and Frances, 1997: 124). Back home in Australia, there was concern that the behaviour of men either going to or returning from overseas postings would further spread immorality, and ultimately disease. Thus new regulations emerged in various states, including the arrest and imprisonment of girls and women thought to be infecting soldiers, and some women's groups advocated raising the age of consent for women to 21, reflecting a mistrust of 'flapper' girls (Scates and Frances, 1997; Shute, 1995).

In Germany, wartime military authorities tried both to regulate the behaviour of prostitutes and to prevent the spread of disease by women. Any member of the military found to have a venereal disease was required to reveal the identity of any woman who might have transmitted the disease. Any woman accused of having sex with several men within a month – regardless of whether she accepted payment for this – could find herself a 'registered' prostitute after two warnings (Usborne, 1988: 392). Here as elsewhere, the blame and punishment fell upon women rather than men. German commentators perceived that illicit sexuality was on the rise, not from professional prostitutes but so-called 'secret' or 'wild' ones. The number of women arrested for this and found to have venereal diseases increased in major urban centres throughout the war (Daniel, 1997: 139, 142). In addition, as a preventative measure, the Prussian military closed bars with hostesses in Berlin, and military physicians became responsible for examining prostitutes and certifying that they were free of disease (Sauerteig, 1998).

One reason that these measures may have been less than effective was that the main clientele of prostitutes had moved on, and Belgium found itself the seat of wartime prostitution for German troops on the Western Front. The response of the military to this situation was to stress moral education and provide men with prophylactics. This was met with indignation by many sectors of the public who felt that the military was thus encouraging adultery, and it appeared to do little to stem the spread of venereal diseases (Daniel, 1997). Along the Eastern Front, German occupation was feared to be producing a steady moral decline among the region's Jewish population, as local commentators noted the rise of prostitution (Roshwald, 1999: 103–4).

In addition, German popular culture treated as perhaps inevitable relations between women in occupied territories and soldiers. As one song put it:

Mad'moiselle! Oh, Mad'moiselle!
I'll annex you, if you please
We're in Belgium, after all
Where such things are done with ease.   (quoted in Jelavich, 1999: 34)

It is hardly surprising that attitudes towards the relationships that did form between occupying forces and occupied women diverged widely depending on both gender and national perspective.

Russia, as elsewhere, saw a decrease in the numbers of official prostitutes. Brothels remained under police control and street prostitution was severely punished, but a large proportion of the male clientele was now unavailable. Even so, court records reveal that if professional prostitution declined, many women and teenagers became part-time prostitutes in order to support themselves or their families (Bordiugov, 1996: 551).

Although a late-comer to the war, many Americans, and especially American progressives, felt a particular responsibility to ensure the moral safety of their troops. Strict rules governed the behaviour of soldiers in training camps and then overseas, although, what soldiers actually did is another story. None too subtle messages to the troops reinforced this. Posters on the walls of training camps urged the soldier to think of the folks at home and, by staying 'morally clean', not to ruin his life. Messages to women urged them to remain pure and thus to keep men so. The state took measures to try to ensure this, creating alternative recreation and useful work for 'girls' to keep them away from soldiers and their camps. The army was also empowered to create 'moral zones' around training camps where vice, especially prostitution, was to be eradicated. Reformers in America, like those in Britain and elsewhere, also faced the problem of girls who 'lost their heads' at the sight of men in uniform. Such women, as well as those 'hardened' prostitutes who might harm soldiers, increasingly met with repression – commitment to reformatories for women, lest they infect and corrupt soldiers. If women were imprisoned, these men usually escaped with fines (Bristow, 1996: 920).

The problem of what to do about interactions between European women and American troops was seen as even more of a problem when it came to African American troops. For these men experienced a double-standard not only of sex but of race. Although both black and white American men were subject to the same draft, they joined a racially-segregated army. Thus, recreation facilities and programmes for black troops also remained separate and unequal. The government further placed more severe restrictions on their behaviour and that of the women with whom they interacted than they did on white troops and white women. Government officials assumed that immorality was more prevalent and harder to control in the African American community thereby making such distinctions necessary (Bristow, 1996).

Once African American troops went to France, the government continued to police interactions between black soldiers and the French population, especially women. An August 1918 document entitled 'Secret Information Concerning Black Troops' was circulated by the army and explicitly condemned contact between these troops and French women, a sentiment that was publicly denounced by the French government. In addition to the government's response, individual French men and women praised these soldiers and interacted easily with them (Stovall, 1996: 14–18).

Thus racial bias complicated government policy towards interactions between troops and women not just in segregated America but also in Europe. Despite French rejection of some of the more overt biases of the American army, the government kept close watch on its own colonial troops and workers. For in addition to acting as combatants, colonial military reserves provided labour for wartime factories. These men were still subject to military discipline and housed in barracks, and their inter-actions with the rest of the workforce, especially with French women, were carefully controlled (Downs, 1995). Having workers from Africa and Asia in factories alongside French women resulted in liaisons that were particularly unsettling as they raised fears of both sexual relations and of a resulting diminished regard for white women and thus French superiority overall (Stovall, 1998: 747). One response was to try to isolate non-white troops.

Race became a factor in how French authorities deployed military discipline. Many of the same racist stereotypes about non-white troops, whatever their role, can be seen in European militaries' treatment of their colonial soldiers as they became a presence in Europe. This was especially the case in France, which made extensive use of colonised indigenous soldiers, and its government was determined to police the relations between non-European troops and European, that is to say white, women. This explicit interest in controlling their behaviour extended well beyond the concern about the spread of disease that became so important when applied to white troops. France used over 140,000 West African troops, predominantly from Senegal, as combatants. Such troops inspired both admiration for their alleged warrior instincts and fear that these same 'savage' qualities made them a potential sexual and moral threat to French civilians. Thus, officials adopted a dual strategy: the rehabilitation of the image of Africans, notably the Senegalese, in popular media and the restriction of their movement within France. Wartime media stressed the loyalty of such troops, repeatedly calling them 'great children' devoted to France as a motherland (Lunn, 1999).

While cultivating a more sympathetic image of African troops, government officials also severely limited the contact between *tirailleurs* and French civilians by placing these troops in 'isolated' camps where leave was minimal and soldiers could only enter local towns for a few hours a week. Nor did concern about interaction between African soldiers and French women abate when the men were wounded; there was a not entirely successful effort to provide separate hospitals for Senegalese troops and to remove female nurses from them. Of primary significance for the government was restricting contact between women of 'good' character or standing while making brothels accessible to all troops (Lunn, 1999). The official line might have been acceptance but surveillance. The writings by and for French soldiers in trench newspapers are more ambivalent. In these texts, black colonial soldiers were depicted as especially alluring for French women, even irresistible. Thus while urging acceptance of colonial troops, fear of both them and their effect on women remained (Melzer, 1998).

Despite efforts to remove the possibility of contact between Senegalese troops and French women, this was occasionally circumvented. Some wounded men developed friendships with nurses or other soldiers from mainland France who then invited them to meet their families. The previously-discussed role of the *marraine de guerre* was not restricted to women who corresponded with and cared for French soldiers. Although French women were formally warned about the differing values of African troops, some women adopted these soldiers as their *filleuls*. Familiarity with the French language obviously sifted out those who could correspond with these women or not, thus *originaires* (Senegalese troops from four areas who served in regular French units) were more likely to have this often more intimate contact. In a few cases, such contacts led those involved to seek marriage, something one historian describes as evidence of a 'social equality' that was 'unimaginable' before the war (Lunn, 1999: 175). It also represented the potential for the overthrow of a system that relied on racial and gender inequities.

Senegalese troops were not the only Africans deployed in Europe and subjected to different standards from their metropolitan counterparts. When members of the South African Native Labour Contingent reached France to serve in non-combatant support roles for the military, they were kept in isolated compounds by order of the South African government precisely to prevent any mixing between them and the French. Nonetheless, members of this contingent recalled the friendliness of white women, and the altered conditions of wartime France allowed some casual as well as more serious relationships between black African men and French women to arise. So much so that after the unit's demobilisation, the chief censor intercepted and destroyed letters sent to these men by French women (Grundlingh, 1987: 57).

The issue of wartime sexual behaviour emerges when considering other imperial relationships, for instance those between Britain and India. The use of Indian troops by the British army raised new anxieties in an already-charged atmosphere of concern about contact between 'diseased' women and the fighting forces. The result was a heightened policing of both groups – white working-class women presumed to be prostitutes and 'black' colonial troops – 'for the sake of the empire' (Levine, 1998: 110). Military leadership felt these had to be controlled, to prevent not only the spread of disease but also of miscegenation. Officials were concerned about the welcome extended to Indians by the women of Marseilles, for instance, and made efforts to restrict these troops to the base camp set up there and prevent them from entering the city. This caused a good deal of resentment since the French allowed African troops under their command stationed in Marseilles the same access as any other forces, and Indians wrote home that they felt like prisoners. Nonetheless, restrictions remained in place and punishment for violations, at least on paper, were severe (Greenhut, 1981: 72).

Concern about interaction between Indian troops and European women was even more pronounced when it came to British women serving in the war zones, and emerged in debates about the provision of British nurses to hospitals for them in France. This extended to attempts to prevent Indian wounded from being transported to England for treatment for fears of what damage might be done by having them cared for by British nurses. If there was some concern about loose women leading to scandals, there was more anxiety about preventing the direct care of Indians by British women as it was thought that this might erode the Indians' conception of the 'honour' of white women, which was seen as upholding the mystery and legitimacy of British imperial rule (Greenhut, 1981; Levine, 1998).

Thus not only was there anxiety about encounters between servicemen and women generally within the main participant nations, but this was further multiplied when it came to the colonial theatres of the war. The interaction between European troops and what were presumed to be less 'moral' colonial women became a particular issue that emerged for countries such as Britain, which sought to safeguard their imperial holdings. Given their alleged inferiority, such women were thought to pose a greater threat to troops, and legislation had to be much more severely and more routinely enforced in order to prevent Britain's forces from succumbing to the ravages of venereal diseases. Disorderly conduct, such as that of Australian troops in and around the brothels of Cairo, raised fears of insubordination as well as disease (Scates and Frances, 1997).

In other non-European theatres of war, prostitution remained an issue of grave concern for military officials, as witnessed by reports of such behaviour in soldiers' camps in Malawi (Page, 2000: 144–5). Women who sold grain and beer to the men in the camps often remained around the camps after completing their sales. Given that these soldiers, like those in training camps in all belligerent nations, were separated from their wives and families or else unmarried, officials worried about both prostitution and other forms of sexual encounters. One officer went so far as to issue a warning to local men not to allow women to travel near camps and fights broke out between men in the camps and local men (Page, 2000: 145). Within some African cultures, the behaviour of women while their men were absent also took on a heightened meaning as adultery was thought to lead to the injuring or killing of one's husband (Page, 2000: 92, 98).

Nor did fears of interactions between colonial troops and white women end with the armistice. They extended beyond the immediate war years with the placing of colonial troops as part of the French force occupying the Rhine. Many in Germany and elsewhere saw these troops as carrying with them a particular sexual threat and raged at the 'black shame' imposed upon them (Melzer, 1998; Nelson, 1970). Such complaints fed a war of words in the international media, producing accusations of rape and counter-accusations of racism; this battle also invoked testimonials from German citizens, perhaps especially from German women, who documented their favourable impression of the black troops (Nelson, 1970).

As was the case wherever troops encountered women, the interactions between them raised governments' fears. Usually, women were the focus of concern and, in some cases, of legislation. However, racial attitudes also played an important role in how societies mobilised for war responded to the relationships that arose between men and women. Thus, while the war could bring new opportunities for sexual experimentation for some younger women in France, as it could for those in Britain, it mattered a great deal with whom those relationships or encounters occurred (Thébaud, 1986). As some of the more well-known accounts of the war reveal, the war provided opportunities for lesbian relationships to flourish as well. However, the long-term acceptance of any kind of sexuality perceived as deviating from the norm was limited.

THE WAR AND GENDER DISRUPTION

Regardless of where it took place, wartime mobilisation upset traditional gender arrangements. This was partly because it was seen as removing 'rational' male heads of households and placing 'irrational' women, however temporarily, in charge. Mobilisation also provoked fears about immorality, vice and, as the war continued, about sustaining both military and 'home' fronts. Whether worrying over rates of venereal disease infection and the interaction between soldiers and women, or commenting on women's taking on seemingly new vices, public voices across the participant nations in the First World War linked sexual morality with the maintenance of morale.

Against this backdrop of public outcries over immorality, a sustained emphasis on marriage and motherhood can be found. The publication of

Marie Stopes's *Married Love* in 1918 has rightly been seen as an indicator of a new frankness in discussing female sexuality and pleasure, albeit within the socially-sanctioned context of marriage. The genie – an allegedly new and arguably more widespread awareness of a more active sexuality for women – could not be put back in the bottle. However, the social consequences of engaging in sexual encounters outside marriage endured. Lesbianism was still not accepted, the penalties for abortion became more stringent, for instance, in postwar Britain and France, the status of unmarried mothers remained precarious, and culturally, the double standard prevailed. In other areas, women challenged standards that excluded them from public, political life, as we will see in the next chapter.

CHAPTER SIX

PACIFISM, DISSENT AND REVOLUTION

Even in the confusion of August 1914, the horrors of what a sustained war might bring seemed abundantly clear to several groups of women: those on the left; those feminists for whom pacifism or anti-militarism were central to their beliefs; and those who simply could not sanction sending their beloved sons, husbands, lovers, brothers and friends to fight. It required a good deal of courage to counter the prevailing waves of patriotism that emanated from almost every institution, above all the governments of belligerent nations, during the early, optimistic phases of the war, and so the very existence of a women's anti-war movement is significant. Moreover, a few women saw the outbreak of war as giving them a great if tragic opportunity to show the world what made the political empowerment of women so vital. They insisted that a world that listened to their voices would not, and would never in future, be a world at war.

Getting such a message out was no easy task. Across Europe, governments of participant nations made it extremely difficult to criticise the war. This neither prevented heated discussions within feminist, and particularly socialist feminist, organisations over how to respond to the international crisis, nor, despite censorship, personal attacks, arrests and imprisonment, did it stop individual women from speaking out against the war.

Women organising themselves to advocate an end to the war posed a potential threat to the war efforts of belligerent states. They were joined by other women protesting against war-induced economic and social conditions, such as insufficient food and fuel supplies, rising prices, inadequate wages or a combination of all three. As the war dragged on, the line between economic and political protests blurred, and women marched to demand both bread and peace. In several places, most notably Russia, strikes and street demonstrations ultimately contributed to revolution. Thus, the situation of women protesters everywhere after March 1917 was considerably different. But first, let us turn to the situation early in the war [*Doc. 18*].

WOMEN'S ANTI-MILITARISM AND WAR RESISTANCE, *c.* 1914–16

Feminist pacifist arguments against war appeared even before its outbreak and most centred on three aspects of feminism: the international solidarity that existed among women and feminism's commitment to internationalism, its appeal to women as mothers and caregivers who were therefore inherently opposed to war, and the existence of women's oppression and their lack of basic political and social rights. In various nations, as well as in international women's organisations and their works, and in the voices of individual women, one can find echoes of all three perspectives, separately and intertwined (Grayzel, 1999).

Galvanised into action by the crisis at hand, socialist women leaders like Clara Zetkin of Germany and Louise Saumoneau of France determined that they must protest against the war. These leaders, in part, drew upon the Second International's commitment to internationalism, which sought to prevent members of the working class from sacrificing themselves in a capitalist war. Mainstream socialist parties in nations like France or Germany had not adhered to this principle when they agreed to support their governments' war efforts. However these pacifist women, along with a small minority of socialist men, felt that they must continue to protest against the war.

In March 1915, socialist women, called together by Zetkin, met in neutral Berne, Switzerland. Given the wartime circumstances, it was an impressively international meeting. The majority of delegates came from neutral nations, but representatives from Germany, Britain, France and Russia also attended. Among the resolutions passed at this congress was one stating that the real enemy was the capitalist who gained from oppressing the masses, not the citizens of 'enemy' nations. Furthermore, since men in the war zone no longer had a political voice, it was up to women to speak for them and try to end the war. A 'manifesto' issued by this gathering was soon published and distributed in Germany by Zetkin and in France by Saumoneau, bringing them to the attention of authorities who alternated between a desire to arrest and thus silence them and a wish to avoid turning them into martyrs (Evans, 1987: 133–45).

From 28 April to 1 May 1915, a larger and, in many ways, more representative group of women gathered in The Hague. The impetus for this gathering came from the cancelling of the 1914 annual meeting of the International Women's Suffrage Alliance (IWSA) due to the war. Dutch feminist Aletta Jacobs, along with others, proposed that members of the IWSA still gather in her neutral Holland. Thus an appeal went out 'to the Women of all Nations', asking those who supported women's suffrage and the resolution of international conflict peacefully to come together. British suffragist Emmeline Pethick-Lawrence and Hungarian Rosika Schwimmer attempted to rouse support in the United States, and American Jane Addams agreed to chair the congress. This gathering would eventually give rise to a new organisation, the International Committee of Women for Permanent Peace, which would become the Women's International League for Peace and Freedom and help renew a sense of internationalism among women (Rupp, 1997: 26–7).

The gathering at The Hague was crucial for providing an international underpinning for the women's anti-war movement, but it did not meet with overwhelming approval from women or from national feminist organisations. The war itself had divided the large and active women's suffrage movement in Britain. The militant, publicity-seeking Women's Social and Political Union (WSPU), under the leadership of Emmeline and daughter Christabel Pankhurst, suspended all suffrage activity in order to fight the greater German enemy. At the same time Sylvia Pankhurst, leader of the East London Federation of Suffragettes, which began as an offshoot of her mother's and sister's organisation, adopted a vocal anti-war stance and worked to alleviate the suffering that the war had caused poorer women in particular.

The initial call for women to come to The Hague further highlighted what became an increasingly bitter division within the largest British women's suffrage organisation, the National Union of Woman Suffrage Societies (NUWSS) (Alberti, 1989; Liddington, 1989; Vellacott, 1987). The war did not split the movement neatly into those who had previously used violent protest tactics and now supported military violence and those who worked within the legal system and now opposed the war. Rather, those members of the NUWSS who felt that feminism had to combat physical force with 'moral force' felt that it was the essence of their movement publicly to support all efforts to suspend the violence that had broken out among nations. Several leading members of the NUWSS Executive Committee, including both of its secretaries, resigned over the organisation's failure to endorse the gathering at The Hague and actively support peace initiatives. As Helena Swanwick, one of those leaders who resigned from the NUWSS, phrased it, the NUWSS should be working for 'the abolition of militarism as the arch-enemy of women's enfranchisement' (Letter to the Editor, The Common Cause, 30 April 1915).

Ireland's women's suffrage organisations were similarly divided over the war, and for them, the question of Irish nationalism played a crucial role. Some groups, such as the Irish Women's Suffrage Federation, stopped suffrage activity at the war's outset. Others, such as the Irish Women's Franchise League, opposed this option, stressing that the war would not alter Ireland's or women's essential disenfranchisement. Disputes over whether or not to support the war also revealed pre-existing tensions between those who valued women's suffrage over nationalism and vice versa. One concrete expression of this came in the ultimately successful campaign to create a separate Irish branch of the post-Hague International association in 1916, rather than subsuming Ireland's organisation into the British one (Owens, 1997).

France's mainstream feminist organisations unilaterally denounced the meeting at The Hague, claiming that French women could not attend such a gathering while France itself was under enemy occupation. Some individual feminists, such as Gabrielle Duchêne, dissented from this position and even publicised their stance in the international suffrage journal *Jus Suffragii*, although this view was censored in the French version (Bard, 1995). Others, such as Jeanne Mélin, would express their support privately for the aims of the Congress and endeavour to attend, believing that feminism, inter-nationalism and pacifism were all of a piece, and the war had not changed this (Bard, 1995: 93–4; Grayzel, 1999). However, the leaders of the largest French women's organisation, the Conseil National des Femmes Françaises (CNFF) proclaimed that the war had united men and women and they did not 'know how to talk of peace' (*La Française* 1915; also quoted in Hause with Kenney, 1984).

In Germany, as in Britain and France, the feminist movement was divided over how to respond to the war and to peace initiatives. Gertrud Bäumer, head of the Bund Deutscher Frauenvereine (BDF), led the majority of feminists in supporting the war effort. Several other leading German feminists, including Anita Augspurg, Lida Gustava Heymann, and Helene Stöcker, publicly opposed the war and became part of the delegation to The Hague Congress (Gelblum, 1998; Evans, 1987).

Not only did the invitation to come to the Peace Congress reveal already present divisions within the ranks of feminists in Germany and Britain, but belligerent states also made it difficult for those women who wanted to attend to do so. The German government stopped all but twenty-eight women from crossing its border. In Britain, the government refused initially to issue permits to many of the women and that, combined with the closing of all shipping in the North Sea for ten days before and during the Congress, meant that only three members of the British delegation participated.

Despite these obstacles and the absence of Russian and French – although not Belgian – participation, the 1915 Women's Peace Congress at The Hague allowed women of both belligerent and neutral nations to speak together despite the wartime crisis. This in itself was remarkable. Along with discussing the prospects for peace, delegates also articulated a solidarity of women against war, as mothers and the nurturers of children and as the war's victims, suffering not only potential death but 'unspeakable horrors' such as sexual assault (Rupp, 1997: 86). At the end of the meeting, delegates sent a message to the world urging continuous mediation until a peace settlement could be reached and arguing that women must have a voice in any such settlement (Bussey and Tims, 1980: 20–1).

As might be expected, the press treatment accorded the Women's Peace Congress was mostly but not unanimously hostile. Mockery rather than overt anger was common, with many commentators asking how could women presume to know the realities of war and international politics that they were discussing. According to these accounts, even though conference participants and sympathisers were well-intentioned, silly, or deluded, they were still dangerous (Wiltsher, 1985). Hostility was especially strong in belligerent nations, an indication that officials feared the appeal of women to other women.

After the Congress concluded, Jane Addams and Aletta Jacobs were selected to head one of two delegations of women; their task was to approach the leaders of participant and neutral nations and urge them to pursue an immediate, negotiated settlement to the war. Addams, for instance, personally met United States' President Wilson in August. By October 1915, these women were ready to issue a statement to the effect that a conference to negotiate the end of the war should proceed as soon as possible and should be urged by the leaders of neutral states (Bussey and Tims, 1980: 22–4) [*Doc. 19*].

The creation of a women's organisation to promote peace, the International Committee of Women for Permanent Peace, can also be seen as a significant result of the April congress, and in Britain, for instance, many of the women who had resigned from the NUWSS Executive, such as Helena Swanwick, became its active leaders. In France, a new feminist initiative for peace emerged under the leadership of Gabrielle Duchêne. It became known for a pamphlet it published in 1915 calling peace 'an urgent duty for women' (Bard, 1995: 100–1). Across national boundaries, groups of women mobilised other women for peace by using similar appeals. They called upon women as mothers, as the victims of war, as persons denied fundamental political rights like voting, and as exploited workers to rally them to oppose the war. Such efforts in themselves provoked responses in official quarters, as the French government report on an investigation into these groups and their members in October 1915 showed [*Doc. 20*].

In more local efforts, women organisers and activists drew attention to the powerful connections between the costs of prosecuting the war and the expenses that then shifted to working-class families. Sylvia Pankhurst tried to organise a 'no rent' strike in her constituency in East London to protest against rapidly rising costs as a result of war. One of the most vivid examples of this type of political protest can be found in the Glasgow rent strike of 1915. This was an action both by and for poor women, and was set in motion when landlords raised rents in response to the arrival of labourers seeking work in war-related factories. Housing was already scarce and many of those threatened with eviction were the wives of servicemen, so tensions grew extremely high. With the backing of the local Independent Labour Party and their menfolk, these women forced the government's hand by forming pickets and refusing to allow evictions to proceed, and also by making use of the courts to seek redress. The movement spread beyond Glasgow, and eventually the government intervened. By late December, Parliament had passed the Rent Restriction Act covering the entire nation and alleviating the crisis (Smyth, 1992).

Such a protest suited the more overt anti-war activity of organisations that combined feminist and socialist principles, such as the Women's Peace Crusade (WPC) which also emerged in Scotland. The Women's Peace Crusade was a direct response to the introduction of conscription in 1916, a move which brought more working-class women into the anti-war movement because they wanted to keep their men out of the war. It explicitly called upon women socialists to take action against the killing of their (working-class) men, and it organised open-air meetings for women to express these views. In Glasgow, which became a centre of the WPC, it mounted an impressive public campaign for a negotiated settlement to the war, and it responded even more vigorously after the Russian Revolution, organising large meetings across Scotland and the north of England, and being banned from doing so in London (Liddington, 1989; Smyth, 1992).

British feminists who were not members of the WPC also found themselves actively involved in anti-conscription activities. Catherine Marshall, one of those who resigned from the NUWSS over the war, became a key figure in the No Conscription Fellowship. She took over the organising work as many conscientious objectors found themselves in jail when they refused to do anything to help the war. Other women encouraged conscientious objectors and publicly protested their mistreatment in prison (Liddington, 1989; Vellacott, 1987).

Political actions to protest against wartime conditions were not restricted to nations in the thick of war. In Australia, the city of Melbourne witnessed its own women-led demonstrations over the war-induced rise in the cost of living in 1917 (Smart, 1995). As Australian women had gained the vote in 1901, they had a greater political voice than had women in most other participant nations. Socialist women here widely denounced conscription during two referenda on the subject – in 1916 and 1917 – and were in turn attacked for their views (Damousi, 1995). The outcome of the conscription campaigns, both of which ended in victory for the non-conscription side, can, in part, be attributed to the role of women voters. On one level, the words of socialist activist Vida Goldstein that 'as the Mothers of the Race, it is your privilege to conserve life, and love, and beauty, all of which are destroyed by war' must have resonated with her audience (quoted in Scates and Frances, 1997: 83) [*Docs 21 and 22*].

As was true in Britain, the war proved divisive for the Canadian women's suffrage movement with the Canadian Suffrage Association urging arbitration to end the war and sponsoring pacifist speakers while the National Equal Franchise Association advocated no discussion of peace until the Allies won. More extensive campaigning against the war was carried out by socialist women (Kealey, 1998). Officially, Canadian women's groups gathered together during the war as 'the National Committee for Patriotic Service' and refused the invitation to The Hague conference. This did not stop Laura Hughes, the niece of Sir Sam Hughes who was the Minister of the Militia, from attending on her own and later organising the Canadian branch of the international women's peace movement to which it gave rise. Hughes and her associates tried to spread an anti-war message by urging women to think about the costs of war and about ways to prevent it in future. Even a few isolated women in rural Canada protested the war's toll and appealed to women's 'mother-hearts' to stop this war and all future ones (B. Roberts, 1985: 23).

In neutral nations, support for the peace movement divided feminists as it had elsewhere. In the United States, some 15,000 women had paraded down Manhattan's Fifth Avenue in a Women's Peace March on 29 August 1914, and a Women's Peace Party emerged in 1915. During the presidential re-election campaign of 1916, leading feminist pacifists such as Jane Addams and Emily Greene Balch worked for Wilson, who promised to keep the United States out of the war, while Alice Paul and her supporters backed Charles Evans Hughes, who said he wanted both to grant women the right to vote and to get America ready for war if necessary (Wiltsher, 1985: 154). By 1917, American neutrality was in jeopardy and many of those suffragists who had split over the election came together to try to maintain America's bystander status. This proved short-lived and, again, the feminist movement was divided. At the time of American entry into the war in April 1917, the main suffrage group, the National American Women's Suffrage Association (NAWSA), under the leadership of Carrie Chapman Catt, had avowed its full support for the war while the National Women's Party (NWP) under Alice Paul neither actively supported nor opposed it. Membership in the Women's Peace Party quickly fell (Berkman, 1990: 147–8). Those who remained committed to an anti-war stance soon found themselves both busier than ever and under more direct threat from the government. No belligerent state was willing to let those who opposed the war, whatever their motivation, continue to speak out.

THE PROSECUTION OF WOMEN'S ANTI-WAR ACTIVITY

As was the case with their male counterparts, women protesting against the war found themselves viewed as dangerous to their wartime nations. Both Clara Zetkin and Louise Saumoneau were imprisoned for spreading the message of the 1915 socialist women's Berne Congress. Ridicule in the media was a common reaction to the less provocative message of the Women's Peace Congress at The Hague, but women delegates also came under attack as disloyal to their nations.

Women who participated in organisations formed in the immediate aftermath of the April 1915 Peace Congress generally carried out their work with little interference. However, the climate of the war changed after the tremendous casualties of 1916 and the revolutionary unrest of 1917. After this, new political regimes appeared in Britain and especially in France that were determined to sustain the war effort to the bitter end, and they lost little time in attacking women activists who directly worked to halt the war. The French government was concerned enough with women spreading 'alarmist noises' – for instance, repeating rumours of German attacks – to interrogate those reported of doing so by their neighbours (Grayzel, 1999: 185).

The French state had already devoted considerable resources to keeping track not only of the 'esprit' of its civilian population, but also of the actions and writings of individual women. A list of pacifists compiled by the Sûreté in 1916 includes several women and provides brief descriptions about them, noting their affiliations with specific organisations ranging from political parties to unions and feminist groups. The list includes women such as Marcelle Capy, author of 'A Woman's Voice during the War', and Louise Saumoneau, described as 'not hiding her germanophile sentiments'. The document summarises Saumoneau's distribution of circulars addressed to 'proletariat women' and asking them 'where are your husbands? where are your sons?' and records her arrest at the start of October and release in late November 1915 (F7/13371, Archives Nationales, Paris). Saumoneau's arrest did not lead to a long imprisonment, in an effort to stop her publicising her views. However, her continued distribution of anti-war tracts – including the 'Berne Manifesto' – still upset the government. Much harsher action would be taken in the troubled year of 1917 (Sowerwine, 1982).

One activist who appeared on the 1916 government list and found herself prosecuted for more serious offences was the French feminist schoolteacher Hélène Brion. In November of 1917, she was arrested and charged with a treasonous violation of the law, but she was more publicly denounced as embodying the new crime of 'defeatism'. 'Defeatists' advocated a negotiated settlement to the war rather than an all-out fight to victory, and the newly-arrived head of state, Georges Clemenceau, was determined to root this out. The press coverage of her arrest was extensive and made her gender as much as her political tendencies and occupation an object of scrutiny. Thus, Brion found herself denounced not only for her dangerous views and influence on children, but also for wearing 'masculine costume' – as a front-page photograph in *Le Matin* displayed and thus implied her radicalism and deviance from gender norms (Grayzel, 1999; Wishnia, 1987).

Imprisoned for four months, Brion found herself on trial before the First Council of War in late March 1918. While prosecutors focused on her dissemination of anti-war literature, Brion seemed to observers instead to see herself victimised by those opposed to her feminist principles. She made a defence of these the cornerstone of her response to the trial. As she proclaimed: 'I am above all and before all else a feminist ... and it's because of feminism that I am the enemy of war' (Brion, 1918: 8). She made this connection even more explicit as she denounced the hypocrisy of a state that could accuse her of a political crime when, as a woman, she had no political rights, specifically no voting rights (Brion, 1918: 5).

Brion was not the only woman tried for treason during the war. In Britain, Nellie Best, an activist associated with Sylvia Pankhurst, was sentenced to six months imprisonment in March 1916 for interfering with recruiting (Liddington, 1989). Alice Wheeldon and her daughter Hettie, involved in aiding fugitive conscientious objectors, were charged with plotting to assassinate Lloyd George in early 1917 (Liddington, 1989). Novelist Rose Allatini's 1918 work, *Despised and Rejected*, was banned under the Defence of the Realm Regulations as being prejudicial to military recruitment and conduct (Grayzel, 1999). The German government banned activists like Lida Gustava Heymann from public speaking and more radical women like Zetkin and Rosa Luxemburg were arrested and imprisoned, although Zetkin was later released from prison on the grounds of ill health (Evans, 1987). Speaking out and organising women against war proved risky.

In France, as elsewhere, questions about the effectiveness of appeals to women, especially to working-class women, to help end the war remain. On the one hand, the government can be seen as responding with excessive force to campaigns which had limited hopes of success anyway, since the pacifist movement was largely confined to 'intellectuals' within the working class (Dubesset et al., 1992). On the other hand, the potential disruption caused by this movement, perhaps particularly when it appealed to women as mothers, meant it had to be contained.

Prosecution in the United States focused on radical women. With the enacting of the Espionage Act of 1917 and the Sedition Act of 1918, free speech, particularly speech critical of the United States and its war aims, became an endangered species. Although a minority of defendants in cases brought under these acts, women found themselves suspect as much for violating appropriate gender roles as for acting against the war. In one of the most famous of these cases, socialist Kate Richards O'Hare was indicted in June 1917 for suggesting that 'war corrupted motherhood'. As the government asserted at her trial, the war would only be won if there were enough soldiers, and O'Hare's public speeches had proclaimed that calls to women to mother sons and send them to war reduced them to the status of mere 'breeding animals on a stock farm'. Prosecutors tried to show that the presence of draft-aged men or their mothers at such a talk could negatively affect the war effort. In the end, O'Hare was convicted and harshly sentenced to five years in federal prison (a sentence she only began to serve in 1919 when the Supreme Court upheld her conviction and one that ended in 1920 when Wilson commuted it) (Kennedy, 1999: 18–19).

O'Hare's was an exceptional case, both because of her standing in the socialist community and because, as a wife and mother, she used these familial, gendered positions as the basis from which to argue that she was defending a better vision of motherhood. In contrast, other radical women prosecuted for anti-war activity in the United States had led much more unconventional lives. Some had even more radical politics, such as anarchist Emma Goldman, who came to symbolise the threat of immigrant women and found herself first imprisoned and then deported (Kennedy, 1999). Almost all of the women prosecuted by the government found themselves on the defensive as *women* who dared to speak out and question the war.

In addition to this activity, American women played a key role, as they did in Britain, in trying to maintain civil liberties, particularly the rights of draft resisters. Once the United States entered the war, a small coalition of activists, including Emma Goldman, helped create the No-Conscription League, an organisation that fell apart with the arrests of Goldman and her compatriot Alexander Berkman. Others, led by Fannie May Witherspoon, established the New York-based Bureau of Legal Advice to assist pacifist organisations as well as individuals seeking exemptions from the draft. The Bureau also took on many so-called dependency cases, involving wives and children who were left destitute because their men were in the service and the financial support from the army was either not forthcoming or insufficient. Often the most desperate of these cases involved immigrant women and were resolved by the Bureau's women workers. All such workers ran the risk of popular violence as the war continued (Early, 1997).

One way to evaluate the importance of the activities of such small numbers of women internationally is to consider the disproportionate response that they invoked. It is a sign that the voices of women mattered that, without wishing to create martyrs, various governments felt obliged to prosecute vigorously the women who spoke out against the war. Moreover, they allow us to see that women did not speak with one voice. At a time when most women did not have the right to vote, they found ways to participate in and to shape the political process.

STRIKES, PROTESTS AND WAR-WEARINESS, 1917

By the winter of 1917, the war had reached a crisis point. Mutinies occurred across the Western Front, revolution struck Russia, protests about scarcities grew, and strikes threatened vital war production. All but the mutinies directly involved women, and all show how interconnected the lives of civilians and soldiers truly were.

France experienced a huge upsurge in both military and civilian unrest during the spring of 1917. While men mutinied in the war zone, strikes proliferated in the munitions factories in and around Paris, places where women workers were, by this time, in the majority. Often viewed by contemporaries and some historians as apolitical, the strikes were not, and striking women workers decisively linked complaints about wages and working conditions with criticisms of the war itself. Women initiated these work stoppages themselves, protesting against their low wages and proclaiming their desire for Sundays off. Most ominously for the government, when they took to the streets at the end of May 1917, they demanded that the government bring their soldiers home and send the presumed cowards – men avoiding the draft through factory work – to battle in their stead. That some 30,000 women had stopped producing armaments to demand money, their men and ultimately an end to the war gravely alarmed the government. It intervened by a combination of granting some concessions in wages and work and by getting rid of the 'ringleaders' of the movement (Downs, 1993: 123, 130).

Even in non-belligerent European countries like Spain, the war affected the availability of food and fuel, and this in turn had an impact on the living standards of the working class. Shortages of items necessary for families' survival prompted women to take collective action in various places, including Cordoba, Madrid, Alicante and most notably Malaga and Barcelona (Nash, 1995). In January 1918, reacting to the rising cost of bread and coal, groups of Barcelona's women took to the streets and its women factory workers went on strike. In the end, this wartime agitation was quelled only by the use of military force (Kaplan, 1982).

Economic hardship also severely affected women in Germany. Given the severity of the blockade's effects, German women, many of whom were now heads of households, had enormous difficulty in obtaining enough basic foodstuffs for themselves and their families. They became front-line soldiers of an economic war (Davis, 2000). Although they have too often been viewed as apolitical, it becomes clear that the food riots that occurred in German cities in 1917, like the strikes by women workers in France, had clear political implications. Protesting against the shortage of vital food stuffs such as potatoes, German women, especially 'war wives', took to the streets (Daniel, 1997: 183–4). The strikes that began in Berlin metalworking factories and then quickly spread were accompanied by street demonstrations, but these kinds of protests themselves were not new. Vocal reactions occurred as soon as the shortages of food had become evident earlier in the war. What was different about 1917 was that it represented the final eroding of faith in the government as food scandals shocked civilians. The year began with women war factory workers demanding equal rations to male munitions workers. In addition, consumers became enraged by stories of hoarding and profiteering recounted in the press, and the government became newly concerned with the possibility of hungry and newly radicalised women taking to the streets (Davis, 2000: 190, 193–5).

Certainly, in Germany, as elsewhere, news of the first Russian Revolution of February 1917 alarmed authorities, given the level of popular discontent. As the rationing of food was further tightened, war workers went on strike in mid-April; the majority of those doing so in Berlin were women (Davis, 2000: 199, 202). As food and fuel became scarcer and concern about survival during yet another winter of war emerged, street protests continued through the summer with increasing violence and the theft of food (Davis, 2000: 210–11). Conditions did not improve throughout the year, leading to further disillusionment and the arrival of mass strikes in Berlin as the new year of 1918 dawned. We will hear more about what happened next below.

PROTESTS AND RADICALISM IN ASIA

In Allied Japan, while it initially benefited from a wartime economic boom, shortages of some basic foodstuffs and a downturn towards the end of the war also prompted riots. Beginning in July 1918 and lasting for much of that year, women helped lead demonstrations and even rioted over the rising cost of rice (Hane, 1988: 23–4). There were also more overtly political protests by socialists, including women, about the government's suppression of these protests and about the war itself (Hane, 1988: 125). French efforts to recruit labour from Indochina led to protests by women, who accused local authorities of forcing enlistment by threatening the families of those who did not 'volunteer'. Large-scale revolts both here and in China, where France also recruited labour, sprang up during the war (Stovall, 1993). The war years in China also saw the rise of the May Fourth movement, which included a consideration of women's status and culminated in political protests in 1919 reacting to the Treaty of Versailles (Gilmartin, 1999).

As we have seen, the war's economic and political effects were far-reaching, and they had an impact on men's and women's lives and actions in the European colonies of participant nations. One notable example is India, where the war saw an intensification of efforts to gain self-government, as the British sought both its troops and material support. In efforts to recruit troops in India, the state turned to financial incentives, for instance by offering a life pension to war widows (Chakravorty, 1997). This support for women left widowed by war was especially important in the context of a culture where widows did not remarry, an issue that was itself cautiously raised in Hindi women's magazines during the war (Talwar, 1990).

The contradiction between recruiting Indian troops for combat in Europe while the Arms Act legally denied them the right to bear arms in most of India itself also aroused protest. In 1916, Sarojini Naidu, one of the activists in the Ladies' War Relief Association, which believed that support for the war would further strengthen India's case for independence, spoke out against this Act. Naidu argued that women were uniquely qualified to speak on this issue, since they were the 'mothers of men whom we wish to make men and not emasculated machines', thus demanding that 'the birthright of their sons should be given back to them' (Naidu, 1919: 78). She would reiterate these themes throughout the war, stressing in December 1917 that Indians' 'self-respect' was at stake, since 'the primary right of man to defend his honour, to defend his women and to protect his country have been taken away from him' (Chakravorty, 1997: 71) [*Doc. 23*].

Naidu was not alone in believing that active support for the war would demonstrate India's loyalty and worthiness for self-government. Others active in Indian political life, particularly those such as Annie Besant, who also promoted home rule, saw the two as interconnected: 'the price of India's loyalty is India's freedom' (Chakravorty, 1997: 65). Eventually, Besant's activism would lead to her arrest in June 1917, which was met with public outcry, and her release in September of that year.

These increasingly active movements for national self-determination during the war themselves provoked debate over the role of women and women's political rights within them. Naidu would lead the All-Indian Women's Deputation to India's Secretary of State (E.S. Montagu) in 1917. She would continue to agitate not only for constitutional reform but also for this to include a suffrage that would be extended to women (Pati, 1996). However, the British government failed to take seriously demands for home rule or any sort of autonomous rule, thus paving the way for Gandhi's leadership and a new phase of agitation.

Regardless of where they took place, protests and strikes had the serious potential to disrupt what was an international war effort. They further demonstrated how intertwined the actions of civilians and combatants were, and in some instances suggest the importance of women's wartime labour to the war's success. Just how significant this was can be seen in situations where popular protest led to more overt rebellion, such as in Ireland, Russia and Germany.

WOMEN AND REVOLUTION: IRELAND, RUSSIA AND GERMANY

Radical, socialist and Marxist women across Europe generally opposed the war, and a few would see in its longevity the opportunity to advocate revolution. They would urge working-class women especially to see the connection between their families' deprivations and the sacrifices of their menfolk and the futility of a war brought about by the greed of their unjust governments. Rather than urging such liberal changes as the granting of votes to women in order to rectify the situation and reform the government with the addition of more peaceful, feminine voices, these women promoted the destruction of the current system and its replacement by a new order. Some of the rebellions that occurred in the context of the war were primarily economic, about war on a class-based society versus capitalism. The notable case of Ireland involved nationalism as well.

Ireland

The role of women in Irish nationalism and the Irish Rebellion of 1916 demonstrates one potent example of women's decisive participation in revolutionary, military actions concurrent with the war. As discussed earlier, support for the war divided the Irish women's suffrage movement as it divided Irish men and women in general. Conscious of the potential for conflict with Ireland, the British government treated its subjects there as a special case when it came to the war. While encouraging Irish men to enlist, it excluded them when it first decided to impose conscription in 1916. More significantly, the most fervent Irish nationalists saw an opportunity to gain independence for Ireland while Britain was distracted by the war.

Prior to Easter 1916, as the plans for armed revolt emerged, nationalist women served as couriers and gunrunners, using their gender as a way to avoid suspicion. Then in April 1916, the Easter Rebellion broke out. Within the context of the bloodletting and violence of the war overall, it was neither particularly ruthless nor widely successful. It began with the seizing of public buildings such as the General Post Office, which became the headquarters, and other strong points in the city of Dublin. For a week, the insurgents held out, until they were forced to surrender. Most of the 500 killed and 2,500 wounded were civilians caught between government forces and rebels (Jeffery, 2000).

While they were a minority of active participants, women served in a number of vital roles during the uprising, ranging from nursing to taking up arms. Most notably, Countess Constance Markiewicz, head of the Irish-women's Council, found herself second in command of St Stephen's Green, one of the rebel's initial strongholds. Nor was she the only noteworthy female combatant deemed especially dangerous by the British government.

She was tried for treason like the other leaders, but the women participants were not executed as the men were. Instead they received prison sentences (Ward, 1995).

Popular accounts of the responses to the rising suggest women were divided over whether or not to support it. Several reports discuss the vocal objections to the rebellion of 'separation women', those dependent on the separation allowances given to them by virtue of having men fighting for Britain. Thus, their antagonism may be seen as twofold: economic, because they feared the loss of this income if the British government were no longer around to supply it; and political, because they felt the uprising betrayed their men who were actively engaged in fighting or who were already dead (Jeffery, 2000).

In the radicalised aftermath of both the rebellion and, according to many, the unnecessarily harsh British reaction to it, nationalist women became a crucial source of support for the families of those either dead or in jail, and for organising propaganda to further the cause of Irish independence. Such women also became active in attacking conscription, once Britain decided it could no longer afford to exempt Ireland from its provisions in 1917. This scheme relied upon legislation that made it illegal for employers to hire men between the ages of 16 and 62, and thus assumed that women would replace them. Instead, the largest Irish women's organisation pledged 'not to fill the places of men deprived of their work through enforced military service' (Ward, 1995: 128). In the conflict and civil war that followed, women served in roles ranging from nurses to spies on both sides. One can argue that perhaps the only thing that united women in Ireland in the tense years between 1916 and 1923 was a common mourning for the dead.

Russian Women and the Revolution

In the meantime, Russia had proved the most volatile of all the European nations. As conditions worsened for soldiers and civilians alike, mutinies and strikes turned into open revolt. If the most famous leaders of the Russian Revolution were men, women too had their part to play in the over-throw of the Tsar's regime. This was not necessarily predictable at the war's outset. Like women in all belligerent nations, those in Russia became a vital part of the war effort. Leading feminists had urged Russian women to commit themselves to the national cause and, as we have seen, women had taken up the full range of wartime activities from nursing to soldiering, while the number of women factory workers grew rapidly (Stites, 1990: 278–83). The potential for female activism was also present, personified by *soldatki* or soldier's wives (and other female dependents) who suffered material hardships on account of the loss of male breadwinners and other wartime conditions. The war radicalised them into a distinct group that demanded prompt payment of their stipend and adequate food supplies. Groups of *soldatki* displayed overt antagonism to the state in the form of food riots in 1915 and these increased in 1916. As was the case in Germany, the lack of a system for rationing food supplies fairly undermined the authority of the government and those who enforced its laws. By the end of 1916, food riots became increasingly political; a group of soliders' wives protesting in the Don region attacked a portrait of the tsar, shouting 'Trample him; he's taken our husbands off to war' (Engel, 1997: 716).

Certainly by the beginning of 1917, the food situation in Russia had become dire. Since women were in charge of shopping for food – which by this time meant standing in long queues – as well as feeding their families, they began to protest both the shortage of basic foodstuffs like bread and their rising cost. Rural women might have had better access to food than urban women, but still with ten million or so peasant men mobilised into the army, rural households lost a great deal of income as military allotments could not make up for the men's absent wages. As contemporary observers noted, the talk in the street turned from discussing shortages and the need for bread to questions of justice (McDermid and Hillyar, 1999). In this volatile situation, women workers began to strike and other women to riot (Clements, 1994) [*Doc. 25*].

Several historians have agreed that these riots helped set off the February Revolution, regardless of whether the instigators had any planned desire to overthrow the regime. This popular discontent spilled over on International Women's Day (23 February in Russia) when women workers abandoned their factories and went on to the streets demanding 'Bread for the workers!' and 'End the war!'. Soon they were throwing rocks at bakeries and factories and calling out to male workers to join them, and a mass protest began. Within three days, the strike turned into a general one, troops which had been summoned to stop the protests had mutinied and, in a little over a week, the rule of the tsar was over (Clements, 1994; McDermid and Hillyar, 1999).

The Revolution began with women in Petrograd, but quickly spread to other major cities. The months between March and October show women responding in a variety of ways to their new circumstances. Women of the nobility, as might have been expected, feared and rejected the Revolution. As far as the intelligentsia and the 'official' feminist movement were concerned, those who had been arguing primarily for liberal reforms supported the new Provisional Government, one that gave women the suffrage on equal terms as men in July, while others continued to support the more revolutionary aims of the Bolsheviks. Among working-class urban women, Bolshevism appealed to a few but many were unable to concentrate on politics at the expense of their own and their families' survival in a time of mounting economic dislocation and distress. Still, sporadic strikes and street protests by women workers demonstrated their disappointment with the first Provisional Government and their increasing radicalisation (McDermid and Hillyar, 1999: 158–62). In general, peasants, including women, welcomed the overthrow of the tsar and the seizing of noble land, but again their overt political participation was limited (Clements, 1994).

All through the upheavals of 1917, Bolshevik women leaders reached out to working-class women (Wood, 1997). If women had set the wheel of revolution in motion, it now seemed to be running on its own. One key issue for many women, despite the differences suggested above, came from their concern for their menfolk, which prompted their desire to stop the war, and their need to take care of their families. One way in which the Bolsheviks consolidated their appeal to the so-called masses (i.e., the urban workforce, the majority of whom were now women) was by insisting on their commitment to end the war. This was something neither feminist nor liberal nor moderate socialist groups were willing to do (McDermid and Hillyar, 1999).

At the time that the Bolsheviks easily seized power in the October Revolution, women returned briefly to centre stage; only here they were among the last defenders of the old order. Members of the Petrograd Women's Battalion of Death, discussed in Chapter 4 above, remained loyal to Kerensky and the Provisional Government. Other women's battalions had participated in the failed June offensives and despite increased public hostility to them (as to others who wanted to continue the war), they offered to defend the regime to the last. Thus among the 3,000 troops based at the Winter Palace in October were about 200 women, all of whom were easily defeated. Still, it is interesting that in most 'eyewitness' and historical accounts the very presence of the women has been used to suggest that the regime itself must have been on the verge of collapse. The reasoning behind such accounts reaffirms the belief that women combatants could only be used by the most desperate of governments. These stories also underscored the unsuitability of women for such actions by reporting that they became hysterical and were then subject to mass sexual assault by Bolshevik forces, all of which turned out to be false. This also ignores the role played by women in support capacities as well as combatant ones during both the October Revolution and the bloody civil war that followed (McDermid and Hillyar, 1999) [*Doc. 12*].

Revolutionary Upheaval in Germany

As we have already seen, shortages of food and fuel, and other hardships associated with the war, radicalised many working-class German women. Their actions had turned increasingly violent in the summer of 1917, and

1918 began with a mass strike in Berlin, which included many women munitions workers. Furthermore, the nature of these protests changed from street demonstrations to illicit activity as thefts and other attacks on property rose during this last year of war (Davis, 2000: 211, 219). Working women, while unlikely to be as active as men in unions or political parties, proved themselves willing to take to the streets demanding food, better wages and peace (Dobson, 2001). By the autumn of 1918, discontent was rife and the costs associated with the failed German offensive would only help further to make a case against the state itself.

Such discontent would contribute to the revolutionary upheaval that shook Germany at the war's end. The war alone, as was the case in Russia, was not the only cause of the revolutions that occurred in Germany; long-term grievances by both male and female workers against the elites are also important factors (Dobson, 2001). However, both wartime conditions of food and fuel shortages and a widespread dissatisfaction with the political regime shaped by radical political leaders in the climate of defeat proved a fateful combination. Among the national radical leaders Rosa Luxemburg, co-founder with Karl Liebknecht of the Spartacus League, which called for internationalism and workers' political empowerment, stands out. Luxemburg had opposed the war from the outset and denounced German socialists who put the nation before all workers. She was imprisoned for her anti-war activities but never lost faith in the rightness of her cause, and she continued to write, smuggling out articles and pamphlets, and to espouse her own brand of internationalism (Bronner, 1993) [*Doc. 24*].

Even as the German army began to organise for its final offensive in 1918, pamphlets produced by the Spartacus League received a more favourable popular response. Nor were they alone. As the economic and political situations worsened, many Social Democrats also began to advocate more radical measures. Luxemburg and her compatriots saw their opportunity and seized it. Calls for a new mass strike began in the summer, even as the government tried to impose new punishments in response. Instead, demonstrations in the capital city increased in September and October. Civilian morale, already low, plummeted and revolution broke out in Munich on 7 November. On 9 November, men and women workers left their factories and gathered with the population of Berlin and sailors from the North, and the police did not stop them. A republic was declared in the wake of Kaiser Wilhelm's abdication (Davis, 2000). Two days later the armistice was signed, bringing an end to the fighting.

Despite the fact that socialist parties took power in November 1918, unrest continued in Germany. The socialists themselves were split between those who wanted a full-scale socialist revolt and those interested in increasing democracy and workers' rights but not, for instance, the nationalisation of all industry. Those trying to lead the revolution inevitably clashed with those in power trying to restore order. After renewed violence in December 1918, Rosa Luxemburg and Karl Liebknecht mobilised for a second revolt in January 1919. After only four days, this uprising was crushed, and Luxemburg and Liebknecht were arrested and brutally killed. The possibility of a full-scale German revolution and a new order like that in Russia was over. Many factors contributed to the revolutions that beset Germany at the war's end and in its immediate aftermath; one of them was surely the radicalisation of women because of the economic impact of the war.

Women's visible anti-war and revolutionary actions during the period 1914–19 raise a number of interesting questions for historians. They indicate that not all subjects of participant nations supported the war, and they raise questions about gender stereotypes that made it easier for women as 'mothers' and as 'naturally' peaceful to speak out against war. Yet obviously for nations at war, women protesters were seen as potential and indeed actual traitors. The violence of women protesters in revolutionary agitation against wartime conditions (food and fuel shortages, the lack of employment, the suffering of their families) also became outcries against their very governments. Some women could and did represent an 'enemy within' – a volatile and essential constituency of some of the most important political and social protests of the times – even though they themselves did not enjoy the full rights of citizens.

PART THREE   EFFECTS OF WAR

the Sheffield

Peaks Learning Resource Centre

CHAPTER SEVEN

ASSESSING THE CONSEQUENCES OF THE WAR FOR WOMEN

One area of intense debate among historians of women has been the war's effect on gender roles. After all, the war brought about tangible evidence of a changed world where women could wear khaki uniforms, drive trains, trams and ambulances, and take on industrial tasks previously defined as beyond their capabilities. Furthermore, many women found themselves enfranchised after the war. Yet the end of war and demobilisation displaced most waged women workers from their wartime occupations – particularly in fields that had traditionally been the province of men. What then can be determined about their overall social standing? Can we find significant improvements for women as a whole in the postwar world?

A short answer would be 'it depends'. Unsurprisingly, the impact of the war on individual women varied enormously. It was dependent upon class, nation, region, ethnicity, age, war experience and loss. One extremely large group of women directly affected by the war were the widows that it left behind. Despite such variations, some things held true for many women. In numerous places in the West, they, as a group, had new political rights and some new, if limited, social and economic opportunities. Yet almost without exception, they still had to cope with being regarded as the primary care-takers of their families. Indeed, in a number of postwar states, motherhood remained as firmly entrenched as ever in defining women's most essential function.

WARTIME AND POSTWAR CHANGES IN WOMEN'S POLITICAL RIGHTS

On the eve of the war, most women globally lacked the fundamental democratic right to vote. Campaigns for women's suffrage began in earnest in the mid-nineteenth century and in some places, particularly Britain, a growing women's suffrage movement had catapulted the issue to the forefront of politics by mid-1914. The war can thus be seen as interrupting what might have been a fairly rapid granting of a woman's vote in Britain, but such speculation does not get us very far. Instead, in most participant nations – with the exception of France (about which more will be said later) – the end of the war and the immediate postwar era saw an extraordinary rise in the numbers of women who possessed this basic political right.

What was the war's effect on women's politics and was it the cause of the passage of legislation granting women the vote? These issues have proven very controversial. Certainly, the kinds of war work and war service performed by women provided both a rationale and an excuse for male legislators to grant women the vote, but not all governments took that step. Again, we will never know how long granting the vote to women would have taken without the war. Still, even a cursory glance at the list of the nations that gave some measure of national women's suffrage either during or in the aftermath of the war – Austria, Belgium, Britain, Canada, Czechoslovakia, Denmark, Estonia, Germany, Hungary, Iceland, Latvia, Lithuania, Luxembourg, the Netherlands, Poland, Sweden and the United States – suggests that we must at least consider the war's influence on women's enfranchisement.

The issue of the war and women's suffrage was raised almost as soon as the war began. Certainly the women's suffrage organisations which split between those opposing and supporting the war were well aware of the stakes. An oft-quoted line from the leader of the main women's suffrage organisation in Britain, Millicent Garrett Fawcett, was that women must 'show ourselves worthy of citizenship' (Pugh, 1992: 8). Still, others saw that war opened up questions of its costs and the lack of compensation for voteless women, who had no say in its outbreak or outcome [*Doc. 26*].

Immediately prior to the war, Britain had witnessed an intense wave of militant – law-breaking and provocative – suffrage activity spearheaded by the Women's Social and Political Union (WSPU) under the leadership of Emmeline and Christabel Pankhurst. Other versions of militancy were practised by groups like the Women's Freedom League, while the largest British women's organisation, the National Union of Women's Suffrage Societies (NUWSS), advocated less confrontational policies like lobbying. The outbreak of war in August 1914 disrupted the suffrage movement in its entirety at a moment when women seemed very close to receiving the vote (Holton, 1986). Instead, as we saw in Chapter 6 above, support for the war divided members of the women's movement – militants and non-militants alike – fairly dramatically.

As we have seen, the outbreak of war saw militants like Christabel and Emmeline Pankhurst demanding that women have the right to serve Britain and launching anti-German campaigns. The NUWSS sponsored women's hospitals and a range of charitable works. All the while, activists within the NUWSS were monitoring and debating the political climate regarding women. When discussions began in 1916 about reforming the franchise to ensure that every fighting man could vote, they insisted that any such talk of reforms had to include women as well. Debates in the House of Commons led to the successful passage of the Representation of the People Bill in June 1917, with provisions that enfranchised most women over the age of 30. In 1918 the House of Lords assented as well and for the first time some British women had won the right to vote.

After years of struggle, why did feminists accept only partial women's suffrage, not suffrage on the same terms as men? In part because they believed, correctly, that once women had some form of suffrage further reform would follow. They also proved willing to compromise and unwilling to cause a public stink during the war. Some have suggested that it was ironic that the franchise failed to extend the vote to those women workers under age of 30 who had so valiantly served the nation and proved themselves 'worthy of citizenship'. Suffragist leaders acknowledged this but suggested, in the words of Millicent Garrett Fawcett, that what British women had obtained was a 'motherhood franchise' (Grayzel, 1999: 213). What soon became clear was that women's voting did not translate into greater numbers of women in office. The first woman elected to Parliament in December 1918 was Constance Markievicz, who along with other Irish nationalists popularly elected boycotted Westminster in favour of a provisional Irish Parliament.

While the British suffrage movement has received a good deal of historical attention and was one of the most visible of all prewar suffrage campaigns, we must remember that several Commonwealth states had granted women's suffrage prior to the war. New Zealand became the first nation to enfranchise all of its female citizens in 1894, and women across Australia gained a federal vote in 1901 when various states joined in a federation. Thus, there the question becomes did the presence of women in politics have any effect on the national wartime policy? Certainly, the 1916 and 1917 referenda on conscription in Australia, both of which lost by slim margins, had campaigns that explicitly targeted women. Debates about conscription divided along class and ethnic lines, with working-class institutions and Australians of Irish descent tending to oppose the draft, while the middle classes and those of English or Scottish descent tended to support it. Women were among the most vocal anti-conscriptionists, although since votes did not distinguish between men and women, there is no way of knowing how women's voting affected the outcome. Certainly, women were perceived as having contributed to the successful effort to keep Australia's armed forces voluntary (Scates and Frances, 1997).

The granting of votes to women in Britain needs to be put in the context of the eligible women voters in Europe. Only Finland and Norway had enfranchised women before the war. In these two cases, nationalism played an important role, as it did in the enfranchising of women in newly-created states such as Hungary, Poland and Czechoslovakia in the immediate aftermath of the war. Of the states that were created from the dismantling of the former central European empires, only Yugoslavia did not grant women the vote (Evans, 1979).

The first belligerent nation to grant women suffrage (and thus move to truly universal adult suffrage) during the First World War was Russia, on 20 July 1917. In its deliberations over how to reform the franchise, the Provisional Government decided to give the right to vote in elections to the Constituent Assembly to Russians of both sexes over the age of 20 (Stites, 1990: 294). The motivations for this are complicated. On the one hand, this occurred in a revolutionary context, where the support of women might prove crucial and where the Bolsheviks, as a threat to this government from the Left, had not focused on women as a political category. Maybe this was one way that the insecure Provisional Government hoped to gain support. However, by the time women could exercise this right, the Bolshevik seizure of power had made the franchise a moot point.

Wartime and the immediate postwar months provide the context for the granting of women's suffrage in other participant nations. German women also received their voting rights in the midst of revolution by a decree of the Council of People's Representatives on 30 November 1918, something that had proved impossible to accomplish either before or during the war. On paper at least, the Weimar Constitution of the new German government guaranteed men's and women's equality under the law. In practice, women's political participation in elections generally remained lower than that of men (Bessel, 1993). In North America, women had been granted regional but not federal voting rights prior to the war. In Canada, with some controversy, women with close relatives serving in the military overseas received a vote in 1917. By 1918, this was extended to all women (Evans, 1979). As for the United States, women did not have a federal vote when the war began, although certain states, particularly in the West, did allow women to vote in local and regional elections.

Still, in 1915, the United States' women's suffrage movement was divided into two prominent camps. Carrie Chapman Catt, who had just taken control of the National American Woman Suffrage Alliance (NAWSA), strove to secure voting rights on the state level, including the granting of a federal vote to women by state legislatures. Catt, even before the United States' entry into the war, had pledged that her organisation would support the war effort. Alice Paul led the militant National Woman's Party (NWP), which insisted that passing an Amendment to the Constitution was the policy to pursue, and she further radicalised the movement by launching pickets of the White House in the winter of 1917. Even more controversially, when America entered the war, NWP pickets called upon 'Kaiser Wilson' to give women the democratic rights that he claimed the

Allies were upholding abroad. This outraged even some supporters of women's suffrage, who found such behaviour scandalous at best and treasonous at worst (Cott, 1987).

In 1917, Jeanette Rankin of Montana became the first female member of Congress. She also became one famous example of how sex might affect voting. Rankin, as the first and only woman in the House of Representatives, cast a vote against American entry into the war, saying: 'I love my country, but I cannot vote for war' (Wiltsher, 1985: 174). This placed Rankin in contrast to the leadership of the NAWSA, who tried to rally support for their cause by raising fears about what would happen to a nation devoid of its loyal men, where only 'slackers' and supporters of Germany were around to vote. If this were the case, should not patriotic women be given a voice? Whether this tactic was persuasive or not, and despite Rankin's vote, President Wilson announced in January 1918 that he now actively supported women's suffrage. The House of Representatives almost immediately passed the Constitutional Amendment granting the vote to women. It then had to work its way through the Senate, which passed the measure in June 1919, and be ratified by the states, a process that concluded when the thirty-sixth state voted to adopt it in August 1920.

Of all the participant nations, France proves an important counterpoint since it alone of the main Allied nations did not grant women a vote in the war's aftermath. As was the case in other countries, women's suffrage was debated during and after the war in the French legislature (Bard, 1995; Hause with Kenney, 1984; P. Smith, 1996). In the midst of the war, a controversial measure offering women 'suffrage for the dead' received considerable publicity in 1916. This measure would give a woman who had lost a close male relative to the war the right to vote in his place. The idea of women earning such a right through an ultimate wartime sacrifice proved controversial. Several feminists denounced the idea of women gaining the vote in this manner rather than through a recognition of their equal status to men. Another alternative to suffrage for the dead was offering widows, who were now heads of households, a 'familial vote'. Neither measure was adopted. When women's suffrage of any variety was debated in the immediate postwar period, the bicameral French legislature split, and in May 1919 the Chamber of Deputies endorsed women having the right to vote on the same terms as men. It was in the more conservative French Senate that the measure was ultimately defeated in November 1922. As one senator declared in these debates, an 'imprudent' measure such as women's suffrage endangered 'the race', 'the family' and 'the Republic' (Grayzel, 1999: 222).

How then do we assess the war's effect on this and other outcomes of the campaign for women's suffrage? France was far from granting women's suffrage before the war, while Britain in the summer of 1914 arguably was not. The feminist movement itself was divided over support for the war, intensely so in places like the United States at the outbreak of fighting in Europe. Feminists in both neutral and belligerent nations sought to use their war service and patriotic nationalism as evidence of their qualifications for the full rights of citizenship. However, it is not clear that such arguments were ultimately persuasive or that they convinced anyone who was not already sympathetic to the cause. Some historians have argued that the granting of women's suffrage occurred because politicians believed that women would exert a 'stabilising' influence over politics. Hence, the red scares in First World War America, as well as the desire to prevent the spread of Bolshevik-type revolution in Central Europe, were used as the reason for giving women a vote (Evans, 1979). At the same time, it was the fear of women's conservatism and Catholicism, among other things, that prevented members of left-wing parties in France from supporting women's suffrage and enabling its passage (P. Smith, 1996). One thing, however, was clear: women's gaining the right to vote in the midst or aftermath of war was only partially related to their wartime services and sacrifices.

THE EFFECT ON WOMEN'S EMPLOYMENT

In terms of labour patterns, we find enormous variation among belligerent nations. In general terms, the shift in the kind of work performed by women had definitely altered; few women wanted to return to domestic service, for instance, and a greater number of occupations were opened up to women. These included the professions in several parts of Europe. For example, postwar legislation granted British women the right to enter professions such as law and the Civil Service, thus benefiting some middle- and upper-class women. However, the process of demobilisation in much of Europe returned men to their prewar positions and thrust many women out of the workplace. Some women may have gone willingly out of the waged workforce, but not all.

Britain provides a stark case study of what happened to women's paid employment. By March 1918, many thousands of women had been dismissed from munitions factories with one week's notice. On the eve of the armistice in November 1918, women munitions workers marched in London and Glasgow to protest their being laid off, but that had little effect. By 1921, the percentage of women in the labour force was 2 per cent lower than in 1911. Women factory workers were not the only ones who lost their jobs. Women were dismissed from war work ranging from being tram conductors to typists in the Civil Service as preference for employment was given to male war veterans (Beddoe, 1989: 48–9).

Along with the granting of the vote to some categories of women in 1918, other barriers to women's participation in public life, particularly the professions, fell in the immediate postwar period. Women received the right to stand for office as Members of Parliament in November 1918 and the 1919 Sex Discrimination (Removal) Act aimed to put an end to barriers preventing women from entering the professions. This allowed women to become lawyers, for instance, although in very small numbers. Despite these positive signs, for many women, especially working-class women, the postwar era offered little opportunity and a good deal of economic hardship.

Women whose employment had been terminated by wartime factories encountered difficulties finding alternative work. Many of them had no intention of either returning to or engaging in domestic service, an area where employment was available. As a result, women who had received unemployment insurance had their benefits cut off when they refused to take jobs as servants at greatly reduced pay. Attempts to appeal such denial of benefits, for instance by women with children who refused domestic service jobs that would have required them to live in and thus place their children elsewhere, almost invariably led nowhere. The message being sent by the government and employers was that women could not expect the same kinds of opportunity for work at the higher wages that they had enjoyed during the war (Beddoe, 1989; Braybon, 1981).

Former women war workers also found themselves criticised harshly in the popular press. As low-wage jobs as domestics and in laundries went vacant, the press complained that women factory workers receiving benefits were selfishly enjoying a holiday at government expense, that they were greedy and wanted high wages so they could waste money on fancy clothes. Any evidence of male unemployment, particularly of veterans unable to find work, was seen as demonstrating that women were depriving men of work by refusing to leave it and return home. While all women were castigated for working, married women, who presumably could be supported by a husband, were especially taken to task for doing so. Such criticism showed no understanding of the fact that women might not only want to continue to perform waged work, but also that necessity compelled many of them to do so. If the war left many widows, it also left women to support injured men (Beddoe, 1989; Braybon, 1981).

In France, officials such as the Minister of Armaments (now Reconstruction), Louis Loucheur, urged women wartime factory workers to return home as their new patriotic duty (Downs, 1995: 188). There was enough anxiety about the unrest that might result from a mass of unemployed, hungry women that the government offered those willing to stop work in the state arsenals voluntarily by 5 December 1918 a month's severance pay. This helped encourage some, although not all, women to leave, and of those who did so, not all took the money offered. Private industry had no qualms about simply discharging the women it no longer needed, and many women suffered accordingly from rapid demobilisation (Downs, 1995: 202–3).

For some women, however, the period of unemployment was not long. French manufacturers in the postwar era realised that because heavy wartime losses had left them with a labour shortage, they would have to employ women. If some women war workers faced immediate postwar unemployment and difficulties, many of them would be able to continue to work in factories. However, the kinds of work that they could do changed. Manufacturers wanted to employ cooperative women workers in a variety of 'light' occupations and repetitive work on the assembly line, and their participation rates in metalworking tripled between 1914 and 1939 (Downs, 1995: 227). Whatever work women performed was paid less well and was deemed to require less skill than work done by men. Perhaps most significantly, it was not meant to interfere with their more fundamental task of also literally regenerating the nation through having children.

Germany had trouble attracting women to wartime waged labour, but here too the situation of women engaged in wartime work at the end of the war is worth considering. Since working and living conditions overall had declined, the fact that women's wages began to approach men's by the war's end in real terms meant little. In addition, despite the positive impression of women's waged wartime work, as circulated in the media, such work was always assumed to be temporary. Prior to government decrees concerning demobilisation, employers and unions together had agreed that workers returning from military service should resume their prewar positions and this meant that women should be dismissed, beginning with those deemed 'not dependent on their earnings' (i.e., those with another source of income presumably from a male breadwinner) (Rouette, 1997: 55). Demobilisation saw hundreds of thousands of women leaving or being forced to leave the waged workforce so that jobs were available for returning veterans (Daniel, 1997: 281–3; Davis, 2000: 242–3). The number of female factory workers in Danzig, by February 1919, for example, had been reduced by 90 per cent from its October 1918 levels (Bessel, 1993: 140). Most significantly, postwar social policy made it increasingly difficult for married women to find waged work, which was considered 'unsocial'. In practice, postwar unemployment agencies steered women away from industrial work and towards domestic service and agriculture (Rouette, 1997: 56–8).

Despite its late entry into the war, the United States had witnessed women taking on new occupations, and in the immediate aftermath of the war in 1919, women in some of these new jobs, such as telephone operators, went on strike over their wages and working conditions but gained little in return (Greenwald, 1980). Overall, and similar to other nations, American women's advances into previously masculine industrial workplaces and occupations did not extend long past the war. Between

1910 and 1940, the percentage of women in the waged workforce held steady at around 25 per cent (Cott, 1987: 129).

At least in the West, women's employment in the tertiary sector – public service and the service professions such as social work, banking and commerce – rose substantially as it employed more and more women in the postwar world (Thébaud, 1994: 70). In Japan, the war had opened up opportunities for women as teachers and nurses, and this continued in the interwar era, as did other opportunities for white-collar work (Nagy, 1991). Part of the changes in Europe for women's work in tertiary occupations had to do with legislation, such as that discussed in the British case above or in the case of the Italian Sacchi Law of 1919 that allowed women to hold state jobs outside the military, judiciary and diplomatic corps (De Grazia, 1994). A Spanish law in 1918 similarly granted some women access to the professions. In addition, some prewar national patterns also held true. Relatively few married women worked in postwar Britain whereas many married women did so in France. Textile work remained the mainstay of women's industrial labour in both countries as well (Sohn, 1994). The extent to which individual women had better employment opportunities in the postwar world thus depended on nation, class, education, age and other factors; there was no clear sense that the war had benefited women overall.

SOCIAL WELFARE POLICY AND CULTURAL CHANGE

One of the war's most vivid legacies was its injured men, grieving women and fatherless children. In response, states created policies that were designed to help these families cope. Agreeing that they had a responsibility to safeguard those who had made sacrifices for the nation, and to ensure the health and well-being of the next generation of citizens, several governments enacted measures that contributed to the development of what became known as the welfare state.

Almost all participant nations had transformed state welfare policy by deciding to issue separation allowances directly to servicemen's wives and widows. Although women were granted these allowances in Britain and Germany as 'dependents' of their husbands, most came to consider them as their right. British separation allowances were based on the idea that wives and children as dependents ought to be maintained, if not by a male breadwinner, then by the state. France instead only granted benefits to children as a right, and paid money to servicemen's other needy dependents to maintain a standard of living (Pedersen, 1993). These allowances, which often varied depending on the number of children in the household, helped improve the living and health conditions of the children concerned (Bock, 1994).

New attention to maternal and infant health can be seen in several other concrete measures. One was Britain's 1918 Maternal and Child Welfare Act, which established clinics for needy mothers, expectant mothers and children. Another was the passage in the United States of the Sheppard-Towner Maternity and Infancy Act in 1921. This Act federally subsidised preventive health services for mothers and children. Wartime Germany already witnessed the expansion of the state into the realm of family as the Auxiliary Services Law of 1916 increased welfare services aimed at women. Welfare provisions remained a mixture of the private and charitable and the state through both the war and the Weimar periods (Hong, 1996). In Weimar Germany, existing insurance benefits were expanded in 1919 and again in 1927, and eventually included maternity leave for all women workers, in addition to a grant to replace wages and provide free medical care to expectant women (Bock, 1994).

In May 1920, France enacted its first Mother's Day, creating medals to honour women with many children. Its concerted efforts to promote maternity included several postwar legislative initiatives. Later in 1920, new legislation banning propaganda that would encourage the use of birth control or abortion was passed with overwhelming support (M. Roberts, 1994). Both measures, and indeed much of the public rhetoric of postwar France, were explicitly pronatalist. By the early 1920s, the French government established family allowances based on the principle that the redistribution of income to families with children was a state concern (Pedersen, 1993). This was not compensation to women for their labour in the home, as some British feminists, notably Eleanor Rathbone, had argued in the postwar period. Rather, this funding was meant essentially to reward families for having children. In interwar Europe then, most states enacted some version of children's allowances, mainly state subsidies to help alleviate the costs of rearing children that involved redistributing wealth from those without to those with children. In more democratic states, this money was paid directly to women; in the interwar dictatorships, it was paid to fathers (Bock, 1994).

If the war's end saw some women achieving new political and social rights yet losing economic ground, what about the effect of the war on the understanding of what it meant to be a woman? For instance, in many places in the West, certain fashions had altered during the course of the war, as women cut their hair and wore shorter skirts (or in some cases, trousers rather than skirts). As we have seen in Chapter 5 above, in addition to their changed appearances, women were now seen as having acquired new vices, such as drinking alcohol or smoking cigarettes. Other social issues must be considered, such as the increase in divorce and decline in the birth rate. In the 1920s the number of both marriages and births were on the decline in France and divorce rates rose in Britain as well. Some of the strain on marriages could easily have resulted from the psychological traumas and emotional difficulties imposed on couples by the war, and the deaths of such huge numbers of male combatants no doubt contributed to the falling birth rate. In Germany, the immediate postwar years saw an increase in marriages but also in divorces. What, however, did all of this mean? If one interpretation was that a horde of newly liberated women was now abandoning traditional assumptions about femininity, another was that many postwar women were deprived of the possibility of becoming wives and mothers and had to invent new ways of living without male support (Kent, 1993; M. Roberts, 1994).

As we saw in Chapter 5, public media in many wartime states, by expressing anxiety about women's sexuality, paradoxically allowed for more widespread discussion of it. Despite changes in cultural ideas and even in behaviour, it is worth noting that marriage and motherhood were still understood to be – and to a fairly large extent remained – the norm for many women. Evaluating what the war changed, what prewar and postwar social movements changed, and how widespread were the adoption of new cultural attitudes and elements remains difficult.

MOURNING AND COMMEMORATION

The war's death tolls were enormous and one way to characterise postwar Europe was as a world in mourning. The war left widows, orphans, bereft parents and siblings, grieving lovers and friends. Dealing with these immense losses was an ongoing process but it reached a new urgency at the war's end. In each belligerent nation, the public had to determine how the dead should be commemorated and what role civilians, especially women, should play.

In national and local discussions about the ways to distinguish the grieving, often female, relatives and friends of military men and in attempts to create rituals and provide monuments to commemorate the fallen dead, women's mourning came to have a political overtone. Wartime and postwar efforts to provide spaces in which to mourn the dead highlighted, in many cases, the particular loss experienced by women and mothers, who stood in for the nation at large. Some of the monuments and rituals themselves also made the mourning mother a bearer of memory for the community of her fallen son.

Across Europe, in every participant nation, localities and the nation as a whole had to decide how to remember and thus honour the war dead. One way that nations such as Britain, the United States and France chose to honour the dead was with a national tomb where the body of a unknown combatant could stand for every mother's son killed in the conflict. These national monuments and the ceremonies accompanying their unveiling provided an opportunity to make a symbolic statement about the war and its significance.

In Britain, government officials organising the ceremony to unveil their national monument debated who would be allowed to attend. A Cabinet Memorial Services Committee meeting on 19 October 1920 established that any seats for the interment of the unknown warrior, aside from those for members of the official procession, would be allotted 'not to Society ladies or the wives of dignitaries, but to the selected widows and mothers of those who had fallen, especially in the humbler ranks'. How were particular widows and mothers to be selected? Preference for seating would be given, first, to women who lost all their sons and their husband; second, to women who had only lost all their sons, and third, to widows who had lost an only son. As the secretary of the Memorial Services Committee further elaborated, this would mean that 'you might find the Duchess next the charwoman' (Grayzel, 1999: 229–30).

Thus, officials intended that national ceremonies would help to heal the nation by uniting it across class lines via shared grief. One potent emblem for doing this was featuring grieving women of all stations, particularly bereaved mothers, prominently in local ceremonies. For example, the city of Leicester's war memorial was unveiled on 4 July 1925 'in the name of all those who have lost their dear ones, by A Bereaved Mother' (Grayzel, 1999: 231).

Britain eventually decided to erect a national monument to the women of the Empire who died as a result of their service in the war as well. Below a newly-restored Five Sisters' Window in York Minster, 1,465 names were inscribed, including not only nurses but munitions and motor transport workers, members of the Land Army and every other women's service. At the unveiling ceremony for this memorial in 1925, the Duchess of York spoke of doing honour to these women of the Empire 'in the name of their sisters in all parts of the world' (Programme for Unveiling Ceremony, No. 754, IWM; *Yorkshire Herald*, 24 June 1925).

Given the geographical placement of women during the war in the occupied zones of the north and east of France, monuments here contained rolls of honour that recorded the names of civilian war dead, including women. The names of female victims of air raids in Britain also appeared on war memorials' rolls in places such as Deptford and Camberwell, again suggesting their status as casualties of war.

Of the national monuments, however, Scotland's stands out for its depiction of women's contributions as more than victims or mourners. The Scottish National War Memorial pays tribute in one brass panel to the work of those women who participated in the nursing services. It also has a separate panel that is dedicated to all Scotswomen, 'who amid the stress of war sought by their labours sympathy and prayer to obtain for their country the blessings of peace' (*Scottish National Memorial*, 40) [*Doc. 29*].

Other memorials themselves depicted mothers mourning their sons as a way to symbolise collective grief. In Hangest-en-Santerre in France's department of the Somme, a sculpture features a woman with her arm around her small son; she holds the helmet of a soldier and this image is offered to 'sons dead for France' (Rivé, et al., 1991: 195). Mourning women appear in several other French monuments, heads bowed with grief or sheltering small children (Sherman, 1999: 185, 212). In other locales, allegorical female figures were meant to embody 'pity' – the sentiment of all grieving mothers (Sherman, 1999: 205). In these instances, women became synonymous with civilians, whose duty was now to remember the dead. Other uses of feminine allegories in war memorials carried over from their earlier appearance in posters, as we saw in the discussion of propaganda in Chapter 2. A feminine 'Liberty' or 'winged Victory' appeared on memorials in many Allied nations, such as Britain, Canada and France (Moriarty, 1997; Sherman, 1999; Vance, 1997). Such angels of victory might point the way to battle or to heaven, but among arguably the most powerful monuments, the grieving mother prevails (Grayzel, 1999).

Some French women were active in the commemorative process by becoming the primary fundraisers for local monuments and as mourners, who owed an unredeemable debt to the soldiers who had saved them and the nation (Sherman, 1999). Still other French women took their grief and their status as bereft mothers and wives and defied governmental rules in order to claim the bodies of their sons. In February 1919, a law prohibiting families from removing French corpses from the battle zone in order to bury them closer to home, which had been enacted during the war, was extended for three years. As a result, some women not only protested against the law but also independently and illegally exhumed the bodies of their dead and took them home. Even the officials who were meant to stop such actions expressed sympathy with these women and their grief (Grayzel, 1999).

In Canada, soldiers' mothers were seen as having made a unique sacrifice that entitled them to a greater say in how their sons' deaths were to be commemorated. They could influence what kind of memorial was built and they could stand at the forefront of unveiling ceremonies. In one ceremony in Yarmouth, Nova Scotia, mothers and not fathers were seated directly in front of the monument. In part, this emphasis on mothers reflected the relationship between Canadians and 'Mother Britain', to whom was owed unquestioning duty and love (Vance, 1997: 149–50).

One of the most remarkable examples of a mother actively shaping the process of commemoration is German artist Kaethe Kollwitz's sculpture for her dead son, which remains one of the most powerful monuments of this or any war (Winter, 1995). Kollwitz's younger son Peter was killed in October 1915 and as her diary notes in July 1917, she began to think about making him a gravestone (Kollwitz, 1988: 82–3). Then, she began to plan a life-size monument of bereaved parents for the whole cemetery. She would work on these sculptures on and off until they were installed in July 1932 in the cemetery in Belgium in which her Peter lay buried. The final work features the figures of herself and her husband, literally forced to their knees, hugging themselves, in a transcendent grief. As Kollwitz describes it, on her last afternoon in Belgium she and her husband 'went from the figures to Peter's grave. ... I stood before the woman, looked at her – my own face – and I wept and stroked her cheeks' (Diary entry, 14 August 1932, quoted in Kollwitz, 1988: 122) [*Doc. 28*].

In addition to monuments depicting a universalised grief for a specific loss, the war's monuments to the unknown warrior too could have individual meaning. The symbol of the unknown combatant could stand in for every woman's relative, but especially a son, and this resonated in the postwar era. One fascinating example of this can be seen in May Miller's one-act play, *Stragglers in the Dust* (1930). This African American playwright poignantly shows the grief of a black cleaning woman who tends the tomb of the unknown soldier, her son. Her conviction that the tomb contains her son is dismissed as 'impossible' by two white men, the guard and the father of a shell-shocked veteran who haunts the monument. This same veteran (the 'straggler' of the title) claims to see the black soldier, who saved his life, enter the tomb each night, and the play ends with his death as he follows his fellow soldier into the monument (Miller, 1930).

Allied governments such as Britain, France, Italy and the United States, while having in common the honouring of war dead through the unknown warrior or soldier, adopted different methods for dealing with individual dead servicemen and women. Relatives in the United States were given the option of having their loved one's body repatriated and many chose to do so. Others were placed in official cemeteries (Meigs, 1997). British, Canadian and Australian bodies were not repatriated, and one result was that the places where the war dead fell also became sites of pilgrimages for their families, including many women. So, too, did the cemeteries where they were buried and the war memorials that appeared after the war in France. Women and veterans composed the bulk of those who proceeded to these sites in Northern France in the war's aftermath. Whether given the choice to repatriate bodies or not, the fate of their dead loved ones preoccupied women in the postwar world [*Doc. 30*].

In a country as seemingly isolated from the war zones as Australia, grief and the anticipation of grief proved a way to unite communities and to bring the war home. While soldiers' letters and news of the progress of the war itself were heavily censored, newspapers continued to publish death notices and casualty lists, thereby offering stark reminders of the war's costs. Approximately 60,000 of the over 330,000 men mobilised were killed; some 18,000 bodies were never found (Scates and Frances, 1997: 103).

Since Australian war dead were not repatriated, massive cemeteries arose on former battlefields. Unlike in other countries, families could choose what appeared as inscriptions on gravestones. These could range from the patriotic 'For duty done' to the despairing 'Another life lost/Hearts broken for what?' (Scates and Frances, 1997: 112). Not only did Australian families personalise these markers, but back in Australia, women actively participated in shaping the mourning process. They helped raise money to erect monuments, to determine what they should contain, and to unveil them. In addition, they sometimes appeared themselves on monuments designed to commemorate the war dead (Scates and Frances, 1997).

At the war's conclusion, Australian mothers were granted a special status, and their losses were acknowledged as being particularly acute. Australian women could even publicly display such grief through wearing badges with a star for each son or brother lost in the war. Mourning mothers claimed a public voice both to display grief and, over time, to demand compensation. In this effort, they were joined by war widows, as both categories of women found themselves economically disadvantaged, and in some cases reduced to dire poverty by the loss of the income of male breadwinners (Damousi, 1999).

Thus women's war losses could be as much material as emotional. Estimates for the numbers of war widows in some European nations are as follows: 600,000 in France, over 500,000 in Germany, and 200,000 each for Britain and Italy (Damousi, 1999: 71). Despite government pensions, for many of them and their children, the postwar world was a much grimmer place economically, socially and emotionally. Many war widows experienced great economic hardships as pensions proved inadequate to sustain families. Instead, in many parts of Europe, notably Germany, Britain and France, private and voluntary charitable organisations, many of them religious in nature, stepped in to help fill the gap between what the state could provide and what these women needed (Winter, 1995). Some English widows forced to accept poor relief found the experience humiliating and tried to avoid it, even if it meant overwork (Lomas, 1994). For Italian widows, aid was often linked to appropriate behaviour and waged work was discouraged. Here, too, widows' postwar economic and social situations were noticeably worse (Lagorio, 1995).

In Germany, as elsewhere, the government made an effort to support war widows who were mothers and thus defined as rendering vital service to the nation. Yet a consensus on providing the financial support necessary to perform this role adequately without a male breadwinner evolved quite slowly; pensions proved inadequate and the postwar job market made it difficult for women to supplement their incomes. For numerous women, then, their prewar standard of living was gone forever. Furthermore, in a postwar world that construed women as suffering mourners of dead heroes, there was little room to display and thus understand the messy and discomfiting reality of these heroes' families (Hausen, 1987).

While evidence is available for the numbers of widows, there are no statistics for the number of single women who lost a lover or potential husband and partner. We do not know how many women lost fathers or brothers whose emotional as well as material support was incalculable. Some wartime and postwar literature by women attempted to deal with this sense of grief. Vera Brittain returned to her studies at Oxford after the war a very changed woman; she had already described her brother's battle wounds as inflicting 'scars upon her heart' and the war had cost her not only his life but that of the man she loved. In 1920, she wrote a lament for the war's 'superfluous' women, those of her generation who had lost their men in the war; its poignant ending asks 'But who will give me my children?' [*Doc. 27*].

CHAPTER EIGHT

CONCLUSION

It is difficult to evaluate the extent to which the political, social and cultural conditions of the immediate postwar years and indeed of the 1920s themselves were due to the war. There may be no simple explanation for any of them. We can only understand what happened to the war's women by looking at them in a comparative perspective that acknowledges the diversity of their experiences. Was a French woman in 1919 cutting her long hair into a bob showing her liberation and modernity or enacting an older form of mourning and grief? Were British women wearing shorter skirts acting out of rebellion, thrift or conformity? The answers to both of these questions could be all or none of the above, depending on the individual.

Certainly, we have seen how the war accelerated the pace at which women across class lines entered public spheres and gained new employment and political opportunities. In some cases this was 'for the duration', but in other cases, women acquired new skills and new voting rights that enabled them to achieve more than had been possible prior to 1914. Concern over the spread of venereal diseases, among other factors, led to more open public discussions of sexuality, including women's sexuality. Examining women's wartime lives across many national boundaries, we should be struck by some similarities in how states viewed women, but also by many differences. One conclusion then is that political borders and states matter, that part of what makes this war such a compelling moment in women's history is that it provides an opportunity for many women to forge a new relationship with their nation-states. This does not mean that they succeeded, for we are left with contradictory evidence of women's progress: for example a nation like Britain passes legislation giving some women the vote during the war but does not enfranchise the vast majority of women war workers.

Women's war experiences varied enormously, but, with few exceptions, they remained different from those of the majority of men conscripted into military service. No nation was willing to break this barrier and draft women to serve in its army. For all the debate at relatively high levels of government over compulsory war service for women in Germany and Britain, nothing came of such measures. Thus, to an extent, everything that women contributed to the war was done on a 'voluntary' basis. Many perceived that wartime women, particularly the young, had choices that their male counterparts, by and large, did not. Perhaps this explains why, for all the praise of women's undeniably important work for their nations at war, the postwar world was unwilling to accord them equal recognition. Despite all the evidence presented here about the centrality of both material production and good morale at home to the whole enterprise of total war, women's roles were quickly relegated to the sidelines.

In part, this occurred because of the bias of those who write military history, who consider what happens on battlefields to be paramount. Even as the nature of warfare itself began to change, with women directly and indirectly under fire, the fact of their exclusion from combatant status made women seemingly easy to ignore. So too did the failure of the war to free the majority of women from being held responsible for their households and children. That the public holiday given over to postwar women became a version of 'Mother's Day' says a great deal about the unwillingness of their societies to alter their fundamental assumptions about women's service to the nation. Denied the status of true 'participant', many women shaped by the First World War continued to sustain their families, in some cases to support them financially, and to cope with grief and guilt over surviving an experience that left so many dead or shattered.

At the same time, women's exclusion from military service empowered a feisty minority of women to protest vigorously against the war and militarism in general. They did so with the tools of their femininity, speaking out as mothers and as the disenfranchised, whose nations were waging a war without their consent. Where women did have the vote, such as in Australia, they played a role in helping to stop conscription and thus the further spread of total war into their society. Yet, being able to protest against a war that they did not have to fight also made women suspect – a threat to their nations that had to be suppressed.

Whatever their ultimate view of the war, the years 1914–18 did not leave many men and women, particularly in the main belligerent states, unchanged. Some women, like Vera Brittain, transformed their grief into activism, condemning war and fighting for justice for men and women in public arenas. Others were ready, when the next wars came, to urge that women be pressed into service, that having once demonstrated their worth to the nation, they were ready to answer the call again. Still others suffered physically, materially and emotionally from the high costs of waging the war.

Some questions raised by the experience of women in the First World War are with us yet. Should women naturally advocate peace not war?

Should women be excluded from combat? What is the appropriate role for women, for mothers, in a wartime state? What does citizenship or even patriotism mean for women when their national service is not compelled as is that of men? Is there a firm boundary between the war front and the home front? By examining how societies grappled at the start of the twentieth century with these unanswered questions, perhaps we can begin to reach some conclusions in our own.

Propaganda posters used images of women to recruit men and women, and to justify what the war was being fought over.

Poster by Howard Chandler Christy (USA), Imperial War Museum, London.

Poster by E. Kealy (Britain), Imperial War Museum, London.

DOCUMENT 2   SURVIVORS' ATROCITY TESTIMONY USED FOR
             PROPAGANDA PURPOSES (1)

Testimony from survivors of attacks by the German army were collected by both the British and French governments. The published accounts were widely read and helped propagate the idea of German atrocities against innocent civilians, especially women, as a motivation for the Allied cause. Such reports later came into disrepute.

a33 Testimony of a Belgian refugee, Pepinster

As I looked into the kitchen I saw the Germans seize the baby out of the arms of the farmer's wife. There were three German soldiers, one officer and two privates. The two privates held the baby and the officer took out his sword and cut the baby's head off. The head fell on the floor and the soldiers kicked the body of the child into a corner and kicked the head after it. When the farmer, who was with us in the dairy saw this he wanted to shout out and go nearer the window. The two men and I prevented him from doing this as we said we should lose our own lives. One of the men put a cloth in the farmer's mouth so that the noise of his weeping should not be much heard. It takes practically no time to get from the kitchen to the dairy by the way we went. We ran round. You could not hear anything that was said in the kitchen. We could see that the wife was crying, but we could not hear her.

After the baby had been killed we saw the officer say something to the farmer's wife and saw her push him away. After five or six minutes, the two soldiers seized the woman and put her on the ground. She resisted them and they then pulled all her clothes off her until she was quite naked. The officer then violated her while one soldier held by the shoulders and the other by the arms. After the officer each soldier in turn violated her, the other soldier and the officer holding her down. The farmer did not see his wife violated: the two men-servants had pulled him down from the bench after the baby had been killed, and they would not let him get up again. After the woman had been violated by the three the officer cut off the woman's breasts. I then saw him take out his revolver and point it at the woman on the ground. At this moment the farmer broke away from the two men-servants, jumped onto a chair and put his foot through the window. The two men-servants and I and the servant girl ran away as soon as the farmer had broken the window and we know nothing more. We ran into the fields and from there saw the farmhouse had been set on fire. ...

Committee on Alleged German Outrages, *Appendix to the Report of the Committee on Alleged German Outrages* (London: HMSO, 1915), pp, 12–13.

DOCUMENT 3   SURVIVORS' ATROCITY TESTIMONY USED FOR
PROPAGANDA PURPOSES (2)

*Report presented to the President of the Council [of Ministers] by the
Commission instituted to verify the acts committed by the enemy in
violation of the law of nations, 17 December 1914.*

The outrages against women and young girls were of an unprecedented
frequency. We have here documented a great number, which represents but
a minute quantity in comparison with those we have been able to turn up;
but, by virtue of a very respectable sentiment, the victims of these odious
acts have generally refused to relieve themselves to us. ...

Interrogation 1 Oct., Sancy-les-Provins
Dame X ... , 27 years
Sunday September 6, a German cyclist came to the house of my mother-in-
law, where I found myself with my four children, my husband having left
for his regiment. This cyclist demanded a bed and wine. I showed him the
bed in which my children were going to go to bed. He seized me by the
wrist and by the chest, dragged me into the next room, and, menacing me
by his placing his revolver against my throat, he forced me to have intimate
relations with him.
    After reading, the witness signed with us.

6 Oct. Jussécourt-Minecourt
Demoiselle X, 21 years, domestic servant
September 8, around nine o'clock in the evening, I went to go to bed
completely clothed, when three Germans broke in the door of my room
with the aid of a bill-hook. They then introduced their hand guns into my
room. Then one other arrived, and all four violated me successively. I swear
that what I have told is the truth.
    After reading, the witness signed with us.

*Documents Relatifs à la Guerre 1914–1915: Rapports et Procès Verbaux d'Enquête de la
Commission I* (Trans. Susan R. Grayzel; Paris: Imprimerie Nationale, 1915), pp. 8, 56, 87–8.

DOCUMENT 4   ON STATE SUPPORT FOR SOLDIERS' DEPENDENTS

*Almost all participant nations used state support for soldiers' dependents as
a way to promote the morale of both military men and civilians. In Britain,
they were also used as a recruiting tool, but the measures put into place to
determine how such dependents would receive aid generated controversy.
Here is a journalist's response to this debate in 1914.*

Although the new scale of allowances for wives and dependents of soldiers and sailors has done something to allay the deep irritation that was felt in many quarters, it has not satisfied anyone who is of the opinion that the defenders of the nation should be treated as something better than 'cannon fodder', to be bought at the lowest market rates.

... [A]ll classes, ever since the commencement, have realised that the present war is one of vital import. Press and Parliament alike have warned the nation that a supreme effort would be required, and that a supreme effort could not be made unless hundreds of thousands, even two or three millions, of men were withdrawn from civil life and turned into soldiers.

... [T]he patriotism of such men, their love of the nation and their readiness to fight for its best traditions and ideals, naturally demanded that the nation should retain their homes and families in health whilst they were saving the country.

[Kenney then laments the inadequacies of the current system and delays in delivering allowances to needy families.]

And, added to all this, soldiers' dependents are now to be put under police surveillance. The Army Council has addressed to Chief Constables, with a covering letter from the Home Office, a memorandum, of which the first sentence runs: 'The Army Council desire to have the assistance of the police in the measures which are being taken to provide for the withholding of separation allowances payable to wives or dependents of soldiers in the event of serious misconduct on the part of the recipient.' Even at this hour, apparently, the pay of soldiers and the allowance to their wives is to be regarded as a dole instead of a national obligation for services rendered. As Lord Middleton frankly put it, 'The dependents of soldiers should receive their allowances, after proper investigation, as a favour, and not as a right.' ... They are sore troubled about the temptations to which women with a regular income of a few shillings a week will be subject. The payment of allowances to 'women supported by soldiers with no legal tie' is a 'fruitless extension of an unsound principle'. Such a procedure, says Lord Middleton, 'will be considered by all who have specially at heart the moral and religious well-being of the country to strike at the root of morality'. Quite so. We must make our soldiers and their dependents moral, if we starve them to death in the process. Besides, if we keep the women who are not legally tied moral, by refusing to pay them their just dues, look what we shall save. Business as usual.

[Kenney proposes an alternative]

[T]he recognition that the payment is made as a right, thus abolishing all police or other inquisition; and the consequent closing down of numerous charitable agencies and the release of their workers for more productive labour. Let us hope that the Select Committee that has been appointed will come to some such conclusion.

From Rowland Kenney, 'Soldiers' Dependents', *The English Review*, December 1914, pp. 112–13, 116–18.

DOCUMENT 5   DEBATING COMPULSORY WAR WORK FOR GERMAN WOMEN

Here is a letter debating the merits of including compulsory war work for German women in light of the 1916 Auxiliary Services Law that would allegedly put all German men to work.

It is also my opinion that women's work should not be overestimated. Almost all intellectual work, heavy physical labour, as well as all real manufacturing work will still fall on men – in addition to the entire waging of the war. It would be good if clear, official expression were given to these facts and if a stop were put to women's agitation for parity in all professions, and thereby, of course, for political emancipation. I completely agree with your Excellency that compulsory labour for women would be an inappropriate measure. After the war, we will need the woman as spouse and mother. I thus strongly support those measures, enacted through law, prerogative, material aid, etc., aimed at that effect. In spite of the strong opposition to such measures, it is here that vigorous action needs to be taken in order to extinguish the influence of this female rivalry, which disrupts the family. Your excellency would please gather from the above that I am not only concerned with the war, but that I am also aware that, for the development of our people *after* the war, healthy social conditions, i.e. in the first place the protection of the family, are necessary.

If I *nevertheless* urge that the requirement to work be extended to all women who are either unemployed or working in trivial positions, now and for the duration of the war, I do so because, in my opinion, women can be employed in many areas to a still greater degree than previously and men can thereby be freed for other *work*. But first industry and agriculture must be urged even more to employ women. Further, the choice of occupation must not be left up to the women alone, but rather, it must [be] regulated according to ability, previous experience and social status. In particular, I want to stress again that I consider it especially wrong to keep secondary schools and universities, which have been almost completely emptied of men by conscription, open only for women. It is valueless, because the scholarly gain is minimal; furthermore, because precisely that rivalry with the family that needs to be combated would be promoted; and finally, because it would represent the coarsest injustice if the young man, who is giving everything for his Fatherland, is forced behind the woman.

Letter of Chief of the General Staff General Paul von Hindenburg to Chancellor Bethmann Hollweg, October 1916. Quoted in Ute Daniel, *The War From Within: German Working-class Women in the First World War* (Trans. Margaret Ries; Oxford: Berg, 1997), pp. 68–9, emphasis in the original.

DOCUMENT 6   AN EXCHANGE ON THE EFFECTS OF WAR WORK ON WOMEN

As women flocked to war work, especially in war-related munitions factories, concern grew that such war work was somehow coarsening women, as this exchange about Glasgow women workers in 1917 illustrates.

A short procession on Saturday revealed to a number of people that a great many of our young munitioners are what Lady Macbeth prayed to be, unsexed from the crown of their bonneted heads to the toe of their masculine overalls. The badinage that many of these youngsters hurled at the spectators was almost incredibly coarse. This issue of the war is not news, but a little advertising of the fact may lead to something being done about it. ...

If ... war work is coarsening our young womanhood, the cause must lie in the special conditions. Our foul-mouthed Army pleads that the excitement of fighting, the dirtiness of the killing job, the divorce from the ordinary decencies of life are an excuse. But the munitioners' work is not exciting; home life is possible for the majority; there are agencies like the 'Welf', which seek to make munitioneering, if possible, a positively elevating influence.

We are bound to believe that the degenerates in speech and conduct that are giving the women war workers their 'name' have been for the most part carried away by vanity, plus high wages which are mainly wasted. They are after a fashion heroines, and have been taught to regard themselves as such – the indispensable aides of the men at the guns, several cuts above common factory workers. They are pampered. The masculine dress has a psychological effect on the susceptible. The youngsters are naturally too conscious of being engaged in a great adventure. ...

Now, we do not say ... that the great mass of munition workers are coarsened or that the vixens who shocked the ears of Glasgow on Saturday are hopeless cases, bound for the gutter when the war is over. That is no more inevitable than that our swearing Army is going to debase ordinary talk for a generation. In both cases, of course, some of the defiling pitch must stick. ...

There are many ways in which the 'shaping' and posturing of the pampered munitioner could be discouraged. In the factories themselves good influences could be deliberately sowed. ... The class from which the workers come could show them in many ways that cursing and indecent talk are not the thing. The whole community could put these young fools to shame if it liked.

... Is the standard of taste in the community, not to speak of the standard of morals, high enough to counteract all these and other horrid issues of the war?

'Foul-Mouthed Bellona', *The Bulletin*, 3 September 1917.

Sir: To one who is proud to control many thousands of girl munition workers, the leading article headed 'Foul-Mouthed Bellona', which was published in Monday's 'Bulletin', comes somewhat as a shock. ...

[N]o one with the knowledge of what women have done and what they will do in the months to come can feel other than that such an article produces in the minds of the community an entirely wrong impression. War work is not coarsening our young womanhood. On the contrary, it is elevating it. ...

It is very possible that out of the many thousands at Georgetown there may have been a small minority on Saturday who misbehaved themselves. In the hurry of gathering great bodies of workpeople together such is inevitable. ...

I have stated on many occasions that the women of Great Britain have saved the country. No sane man would deny that, and no sane woman will deny that it has been done by the loyal help of the men who have taught them their craft.

During the past two years I have been responsible for the placing of thousands of women either outside my control or directly under my control, and almost without exception every one of the great crowds have not only done magnificent work but have set an example to the country of steadiness under great stress, and, what is more difficult, steadiness under wages conditions that are at present probably higher than they have ever been in the history of the country. ... I am not speaking without knowledge when I say that the generosity displayed by the girls towards every kind of charity, the percentage of money they have put into war loans, their appreciation of every little service rendered, their general kindness not only to those in authority but to their colleagues in the factories, especially those who are in distress – all these are phenomenal. The vast majority are not the 'pampered crowd' that they are represented to be, but they have taken their places in the war with a solid determination to provide the means to carry on the war in the absence of our millions of skilled and unskilled men. ...

Cecil Walton, Letter to the Editor of The Bulletin, 7 September 1917.
(Women's Work Collection, Imperial War Museum)

DOCUMENT 7   A NURSE'S EXPERIENCE OF THE WAR

This excerpt from a Canadian nurse's diary gives an insight into what women engaged in this and related professions experienced during the war.

1915
June 7

Some of these new patients have dreadful dreadful wounds. One young boy with part of his face shot away both arms gone & great wounds in both legs. Surely Death were merciful. Many head cases which are heart-breaking, & many many others. The men are all so good & patient, & so grateful for even the smallest attention. These are the horrors of war, but they are too horrible. Can it be God's will or only man's devilishness? It is too awful. Our boy with both his arms gone is only twenty years old. ...

1916
June 4

The news of the fighting Thursday, Friday & yesterday is ghastly. Our troops simply mown down without hope of resistance by artillery fire. Miss Harrisons [*sic*] brother has come in with a head wound. Mrs Giffins [*sic*] brother was last seen by one of these men lying on his face in a trench. Louise McGreer's brother has been in the thick of it. – & there are thousands of others. It is terrible. I went down to the Red Cross today with Mrs Giffin in hours off to see if we could get news of her brother at the Red Cross. We waited for a long time ... but met with no success. ...

June 6

The tales of the loss of life in recent fighting around Ypres increase each day. This is part of a third battle of Ypres. Our Canadian troops lost their trenches & retook them. It is a ghastly affair.

Susan Mann (ed.), The War Diary of Clare Gass 1915–1918 (Montreal: McGill-Queen's
University Press, 2000), pp. 26 and 123.

DOCUMENT 8   REFLECTIONS ON CHARITABLE WORK AND
RACISM IN THE AMERICAN ARMY

Every participant nation saw its female citizens engaged in charitable work to aid soldiers, especially those stationed overseas. Here two African American women describe what such women contributed generally as well as reflecting on the racism of the American Army as it tried to police contact between African American soldiers and the French population, especially French women.

(a)

Over the canteen in France was essentially different from the same thing in the United States where friendships and home ties had not yet been really severed and war was still thousands of miles from the camp. In France, war, with its mystery of pain and suffering was over all. Everywhere were evidence of its mutilation and destruction of life and home. Everywhere there was exhausting work and deep loneliness. In the most joyous hour in the Y hut we knew that there was a nervousness, a tenseness, a deep undercurrent of seriousness that could be found only in an environment of death and desolation.

Over the canteen in France friendships and confidences ripened quickly because of the loneliness of men – because of the haunting and yearning memories of their women-folk at home. A glass of lemonade or a cup of chocolate offered with a sympathetic touch was usually sufficient to break down all barriers. ... We learned to anticipate that from some pocket in the jacket – usually the one nearest the heart – would be drawn forth a wallet or a much worn envelope. From it photographs would come forth. Sometimes it would be the 'best mother,' again the 'dearest wife,' and still again the 'finest girl' or 'cutest kid' that a fellow ever had. ...

Over the canteen in France, the woman became a trusted guardian of that home back in America. To her were revealed its joys and sorrows. Because of that same loneliness – that loss of background – the soldier poured out to the canteen worker his deepest and dearest memories and dreams. She must be ever ready to laugh with him, but she must also be ready to go down into heart-breaking valley with her soldier boy when he would get a bit of bad news – a mother, father, sister or even a wife or child might have been taken away; or, worse still, once in a great while the tragedy of faithlessness was made known to him. But by far, the letters from home were cheerful to have come straight from hearts of women tense with longing and anxiety. ...

Addie W. Hunton, 'Over the Canteen in France', in A.W. Hunton and K.M. Johnson, *Two Colored Women with the American Expeditionary Forces* (Brooklyn, NY: Brooklyn Eagle Press, 1920), pp. 741–2.

(b)

The first post of duty assigned to us was Brest. Upon arriving there we received our first experience with American prejudices, which had not only been carried across the seas, but had become a part of such an intricate propaganda, that the relationship between the colored soldier and the French people is more or less a story colored by a continued and subtle effort to inject this same prejudice into the heart of the hitherto unprejudiced Frenchman.

We had gone to this city under protest, because we felt that since there were only three colored women in France among approximately 150,000 colored soldiers, that our first duty should be to the men at the front, who were without doubt suffering the greatest hardships. But we were told that in this city there was a great need, and that we had better serve out a probation here, before being sent to the more arduous tasks at the front. ...

In one city, the soldiers informed us, colored Americans were confined to certain streets in order that their contact with the French people might have all possible limitations.

Following is a copy of an order gotten out, and a duplicate preserved:

HEADQUARTERS SECOND BATTALION
    804TH PIONEER INFANTRY
    A.E.F., FRANCE
    WARCQ, FRANCE, MARCH 20, 1919

Enlisted men of this organization will not talk to or be in company with any white women, regardless of whether the women solicit their company or not.

    By the Order of CAPTAIN BYRNE

A True Copy

S/L/D/

This propaganda was spread from the streets of the large cities to the topmost peaks of the Alps Mountains, away up among the little shepherd girls, who knew nothing except what others came up to tell them. 'Soldat noir-vilain,' they remarked to the writer one day, while she sat down to gather strength to finish her trip to the little chapel whose ruins stood on the highest pinnacle; even their minds had been poisoned with the thought that 'black soldiers were villains.'

... [The French people] gradually discovered that the colored American was not the wild, vicious character that he had been represented to be, but that he was kindhearted, genteel and polite. One could frequently hear the expression, 'soldat noir, tres gentil, tres poli' (black soldier very genteel, very polite); this characteristic appealed greatly to these people who have always been noted for their innate politeness.

The French women were especially kind and hospitable to their dark-skinned allies. ... When French women learned that the Americans were trying to control the social intercourse of their homes, they deeply resented it.

Kathryn M. Johnson, 'Relationships with the French', in A.W. Hunton and K.M. Johnson, *Two Colored Women with the American Expeditionary Forces* (Brooklyn, NY: Brooklyn Eagle Press, 1920), pp. 182, 185–8.

DOCUMENT 9   THE TRANSITION FROM DOMESTIC SERVICE TO WAR WORK IN THE USA

Many women who worked in wartime factories or for the government during the war made the transition from domestic service, rather than entering the waged workforce for the first time. Here a former African American domestic servant now employed as a common labourer in a railroad yard describes her transition in more general terms.

All the colored women like this work and want to keep it. We are making more money at this than any work we can get, and we do not have to work as hard as at housework which requires us to be on duty from six o'clock in the morning until nine or ten at night, with might little time off and at very poor wages. ... What the colored women need is an opportunity to make money. As it is, they have to take what employment they can get, live in old tumbled down houses or resort to street walking, and I think a woman ought to think more of her blood than to do that. What occupation is open to us where we can make really good wages? We are not employed as clerks, we cannot all be school teachers, and so we cannot see any use in working our parents to death to get educated. Of course we should like easier work than this if it were opened to us. With three dollars a day, we can buy bonds ... , we can dress decently, and not be tempted to find our living on the streets. ...

Helen Ross, Freight House, Santa Fe RR, Topeka, Kansas, 28 October 1918, File 55, Women's Service Section, Record Group 14 [Records of the United States Railroad Administration] National Archives, Washington, DC. Also quoted in M.W. Greenwald, *Women, War and Work: The Impact of World War I on Women Workers in the United States* (Ithaca, NY: Cornell University Press, 1980, reprinted, 1990), p. 27.

DOCUMENT 10 AMBIVALENCE ABOUT MOTHERHOOD AND WAR WORK

This advertisement for Glaxo Infant Formula, appearing in The Woman Worker, *June 1918, demonstrates some of the ambivalence that greeted women's shift from work in the home to work in the wartime factories.*

'Munitions and Motherhood'
Not even a woman can eat her cake and have it, not even she can make the munitions to save the present and tend the children who are to be the future. But the present day requires that women shall leave their homes, where the future should be made, and should take the place of men in the factories. ...

Women can take men's places; but men cannot take women's. That is the humiliating truth for the sex-proud men to swallow to-day. ...

At first we were as blind and reckless of the consequences to the future as we could be. We worked our women seven days a week, ... and we forgot the children altogether. ... To-day we are learning some measure of sense; and its substance is this: –

If women in general, who necessarily include mothers, are to make munitions, serve their country ... in any capacity, high or low, it is necessary for our national future that special steps be taken to guard the children who are the natural, sacred and supreme care of womanhood. Whether it be the child of the munition-worker, or of the most highly-placed woman-worker in the land, the problem is one and the same.

The Woman Worker, June 1918.

DOCUMENT 11 REACTIONS TO THE GERMAN ARMY'S REQUISITIONING OF FRENCH FEMALE LABOUR

In April 1916, partially in response to food shortages at home and locally, the German army decided to requisition labour as well as supplies from the civilian population of occupied France. The deportation of young girls and women from the urban centres of the north, and their accounts of their treatment, provoked outrage in France and elsewhere as the French government tried again to show the barbarity of its German foe, given its treatment of women.

Annex 11
Monsignor Charost, Bishop of Lille, to General von Graevenitz
Numerous removals of women and girls, certain transfers of men and youths, and even of children, have been carried out in the districts of Tourcoing and Roubaix without judicial procedure or trial.

You are a father; you know that there is not in the order of humanity a right more honourable or more holy than that of the family. ... Thus, to dismember the family, by tearing youths and girls from their homes, is not war; it is for us torture and the worst of tortures – unlimited moral torture. The violation of the family rights is doubled by a violation of the sacred demands of morality. Morality is exposed to perils, the mere idea of which revolts every honest man, from the promiscuity which inevitably accompanies removals *en masse*, involving mixture of the sexes, or, at all events, of persons of very unequal moral standing. Young girls of irreproachable life – who have never committed any worse offence than that of trying to pick up some bread or a few potatoes to feed a numerous family, and who have, besides, paid the light penalty for such trespass, have been carried off. Their mothers, who have watched so closely over them, and had no other joy than that of keeping their daughters beside them, in the absence of father and sons fighting or killed at the front – these mothers are now alone. They bring to me their despair and anguish. ... I know that you have no part in these harsh measures. You are by nature inclined towards justice; that is why I venture to turn to you. ... We have suffered much for the last twenty months, but no stroke of fortune could be comparable to this; it would be as undeserved as it is cruel and would produce in all France an indelible impression. I cannot believe that the blow will fall. I have faith in the human conscience and I preserve the hope that the young men and girls of respectable families will be restored to their homes in answer to the demand for their return and that sentiments of justice and honour will prevail over all lower consideration.

signed Alexis-Armand

Bishop

Ministère des Affaires Étrangères, *The Deportation of Women and Girls from Lille*
(London: Hodder & Stoughton, 1916), pp. 15–16.

DOCUMENT 12   AN EYEWITNESS ACCOUNT FROM THE RUSSIAN FRONT

As an English nurse serving on the Russian Front throughout the war, Florence Farmborough witnessed some of the most dramatic circumstances of a tumultuous time. In these excerpts from 1917, she discusses the outbreak of the Russian Revolution and the appearance of women soldiers, as well as noting the power imbalance between (mostly female) nurses and (mostly male) doctors that confronted women in the medical professions no matter where they were stationed during the war.

January 1917

Discontent among the masses in Russia is daily becoming more marked. Disparaging statements concerning the Government are being voiced – at first, they were surreptitious, and now, more bold and brazen, at meetings and street corners. ...

Now that food has grown scarce in Petrograd and Moscow, disorder takes the shape of riots and insurrections. We are told that mobs of the lower classes parade the streets shouting 'Peace and Bread!' They are aware that the war is at the root of their hardships. So it is: 'Peace and Bread!' But as the days pass, hunger gains primary place and the erstwhile docile rabble grows unruly and rampageous. ...

... Some enigmatic movement is afoot in Russia. Who can gauge its meaning and determine its goal?

It is a dull, oppressive winter; the frost and ice do their best to numb our thoughts and hamper our movements. There is no settled work; now and then a couple of wounded are brought in, or a few sick men, but for the most part we are experiencing complete inaction. Tempers become fractious, nerves frayed, and it is no unusual thing to hear lengthy disputes, or peevish, irritable words. We seem to be waiting for *something* to happen. Things cannot continue as they are. Many questions are asked, but none can answer them. 'Will the war continue?' 'Will a separate peace be arranged between Russia and Germany?' 'What will our Allies do in such an emergency?'

It is a grievous situation for us all; I, too, share the tension. ...

11 May 1917 Podgaytsy

Today we left Strusuv for Podgaytsy. Our division is back at the Front and two of its regiments are already in the trenches. Now and then unexpected skirmishes take place – the initiative always with the Austrians – and a few wounded are brought to us. We notice a strange apathy about them; they lack the spark of loyalty, of devotion to God and their mother-country which has so distinguished the fighting-men in the previous two years. It worries us; we do not need to be told that the Russian soldier has changed; we see the change with our own eyes. ...

26 July, Into Roumania

[A]nother story made a deep impression. A Siberian woman soldier had served in the Russian Army since 1915 side by side with her husband; when he had been killed, she had continued to fight. She had been wounded twice and three times decorated for valour. When she knew that the soldiers were deserting in large numbers, she made her way to Moscow and Petrograd to start recruiting for a Women's Battalion. It was reported that she had said:

The Sheffield
Peaks Learning Resource Centre

'If the men refuse to fight for their country, we will show them what the *women* can do!' So this woman warrior, Yasha Bachkarova [*sic*], began her campaign; it was said that it had met with singular success. Young women, some of aristocratic families, rallied to her side; they were given rifles and uniforms and drilled and marched vigorously. We Sisters were of course thrilled to the core.

A woman soldier, or boy soldier, was no unusual sight in the Russian Army. We had even come into contact with a couple of Amazon warriors; one, in her early twenties, who had had a nasty gash on her temple caused by a glancing bullet, had come to our first aid post on the Galician Front. I recalled, how, after bandaging her and feeding her, we had had some difficulty in persuading her to stay the night with us in our barn and return to her company at daybreak. I think that she feared her comrades might think she had absconded.

9 August

Last Monday, an ambulance-van drove up with three wounded women soldiers. We were told that they belonged to the Bachkarova Women's Death Battalion. We had not heard the full name before, but we instantly guessed that it was the small army of women recruited in Russia by the Siberian woman soldier, Yasha Bachkarova. Naturally, we were very impatient to have news of this remarkable battalion, but the women were sadly shocked and we refrained from questioning them until they had rested. The van-driver was not very helpful, but he did know that the battalion had been cut up by the enemy and had retreated.

19 October

I saw one of our young doctors dressing a wound before the dirt and grime around it had been washed off. I gave way to my wrath and told him that he was asking for serious trouble if he had dressed the wound before first cleansing it. He rudely told me to mind my own business; I told him that it *was* my business to see that our soldiers' wounds were cleaned before bandaging. We exchanged many angry, resentful words. I knew that I was right; he knew that he was wrong. But he was a doctor! I was only a Sister!

That night, I worked it out before I went to sleep. I knew that I was growing coarse, bad-humoured and fault-finding. At first, I ascribed it to the pressure of warfare, the many hardships and humiliations, the conditions of our everyday life at the Front, when for days we could not undress, or even have a good wash. I decided that there were, indeed, good reasons for my bad temper; yet I began to feel ashamed of myself. ...

26 October

There has been a big uprising of the *Bolsheviki* in Petrograd. A telegram has come containing the news that some members of the Provisional Government have been arrested by the rioters and that their so-called 'Socialist Organisation' intends to overthrow the Government and take power into its own hands. ...

Florence Farmborough, *With the Armies of the Tsar: A Nurse at the Russian Front in War and Revolution, 1914–1918* (New York: Cooper Square Press, 1974; reprinted, 2000), pp. 254–5, 266–7, 299–300, 302, 326 and 327.

DOCUMENT 13 THE EFFECTS OF THE WAR ON AN AMBULANCE DRIVER ON THE WESTERN FRONT

In this excerpt from Evadne Price's postwar novel, based on the wartime diaries of an ambulance driver on the Western Front, the main character reflects on the effects of the war on the entire generation of women who witnessed its horrors directly.

Whenever I close my aching red eyes a procession of men passes before me: maimed men; men with neither arms nor legs; gassed men, coughing, coughing, coughing; men with dreadful burning eyes; men with heads and faces half shot away; raw, bleeding men with the skin burned from their upturned faces; tortured, all watching me as I lie in my flea-bag trying to sleep ... an endless procession of horror that will not let me rest. I am afraid. I am afraid of madness. ...

For I fear these maimed men of my imaginings as I never fear the maimed men I drive from the hospital trains to the camps. The men in the ambulance scream, but this ghostly procession is ghostly quiet. I fear them, these silent men, for I am afraid they will stay with me all my life, shutting out beauty till the day I die. ...

What is to happen to women like me when this war ends ... if it ever ends. I am twenty-one years of age, yet I know nothing of life but death, fear, blood, and the sentimentality that glorifies these things in the name of patriotism. I watch my own mother stupidly, deliberately, though unthinkingly – for she is a kind woman – encourage the sons of other women to kill their brothers. ... And my generation watches these things and marvels at the blind foolishness of it ... helpless to make its immature voice heard above the insensate clamour of the old ones who cry: 'Kill, Kill, Kill!' unceasingly.

What is to happen to women like me when the killing is done and peace comes ... if ever it comes? What will they expect of us, these elders who have sent us out to fight?. ...

We, who once blushed at the public mention of childbirth, now discuss such things as casually as once we discussed the latest play; whispered stories of immorality are of far less importance than a fresh cheese in the canteen; chastity seems a mere waste of time in an area where youth is blotted out so quickly. What will they expect of us, these elders of ours, when the killing is over and we return?. ...

I see us a race apart, we war products ... feared by the old ones and resented by the young ones ... a race of men bodily maimed and of women mentally maimed.

What is to become of us when the killing is over?

Helen Zenna Smith [pseud.], *Not So Quiet: Stepdaughters of War* (New York and
London: the Feminist Press, 1930; reprinted, 1989), pp. 162–3, 164–7.

DOCUMENT 14   **WOMEN'S HEROISM DURING AN AIR RAID,
JANUARY 1915**

Air raids attacked London, Paris and other locales far beyond the front line. Here the newspaper of the National Union of Women Suffrage Societies notes the appropriately brave behaviour of women during one of the earliest ones.

Nurses' Heroism Under Fire

At a meeting of the Hartlepools Hospital governors, appreciation was expressed of the coolness and heroism of the matron and nursing staff during the recent bombardment. Although shells were bursting all round the building the nurses stayed calmly at their posts tending their patients and removing to less dangerous parts those who were in the more exposed sections of the buildings. Fortunately, the hospital was not struck, though great havoc was wrought among the property all around it. The matron stated that if ever women deserved the V.C. it was members of her staff on that occasion.

The Common Cause, 15 January 1915.

DOCUMENT 15   **WARTIME BIRTH RATES FOR GREAT BRITAIN**

Wartime birth rate statistics for Great Britain (i.e., England, Wales and Scotland), including illegitimacy rates. Nearly all European participant nations expressed concern about population decline and rising immorality as seen in rising illegitimacy rates. These statistics give a fuller picture for the basis of such concerns.

Year	England & Wales (000s)		Scotland (000s)		Ireland (000s)	
	Total	Legitimate	Total	Legitimate	Total	Legitimate
1914	879	842	124.9	115.1	98.8	95.9
1915	815	778	114.2	106.3	95.6	92.6
1916	786	748	109.9	102.1	91.4	88.7
1917	688	631	97.4	90.1	86.4	83.7
1918	663	621	98.6	90.7	87.3	84.6
1919	849	810	106.3	98.8		

B.R. Mitchell, *Abstract of British Historical Statistics* (Cambridge: Cambridge University Press, 1962), pp. 30–3, using *Annual Report of the Registrar General for England & Wales, for Scotland, for Ireland and for Northern Ireland.*

DOCUMENT 16　WARTIME BIRTH RATES FOR FRANCE

Wartime birth rate statistics for France for 77 departments (rather than 87 because of invasion), including illegitimacy rates.

The number of legitimate births was reduced by the war in a proportion that was much stronger than that of illegitimate births.

Year	Born Alive (000s)		Still-born (000s)		Illegitimate (000s)		Children recognised by the father (per 1,000 illegitimate births)
	Total	Illegitimate	Total	Illegitimate	Born alive	Still-born	
1913							159
1914	593.8	50.8	26.7	3.5	85	134	140
1915	387.0	43.2	17.4	3.0	112	166	99
1916	313.0	43.0	15.6	3.1	137	198	102
1917	342.5	48.5	16.6	3.6	142	217	99
1918	399.5	55.0	19.2	4.0	138	209	98
1919	403.5	53.4	20.7	4.0	132	193	120

Note:　Statistics during the war years are for the 77 unoccupied departments.

Michel Huber, *La population de la France pendant la guerre* (Trans. Susan R. Grayzel; Paris: Presses Universitaires de France, 1931), pp. 251–2.

DOCUMENT 17   REGULATION 40D, MARCH 1918

In an effort to prevent the spread of venereal disease from hurting the strength of its fighting forces, the British government tried a variety of regulatory measures culminating in Regulation 40D, which was promulgated in March 1918.

Regulation 40D.

No woman who is suffering from venereal disease in a communicable form shall have sexual intercourse with any member of His Majesty's forces or solicit or invite any member of His Majesty's forces to have sexual intercourse with her.

If any woman acts in contravention of this regulation she shall be guilty of a summary offence against these regulations.

A woman charged with an offence under this regulation shall, if she so requires, be remanded for a period (not less than a week) for the purpose of such medical examination as may be requisite for ascertaining whether she is suffering from such a disease as aforesaid.

The defendant shall be informed of her right to be remanded as aforesaid, and that she may be examined by her own Doctor or by the Medical Officer of the Prison.

In this regulation the expression 'venereal disease' means syphilis, gonorrhoea, or soft chancre.

Defence of the Realm Regulations [Monthly Edition] (London: HMSO, March 1918), p. 68.

DOCUMENT 18   A GERMAN GIRL'S GROWING ALIENATION FROM THE WAR

Here a young German student's war diary shows her growing sense of alienation from the war, particularly when her brother Willi is called up in 1918.

2nd August 1915

It is a year since the war began. How much longer will it last? I ask, as does Mummy. 'Am I really to go on writing this war diary?' ...

I spoke about it to Hans Androwski. He said, 'If you want to know what I think, you should go on writing'.

'Why on earth should I?' I asked in despair. 'You must bear witness', said Androwski. 'If another war comes, people will quite forget this one'.

I was indignant and cried, 'There'll be no more war after this one!'

'And why not?' asked Androwski.

'Because every one will have their bellyfull of war', I cried, 'especially the soldiers'.

'Soldiers will always be soldiers and obey orders', declared Androwski. 'If the Fatherland is attacked they will fight. They will also fight if the government wants them to'.

We argued for at least an hour. Willi took Androwski's side, which made me so furious that I became quite red in the face. In the end they both pressed me so hard that I promised to go on with the war diary but only when something special happened. Unfortunately something is happening right away – that is, the whole town is full of soldiers again. Billeting and more billeting. At one time I would certainly have liked this, but now I should like some peace and quiet and not be always writing. ...

In the evening we all sit on the Wegner's seat in front of the house, drag more chairs out and sing songs with the soldiers or listen to their stories from the Front. Sometimes the soldiers flirt with Gretel's elder sisters, but in a nice way, and the sisters put up with it, because we all know sure enough that the contingent has to go to the Front in a few days' time and the soldiers will probably be killed.

1st February, 1918

Willi had received his call-up papers! The plea of 'Water on the knee' and 'Muscular weakness of the heart resulting from scarlet fever' is no further help to him. The Staff-doctor has passed him as fit for military service. Willi was furious. He said that he and the other recruits were examined stark naked in the ice-cold barracks. The doctor just pressed his abdomen and sounded his lungs, that was all. 'Sound as a bell', he declared.

Willi spat and said, 'The great fop! He just wants fresh cannon fodder for Emperor Wilhelm!'

... 'Don't get shoved into the footsloggers!' said Androwski. 'Not the infantry. The Air Force would be best. Ground staff of course. Office work best of all. Really! Office work. Just tell them you have fabulous hand writing'.

'Just tell them!' mocked Willi. 'You've no idea! Everything there goes by opposites. There's no sense in it at all. Prussian Army. And now I'm stuck in it'.

'Just let Uncle Bruno hear that – or Mummy', I said. 'To them "German national" is still the tops. And if you fall with a cheer for the Fatherland you will die as a hero in their eyes'.

'What kind of new tone is this?' mocked Androwski. 'Miss Piete – the new Pliny. Are you suddenly writing the history of the war from a different point of view?'

I went red again and exclaimed that to-day every one of any intelligence knew what had happened to the enthusiasm for war. I don't want any more soldiers to die. What purpose is served, for what and for whom? What use has it been to the Russians to perish in the Masurian Lakes? They can no longer die for the Tsar. He too is now worth nothing. Millions of dead for nothing – I repeat nothing.

Androwski thought that the millions had by their death brought about the Revolution.

'Through their death?' I cried. 'If that is what it costs I don't want any more Revolution!'

'What then?' asked Androwski, and Willi bit his fingernails irritably.

I couldn't give any answer. Nor could Willi. He stopped biting his nails and grinned foolishly.

'Just tell me', I cried indignantly, 'why millions have to die before you have a revolution? Can it not be brought about by reasoning?'

… We must just make sure that there is never another war in the future. We must never again fall for the humbug with which the older generation has bewitched us. We were still only children, still at school. And everyone at school, led on by the headmaster and the other teachers, shouted hurrah. Our parents and relatives have become poor because they have given up all their money, jewelry and valuables for the war-loan. Grandma maintains us by means of the few marks brought in by the rent paid by the poor people who live in our house on the Berliner Platz. They are even poorer than we are and some can hardly afford the rent any more. Anyhow, Grandma lets old Tiedtke live there rent-free, and our former cook, too. About ten people are cooped up there in two miserable rooms. I think I would rather die. But that is no solution. It is better to live. Definitely.

Piete Kuhr, *There We'll Meet Again: The First World War Diary of a Young German Girl*
(1982; Trans. Walter Wright, Gloucester, 1998), pp. 150–1 and 260–1.

DOCUMENT 19   **DECLARATION OF THE FIRST WOMEN'S PEACE CONGRESS, THE HAGUE, OCTOBER 1915**

This declaration was issued by delegates of the first Women's Peace Congress in The Hague in October 1915 after efforts to promote a negotiated end to the war.

Here in America, on neutral soil, far removed from the stress of the conflict we, envoys to the Governments from the International Congress of Women at The Hague, have come together to canvass the results of our missions. We put forth this statement as our united and deliberate conclusions.

At a time when the foreign offices of the great belligerents have been barred to each other, and the public mind of Europe has been fixed on the

war offices for leadership, we have gone from capital to capital and con-
ferred with the civil governments. ...

As women, it was possible for us, from belligerent and neutral nations
alike, to meet in the midst of war and to carry forward an interchange of
question and answer between capitals which were barred to each other. It is
now our duty to make articulate our convictions. We have been convinced
that the governments of the belligerent nations would not be hostile to the
institution of such a channel for good offices; and that the governments of
the European neutrals we visited stand ready to co-operate with others in
mediation. Reviewing the situation, we believe that of the five European
neutral nations visited, three are ready to join in such a conference, and that
two are deliberating the calling of such a conference. Of the intention of the
United States we have as yet no evidence. ...

The excruciating burden of responsibility for the hopeless continuance of
this war no longer rests on the will of the belligerent nations alone. It rests
also on the will of those neutral governments and peoples who have been
spared its shock but cannot, if they would, absolve themselves from their
full share of responsibility for the continuance of war.

Signed by Jane Addams (United States); Emily G. Balch (United States);
Aletta Jacobs (Holland); Chrystal Macmillan (Great Britain); Rosika
Schwimmer (Austro-Hungary).
New York, October 15, 1915

> Appendix I, 'Manifesto issued by Envoys of the International Congress of Women at
> The Hague to the Governments of Europe and the President of the United States in 1915',
> in G. Bussey and M. Tims, *Pioneers for Peace: The Women's International League for
> Peace and Freedom, 1915–1965* (London: WILPF British Section, 1980), pp. 22–4.

**DOCUMENT 20   SPECIAL POLICE REPORT ON FEMINISM AND
PACIFISM IN FRANCE, 1914–1915**

*Women's anti-war activity aroused the attention of belligerent states, and
such interest intensified after the International Women's Peace Congress at
The Hague in April 1915. Here is a passage from a special police report
designed to reveal the status of the feminist anti-war movement in France in
order to develop strategies to best contain it.*

GENERAL CONSIDERATIONS

The feminist pacifist campaign presents a certain interest: its promoters
know, in effect, that the influence of woman can be very efficacious,

considering that she is called to manifest herself first in the family, then in the feminine element of society where action, less deliberate, is more diffuse, more vehement and more uncompromising than in other settings.

During the first months of the war, while everyone followed with anxious attention the precipitous march of events, feminist groups, like progressive political parties and anti-militarist and pacifist committees abstained from all demonstrations that would have been capable of jeopardising the defence of the country. The first feminist attempts in favour of peace revived at the end of last January: they manifested themselves timidly at first, then a campaign was overtly undertaken by a group of foreign women, at the initiative and under the management of the famous German socialist Klara ZETKIN and some of her Dutch followers, the doctor JACOBS for example, whose sympathies are notoriously germanophile.

This campaign translated itself into the organisation of two international feminine congresses held successively in Berne and in The Hague. ...

It is evident that the conspicuous personalities of feminism who have been associated with the pacifist campaign have not always played a personal role. And so is it necessary to highlight the importance of groupings [which fall into two categories]:

1. The feminist groups, properly called, generally recruit in the middle classes, who envision the improvement of the fate of woman, the extension of her rights in society[,] and who sanction further the establishment of an international regime for permanent peace[,] all the while being careful of the patriotic notions of their members.

2. The socialist groupings, essentially political, see the same goal, but follow the idealistic and doctrinaire principles of the Unified Socialist Party. ...

[The document then discusses the socialist groups and the conference at Berne and feminist groups in relation to the congress at The Hague before concluding that vigilant surveillance of individuals and actions must be undertaken as:]

Some women, workers or middle class, international socialists or simply feminist, by error or duplicity, still take the word from abroad on the subject of realising an immediate peace, which would only profit our adversaries. ...

'Feminism and Pacifism in France 1914–1915', October 1915, Ba 1651,
Archives of the Prefecture of Police, Paris, France (Trans. Susan R. Grayzel).

DOCUMENTS 21 POSTER CAMPAIGN FOR AND AGAINST THE
AND 22   INTRODUCTION OF CONSCRIPTION IN
            AUSTRALIA

*Australian women, who had so recently acquired the vote, were asked to
vote in a referendum as to whether Australia should introduce conscription.
Here are posters directed at them, both for and against conscription*

No. 20

Why a Woman
Should Vote
YES.

BECAUSE

1. Her son and other women's sons in the trenches are begging for relief and rest.

BECAUSE

2. He is on duty day after day, contending with mud, cold, want of sleep, appalling sights and sounds, home-sickness, war-weariness. Will you not send him help?

BECAUSE

3. Although human life is sacred, justice and liberty are more sacred still, and all through history brave men have been ready and willing to risk their lives for a noble cause. You would not like to think Australians preferred their skins to their duty.

BECAUSE

4. You know all this outcry about producing food being preferable to sending reinforcements is a mere party cry—and that the Government will keep enough men in the country to carry on the necessary industries.

BECAUSE

5. Safety of Australia is intimately bound up with the safety of the Empire. If the Allies fall, Australia falls, and Australians will become German slaves, and the women will be treated as Belgian and French women have been treated.

BECAUSE

6. A very small reinforcement has often changed defeat into victory. The battle of the Marne was won and the course of history changed by a single Division. Think how proud you would be if our five Divisions proved the turning point in this War?

YES.

Authorised by Percy Hunter, Chief Organiser, and Archdale Parkhill, General Secretary, Reinforcements Referendum Council, Sydney.

State Library of Victoria. Reproduced in Bruce Scates and Raelene Frances, *Women and the Great War* (Cambridge: Cambridge University Press, 1997), p. 85.

The Mothers

You who breasted your babies,
    what have you to say?
You who suffered the birth-pangs
    shall you lightly slay?
You who were taught to believe
    in life as a sacred thing—
Oh, what shall be your answer
    when you are answering?

Oh, you who loved the toddlers—
    you who shaped their dreams.
What shall be the answer
    when every jingo screams?
Shall you be worse than the tiger,
    in the jungle curl'd,
Shielding its suckling offspring
    against the warring world?

Mothers of All Australia—
    mothers of him and me.
What, when the answer's given—
    what shall the answer be?—
A primitive howl of fury
    worse than that of the wild?
Shall the lioness love her cub
    more than you can love your child?

Mothers, we wait your answer—
    you of the travail-breed;
You who suffer in silence,
    you who have paid indeed!
The life that you brought to being—
    the life that was half your own—
How will you treat it?—answer
    before the dice are thrown!

State Library of Victoria. Reproduced in Bruce Scates and Raelene Frances, *Women and the Great War* (Cambridge: Cambridge University Press, 1997), p. 89.

DOCUMENT 23   CONDEMNING THE ARMS ACT, LUCKNOW, INDIA, 1916

Here is an excerpt from a speech given by Sarojini Naidu in Lucknow in 1916 regarding the Arms Act, which prevented Indian soldiers from carrying arms within India.

It may seem a kind of paradox that I should be asked to raise my voice on behalf of the disinherited manhood of the country, but it is suitable that I who represent the other sex, that is, the mothers of the men whom we wish to make men and not emasculated machines, should raise a voice on behalf of the future mothers of India to demand that the birthright of their sons should be given back to them, so that tomorrow's India may be once more worthy of its yesterday, that their much-valued birthright be restored to the Hindu and Mussallmans of India, to the disinherited martial Rajput and the Sikh and the Pathan. The refusal of the privilege, that gifted privilege and inalienable right to carry arms, is to insult the very core of their valiant manhood. To prevent to-day millions of brave young men willing to carry arms in the cause of the Empire is to cast a slur on the very ideals of the Empire. ... Who but a woman shall raise a voice for you who have not been able in all these years to speak for yourselves with any effect. ... Have we not, the women of India, sent our sons and brothers to shed their blood on the battlefields of Flanders, France, Gallipoli and Mesopotamia? When the hour comes for thanks, shall we not say to them for whom they fought 'when the terror and tumult of hate shall cease and life is refashioned, and when there is peace, and you offer memorial thanks to the comrades that fought in the dauntless ranks, and you honour the deeds of deathless ones, remember the blood of martyred sons', and remember the armies of India and restore to India her lost manhood.

From Sarojini Naidu, Speeches and Writings of Sarojini Naidu, second edition
(Madras: G.A. Natesan, 1919), pp. 78–9.

DOCUMENT 24   ROSA LUXEMBURG'S HOPE FOR A SOCIAL REVOLUTION AS THE RESULT OF WAR

Rosa Luxemburg, one of the socialist leaders in Germany imprisoned for her anti-war activity, writes to the wife of her comrade Karl Liebknecht, of her hope for the transformative revolution that she feels the war may still unleash.

Letter to Sonya Liebknecht, Breslau, Mid-November, 1917
How I deplore the loss of all these months and years in which we might have had so many joyful hours together, notwithstanding all the horrors

that are going on throughout the world. Do you know, Sonichka, the longer it lasts, and the more the infamy and monstrosity of the daily happenings surpasses all bounds, the more tranquil and more confident becomes my personal outlook. I say to myself that it is absurd to apply moral standards to the great elemental forces that manifest themselves in a hurricane, a flood, or an eclipse of the sun. We have to accept them simply as data for investigation, as subjects of study.

Manifestly, objectively considered, these are the only possible lines along which history can move, and we must follow the movement without losing sight of the main trend. I have the feeling that all this moral filth through which we are wading, this huge madhouse in which we live, may all of a sudden, between one day and the next, be transformed into its very opposite, as if by the stroke of the magician's wand; may become something stupendously great and heroic; must inevitably be transformed, if only the war lasts a few years longer. ...

Mary-Alice Waters (ed.), *Rosa Luxemburg Speaks* (New York: Pathfinder, 1970), p. 337 (translated by Eden and Cedar Paul, 1921).

DOCUMENT 25 POLITICAL OFFENCES IN RUSSIA, JANUARY 1917

An Officer in the Okhrana, the police department in charge of political offences in Russia, reports to the Minister of the Interior in January 1917 on the attitude of Russian women.

The mothers of families, who are exhausted by the endless standing in line at the stores, who are worn out by the suffering of seeing their children half-starved and sick, may now be much closer to revolution than Mr. Miliukov, Rodzianko and Company [leaders of Russian Parliament], and of course, they are much more dangerous since they represent a store of combustible material. One spark would be enough for a conflagration to blaze up.

Quoted in Barbara Evans Clements, *Daughters of Revolution: A History of Women in the USSR* (Arlington Heights, IL: Harlan Davidson, 1994), p. 28.

DOCUMENT 26 THE EFFECTS OF THE WAR ON WOMEN'S RIGHT TO VOTE

Here is an early example of how feminists saw the war in terms of its possible effects on granting women the right to vote in Britain.

We are glad to learn that Women's Suffrage Societies of all types are discussing the relationship of women to the war and to the peace which will one day end it. Women belong to the nation as much as men, and they fall as readily into the national attitude. But they were not consulted about the origin of the war, and probably feel that when negotiations begin, their ideas and feelings will be taken into no kind of formal account. This neglect of opinions is one of the peculiar wrongs of their sex, but it also exists as grievance of most democracies. From them springs the modern conception of the nation 'in arms', be it conscript or volunteer. ... Wars, however, are not supported merely by soldiers; behind them stand a great body of non-combatants. ...

Women have their full share of most of these activities. The business of 'taking care' of the nation while its men are at war devolves especially upon them. They are also subjected to a peculiar and double strain. Not only do they experience the most acute mental sufferings which war entails, but they take the largest part in the physical succour of its victims. ...

Meanwhile, in the civil community a host of questions arise to show how close is a people's dependence on women's labour, and how war affects its purpose and direction. The fabric of women's labour usually suffers a sudden ... shock, while their responsibilities as mothers or breadwinners are suddenly enlarged by the disorganisation of family life. Yet the State makes its re-arrangements of these matters with slight reference to women's desires and little knowledge of their necessities. ... No woman sat on the Select Committee of the House of Commons which re-arranged the scale of allowances for soldiers' dependents. If the problem of child-labour, which the farmers have raised, becomes acute, it will be regulated by male authorities. If conscription for foreign service is adopted, the decision will be arrived at by an executive or a Parliament consisting exclusively of fathers or childless men.

The exclusion of women from political life is, therefore, not a smaller, but a greater injustice in time of war and of greater political disturbance in time of peace. ... It is hardly an accident that we should be at war with a State which prides itself on the purely masculine character of its civilisation and its rejection of feminine influence. ... Nowhere within the range of Western civilisation do women occupy a lower place than in Germany; nowhere is the ground-plan of State living and thinking so conspicuously laid out as if male force and male stratagem covered the entire field of human achievement. Such a Germany and its methods are a challenge to the woman's conception of life, and a reminder of what States do and suffer when they found themselves on a half-idea of social conduct. ...

It is, therefore, an appropriate time to discuss the great reform on which all the more enlightened nations in the world will sooner or later reconstitute their political systems. ... [T]here are practical reasons why, when the war is over, and the community meets the full shock of the privations it has caused, we shall want all the co-operation of all the people to fashion it anew. Doubtless, if it is held that women merely double the ideas of the men, their accession to their full share in the management of the State may not greatly affect its structure.

If full citizenship for women endows the State with a finer tact, a more sympathetic intelligence, than the typical 'male' Empire commands, its policy will not only be more firmly based on the common will, but should thereby be given a new moral direction.

We do not mean that women are always and necessarily opposed to war. History shows that their incentive and even their example have spurred men on, in siege and in battle, to the most desperate resistance to invasion. But as mothers and wives, beginning with a strong instinctive aversion from war, they must needs regard it for what it is, the last and worst expedient of civilisation in resisting forces that have completely outgrown control. ... [Q]uickened by experience gained in hundreds of hospitals, as well as in homes where the pinch of war will be felt years after the last trench has been dug and the last soldier carried to his grave. The nations then called into council will have had their fill of force, and of the neo-German idea of it as the first and most natural activity of the State.

... Something new and helpful must be borne in the heart of the world from its long travail in war. Is it too much to suggest that in such a society the chief argument against the enfranchisement of women must fall to the ground?

From 'The War and Woman Suffrage', reprinted by permission from *The Nation*, 13 February 1915 (London: NUWSS, 1915), pp. 3–8.

DOCUMENT 27   **VERA BRITTAIN'S REFLECTIONS ON HER GENERATION OF WAR WOMEN**

Here, Vera Brittain, having returned to Oxford University after leaving it to perform war service, and having suffered the loss of her fiancé, only brother and several close male friends, reflects on the fears and sadness of her generation of war women.

The Superfluous Woman

GHOSTS crying down the vistas of the years,
Recalling words
Whose echoes long have died;
And kind moss grown
Over the sharp and blood-bespattered stones
Which cut our feet upon the ancient ways.

* * * * *

But who will look for my coming?

Long busy days where many meet and part;
Crowded aside
Remembered hours of hope;
And city streets
Grown dark and hot with eager multitudes
Hurrying homeward whither respite waits.

* * * *

But who will seek me at nightfall?

Light fading where the chimneys cut the sky;
Footsteps that pass,
Nor tarry at my door.
And far away,
Behind the rows of crosses, shadows black
Stretch out long arms before the smouldering sun.

* * * *

But who will give me my children?

July, 1920.

From Vera Brittain, *Verses of a VAD*, reprinted with other poems
(London: Imperial War Museum, 1995), pp. 70–1.

DOCUMENT 28   A MOTHER'S GRIEF FOR A LOST SON

After her youngest son, Peter, was killed while serving as a solider, German artist Kaethe Kollwitz poured out her grief to her surviving son in these letters, and also in a sculpture of two grieving parents that would eventually be placed in the cemetery in Flanders where Peter was buried.

Sunday, February 21, 1915

... Why does work help me in these times? It is not enough to say that it relaxes me very much. It is simply that it is a task I may not shirk. As you, the children of my body, have been my tasks, so too are my other works. Perhaps that sounds as though I meant that I would be depriving humanity of something if I stopped working. In a certain sense – yes. Because this is my post and I may not leave it until I have made my talent bear interest. Everyone who is vouchsafed life has the obligation of carrying out to the last item the plan laid down in him. Then he may go. Probably that's the point at which most people die. Peter was 'seed for the planting which must not be ground'.

If it had been possible for Father or me to die for him so that he might live, oh how gladly we would have gone. For you as well as for him. But that was not to be.

I am not seed for the planting. I have only the task of nurturing the seed placed in me. And you, my Hans? May you have been born for life after all! You must have been, and you must believe in it.

The sculptures of a grieving father and mother are for her son Peter.

From Hans Kollwitz (ed.), *The Diary and Letters of Kaethe Kollwitz*, trans. Richard and Clara Winston (Evanston, IL: Northwestern University Press, 1988).

The Father: © DACS 2002

The Mother: © DACS 2002

DOCUMENT 29 THE SCOTTISH NATIONAL WAR MEMORIAL TO HONOUR WOMEN'S WAR SERVICE

Only a few national memorials were established to honour women's services during the war. One notable exception can be found in the Scottish National War Memorial.

'In honour of all Scotswomen'   *Bronzes modelled by Alice Meredith Williams.*

The Scottish National War Memorial. From Sir Lawrence Weaver, *The Scottish National War Memorial* (London: Country Life Ltd, 1929), p. 40. From the collection of the National Inventory of War Memorials, Imperial War Museum, London.

THEY·SHALL·GROW·NOT·OLD·AS·WE·THAT·ARE·LEFT·GROW·OLD
AGE·SHALL·NOT·WEARY·THEM·NOR·THE·YEARS·CONDEMN
AT·THE·GOING·DOWN·OF·THE·SUN·AND·IN·THE·MORNING
WE·WILL·REMEMBER·THEM

'In memory of the Nursing Services'   *Bronzes modelled by Alice Meredith Williams.*

The Scottish National War Memorial. From Sir Lawrence Weaver, *The Scottish National War Memorial* (London: Country Life Ltd, 1929), p. 40. From the collection of the National Inventory of War Memorials, Imperial War Museum, London.

DOCUMENT 30 LAYING WREATHS UPON WESTERN FRONT GRAVES

Among the many tasks of members of the Women's Army Auxiliary Corps was laying of wreaths upon graves in the Western Front. Here two members of the WAAC display some of the tributes sent by grieving families in Britain.

Members of the Women's Army Auxiliary Corp tending graves in Abbeville, France. Imperial War Museum, London. PCS25/6, Negative No. Q847.

GLOSSARY

American Women's Hospitals   Hospitals created by American women medical professionals, mainly doctors, in order to serve the military during the war.

Australian Women's Service Corps   A voluntary organisation of women who trained for military preparedness; the equivalent of the Women's Emergency Corps or Volunteer Reserve.

Bund Deutscher Frauenvereine (League of German Women's Associations) (BDF)   The largest German women's organisation; it supported the national war effort and helped mobilise women for the war, largely through charitable, patriotic endeavours.

'Canary' girls   A term used to refer to munitions workers in Britain who became jaundiced through exposure to TNT and other chemical poisons. The skin of such women took on a bright yellow colour that gave them this name.

'Christy' girls   Named after Howard Chandler Christy, whose illustrations adorned many American recruitment and war loans posters; these images featured women as both ethereal and seductive.

Conseil National de Femmes Françaises (National Council of French Women) (CNFF)   The largest French women's organisation, devoted to patriotic activity in support of the war.

Foyers du Soldat (Soldiers' hearths)   A French organisation established by women to help provide wholesome environments for soldiers on leave and to send packages and letters to them in the battle zones.

International Women's Suffrage Alliance (IWSA)   An association of the main women's suffrage organisations in each member nation.

Marraines de guerre (godmothers of the war)   A term used to identify French women who 'adopted' a specific soldier (a *filleul* or godson), initially one either without a family or unable to contact his own family, in order to send him letters and packages to boost his morale.

National American Women's Suffrage Association (NAWSA)   The largest women's suffrage organisation in the United States; it supported the war effort once America was involved.

National Union of Women's Suffrage Societies (NUWSS)   The largest British women's group organised for suffrage; its members were divided over the war, but those who supported the war effort gained control.

National Woman's Party (NWP)   The more militant branch of the American women's suffrage organisations, led by Alice Paul.

No Conscription Fellowship   A British organisation formed to oppose conscription and then to support conscientious objectors.

No-Conscription League   An American organisation co-founded by Emma Goldman in 1917 that opposed US participation in the war.

Russian Women's Battalions of Death   Women's combatant corps officially formed in the summer of 1917 by the Provisional Government. While meant to goad men into continuing to support the war effort, the main battalion saw some action in the last skirmishes in which Russia engaged before the Bolsheviks took power.

Scottish Women's Hospitals (SWH)   The brainchild of Scottish suffragist and physician Dr Elsie Inglis and supported financially by the NUWSS, it aimed to provide medical services to the military that would be offered by women. It established several hospitals in France as well as in Serbia and Russia, staffed with women doctors, orderlies, nurses and ambulance drivers.

Separation allowances   Funds provided by the government and in some cases augmented by private sources that were paid directly to the dependents of men serving in the military.

Voluntary Women Patrols   An organisation sponsored by the National Union of Women Workers, where British women patrolled the streets, specifically to regulate the behaviour of other women.

White Feather Campaign   A limited method of recruiting in Britain whereby women passed out white feathers (a sign of cowardice) to men out of uniform; it was controversial at the time and after.

Women's Anti-German League   An organisation created in New Zealand in 1916 to urge the government to enact measures against those of German descent living in the country.

Women's Army Auxiliary Corps   Formed in 1917, this organisation gave women official military status in the armed forces for the first time in Britain as they replaced men in non-combatant tasks, for example as cooks, clerks and drivers.

Women's Compulsory Service League   An Australian women's organisation whose members tried to persuade men to enlist and who supported the idea of conscription.

Women's Emergency Corps   A voluntary organisation whose aim was to train British women for military preparedness.

Women's Forestry Corps   An offshoot of the Women's Land Service Corps that brought British women into foresty work, both ensuring a sufficient supply of timber and freeing men in such occupations for active military service.

Women's International League for Peace and Freedom   An organisation created out of the 1915 Women's Peace Congress at The Hague; during the war, its members worked to promote a quick resolution to the war via a negotiated end to the conflict and a just and lasting peace settlement that women would help to define.

Women's Land Service Corps   A national organisation created to get women involved in agricultural work to ensure an adequate harvest for Britain by replacing male labourers serving overseas.

Women's Peace Crusade   A movement that originated in Scotland after the imposition of conscription in 1916 and had close ties to socialism as it urged women to oppose their menfolk's involvement in fighting the war and to insist upon a negotiated settlement.

Women's Peace March   On 29 August 1914, approximately 15,000 women paraded down Manhattan's Fifth Avenue to urge peace instead of war.

Women's Peace Party (WPP)   A national organisation formed in the United States in 1915 to oppose the war and US entry into it.

Women's Police Service   Another British organisation devoted to promoting women's police work and established by former suffragettes.

Women's Royal Air Force (WRAF) and Women's Royal Naval Service (WRNS)   Following the creation of the WAAC, the British government quickly established auxiliary services for women to serve in similar support roles in the navy and air force.

Women's Social and Political Union (WSPU)   The British suffragette organisation that used militant tactics to try to gain the vote and whose leaders, Christabel and Emmeline Pankhurst, offered fervent support for the war effort.

Women's Voluntary Reserve   A voluntary British organisation that tried to train women for military preparedness.

WHO'S WHO

Addams, Jane (1860–1935) American social reformer and activist, who was opposed to the war and became the leader of the 1915 Women's Peace Congress at The Hague and subsequently one of its representatives who travelled to spread its message. She was president of the Women's International League for Peace and Freedom until her death, and won the Nobel Peace Prize in 1931.

Bäumer, Gertrud (1873–1954) German feminist leader of the BDF and very active in mobilising it, and thus women, to support the war.

Bettignies, Louise de (1880–1918) French woman who worked with British intelligence in smuggling out information from occupied France. She was arrested, tried and sent to a German prison, where she died in 1918.

Bochkareva, Maria (1889–1919?) After serving herself in the army, she became the founder and leader of the largest Russian Women's Battalion of Death, an all-female group of combatants, created by the Provisional Government in the summer of 1917.

Brion, Hélène (1882–1962) French school teacher, feminist, socialist and union activist, she was tried for treason for espousing 'defeatism' during the war. Although found guilty, she was given a suspended sentence in 1918.

Brittain, Vera (1893–1970) British writer, feminist and peace activist; an Oxford student, she enrolled as a VAD during the war and is best known for her 1933 autobiography of her wartime life, *Testament of Youth*.

Catt, Carrie Chapman (1859–1947) Leader of the main American women's suffrage group (National American Women's Suffrage Association) at the outbreak of war, she supported US participation in the war and mobilised women to serve the war effort.

Cavell, Edith (1865–1915) British nurse working in Belgium who aided Allied soldiers in escaping; she was arrested, tried and executed by the German army in 1915 and became an Allied martyr.

Duchêne, Gabrielle (1870–1954) French feminist who protested against the war and formed a women's anti-war organisation that she ran from her home.

Fawcett, Millicent Garrett (1847–1929) British leader of the NUWSS since its creation in 1897. She advocated that women demonstrate their value to the nation at war and lobbied for their enfranchisement in the Representation of the People Act of 1918.

Goldman, Emma (1869–1940) American anarchist who was deported in 1917 for speaking out and organising against the war.

Goldstein, Vida (1869–1949) Australian feminist and socialist active in the campaign against conscription and one of the leaders of the women's anti-war movement in Australia.

Inglis, Elsie (1864–1917)   Scottish suffragist and physician who helped create the Scottish Women's Hospitals during the war and ran the Serbian one until her death.

Jacobs, Aletta (1854–1929)   Dutch feminist who helped organise and host the 1915 Women's International Peace Meeting at The Hague and remained active in the Women's International League for Peace and Freedom.

Luxemburg, Rosa (1870–1919)   German socialist who was imprisoned for much of the war for speaking out against it. As a leader of the Spartacist League with Karl Liebknecht, she was murdered in January 1919 as the German revolution was suppressed.

Markiewicz, Countess Constance (1868–1927)   Irish nationalist and a member of both the NUWSS and Sinn Féin; she took part in the Easter Rising of 1916, and went to prison as a result. She became the first woman elected to the British Parliament in December 1918 but refused to take her seat in Westminster in protest, instead joining the parliament being established in Dublin.

Marshall, Catherine (1880–1961)   British feminist who opposed the war, and resigned from the NUWSS over its policies to support it. She worked actively with conscientous objectors.

Mata Hari (McLeod, Margaretha Zelle) (1876–1917)   Dutch dancer and courtesan who was recruited to work for French intelligence during the war, and was then accused of being a German spy. After being found guilty, she was executed by France in October 1917.

Naidu, Sarojini (1879–1949)   Indian writer and advocate for self-government who argued for India to support Britain during the war and for the right of all Indian men to be armed and for Indian women to vote.

O'Hare, Kate Richards (1877–1948)   American socialist, she was found guilty of violating the Espionage Act of 1917 for speaking out against the war.

Pankhurst, Christabel (1880–1958)   British suffragette and leader of the WSPU. She became an ardent supporter of the war.

Pankhurst, Emmeline (1858–1928)   British suffragette leader of the WSPU, which she helped to found in 1903. She became actively engaged in promoting the war effort.

Pankhurst, E. Sylvia (1882–1960)   British suffragette who was also a socialist, she created the East London Federation of Suffragettes, which she led in opposing the war and trying to relieve the suffering it caused.

Paul, Alice (1885–1977)   American leader of the National Women's Party, the more militant side of the Women's Suffrage Campaign.

Rankin, Jeanette (1880–1973)   American Congresswoman from Montana who famously cast a vote against the United States' entry into the war.

Sandes, Flora (1876–1956)   British woman who fought as a soldier with the Serbian army during the war.

Saumoneau, Louise (1875–1949)   French socialist, feminist and anti-war activist. She engaged in pacifist activities from the outset of the war, and was arrested, released and rearrested during the course of the war.

Swanwick, Helena (1864–1939) British suffragist who opposed the war and resigned from the NUWSS over this issue. She was subsequently the leader of the first British section of the Women's International League for Peace and Freedom.

Teodoroiu, Ecaterina (1894–1917) Romanian soldier and her country's 'Joan of Arc', who died in battle in September 1917.

Zetkin, Clara (1857–1933) German socialist and feminist who actively campaigned against the war from its outset and helped to organise the first international meeting against the war of socialist women in Berne in March 1915.

BIBLIOGRAPHY

ABBREVIATIONS:

AHR   *American Historical Review*
IHR   *International History Review*
JBS   *Journal of British Studies*
JCH   *Journal of Contemporary History*
JMH   *Journal of Modern History*
JWH   *Journal of Women's History*
PP   *Past and Present*

GUIDE TO FURTHER READING

Those interested in primary sources regarding women and the First World War in English are in luck. First, there is a useful recent bibliography by Sharon Ouditt, *Women Writers of the First World War: An Annotated Bibliography* (London: Routledge, 2000). Second, there has been a veritable explosion of anthologies dealing with women's own writing on the First World War; several are only in the English language while others include translations. The most diverse in terms of the range of geographic sources and extensive excerpts translated into English, and most impressive, is Margaret R. Higonnet (ed.), *Lines of Fire: Women Writers of World War I* (Harmondsworth: Plume, 1999). Catherine Reilly's edited poetry anthology, *Scars Upon My Heart: Women's Poetry and Verse of the First World War* (London: Virago, 1981) is still a marvellous starting point and Angela Smith's *Women's Writing of the First World War: An Anthology* (Manchester: Manchester University Press, 2000) offers unpublished letters as well as published sources. Other worthwhile anthologies include: Agnès Cardinal, Dorothy Goldman and Judith Hattaway (eds), *Women's Writing on the First World War* (Oxford: Oxford University Press, 1999) and Joyce Marlow (ed.), *The Virago Book of Women and the Great War* (London: Virago, 1998). Other good starting points for women and war literature include Margaret R. Higonnet, 'Not so quiet in no-women's-land', in Miriam Cooke and Angela Woollacott (eds), *Gendering War Talk* (Princeton, NJ: Princeton University Press, 1993), and Dorothy Goldman's two edited volumes, *Women and World War I: The Written Response* (New York: St Martin's Press, 1993) and *Women Writers and the Great War* (New York: Twayne, 1995).

Other printed non-fiction primary sources of interest include: Vera Brittain, *War Diary 1913–1917: Chronicle of Youth* (London: Victor Gollancz, 1981); Stephen Eric Bronner (ed.), *The Letters of Rosa Luxemburg: New Edition* (Atlantic Highlands, NJ: Humanities Press International, 1993); Florence Farmborough, *With the Armies of the Tsar: A Nurse at the Russian Front in War and Revolution* (New York: Cooper Square, 2000); Hans Kollwitz (ed.), *The Diary and Letters of Kaethe Kollwitz* (Evanston, IL: Northwestern University Press, 1988); Piete Kuhr, *There*

We'll Meet Again: The First World War Diary of a Young German Girl, translated by Walter Wright (Gloucester: Walter Wright, 1998); and Susan Mann (ed.), *The War Diary of Clare Gass 1915–1918* (Montreal: McGill-Queen's University Press, 2000). For photographs of women during the war, see Diana Condell and Jean Liddiard, *Working for Victory? Images of Women in the First World War 1914–1918* (London: Routledge and Kegan Paul, 1987).

For the most part, specific works on individual nations can be found in the references. What follows is a brief introduction to some of the most important scholarship on separate topics. For propaganda and mobilisation, see first the two articles by Nicoletta F. Gullace, 'Sexual violence and family honor: British propaganda and international law during the First World War'. *AHR*, 102: 3 (1997), pp. 714–47, and 'White feathers and wounded men: female patriotism and the memory of the Great War', *JBS*, 36: 2 (1997), pp. 178–206. See also Cate Haste, *Keep the Home Fires Burning: Propaganda in the First World War* (London: Allen Lane, 1977), Michael Sanders and Philip M. Taylor, *British Propaganda during the First World War 1914–1918* (Basingstoke: Macmillan, 1982), and Karen Petrone, 'Family, masculinity, and heroism in Russian war posters of the First World War', in B. Melman (ed.), *Borderlines: Genders and Identities in War and Peace, 1870–1930* (New York: Routledge, 1998); Samuel Hynes, *A War Imagined: The First World War and English Culture* (New York: Collier, 1990, reprinted 1992); and Hubertus F. Jahn, *Patriotic Culture in Russia during World War I* (Ithaca, NY: Cornell University Press, 1995). For the images themselves, see Peter Paret et al. (eds), *Persuasive Images: Posters of War and Revolution from the Hoover Institution Archives* (Princeton, NJ: Princeton University Press, 1992), and Walton Rawls, *Wake Up, America! World War I and the American Poster* (New York: Abbeville, 1988).

For social policy towards women as dependents or consumers, see Susan Pedersen, *Family Dependence and the Origins of the Welfare State: Britain and France, 1914–1945* (Cambridge: Cambridge University Press, 1993); Nancy Christie, *Engendering the State: Family, Work, and Welfare in Canada* (Toronto: University of Toronto, 2000); and Walter Hickel, 'War, region, and social welfare: federal aid to servicemen's dependents in the south, 1917–1921', *The Journal of American History*, 87:4 (2001), pp. 1362–91, as well as discussions in Ute Daniel, *The War From Within: German Working-class Women in the First World War* (Oxford: Berg, 1997), and Young-Sun Hong, 'World War I and the German welfare state: gender, religion, and the paradoxes of modernity' in G. Eley (ed.), *Society, Culture, and the State in Germany, 1870–1930* (Ann Arbor, MI: University of Michigan Press, 1996), and the essays in Richard Wall and Jay Winter (eds), *The Upheaval of War: Family, Work and Welfare in Europe, 1914–1918* (Cambridge: Cambridge University Press, 1988).

For more on women's waged labour during the war, these are the essential places to begin: Gail Braybon, *Women Workers in the First World War* (London: Croom Helm, 1981); Ute Daniel, *The War From Within: German Working-class Women in the First World War* (Oxford: Berg, 1997); Laura Lee Downs, *Manufacturing Inequality: Gender Division in the French and British Metalworking Industries, 1914–1939* (Ithaca, NY: Cornell University Press, 1995); Maurine Weiner Greenwald, *Women, War and Work: The Impact of World War I on Women Workers in the United States* (Ithaca NY: Cornell University Press, 1980, reprinted

1990); Deborah Thom, *Nice Girls and Rude Girls: Women Workers in World War I* (London: I.B. Tauris, 1998); and Angela Woollacott, *On Her Their Lives Depend: Munitions Workers in the Great War* (Berkeley, CA: University of California Press, 1994). For other occupations, see Kimberly Jensen, 'Physicians and citizens: US medical women and military service in the First World War', in R. Cooter et al. (eds), *War, Medicine and Modernity* (Stroud: Alan Sutton, 1998); Leah Leneman, 'Medical women at war, 1914–1918', *Medical History*, 38 (1994), pp. 160–77; and Sharon Ouditt, *Fighting Forces, Writing Women: Identity and Ideology in the First World War* (London: Routledge, 1994).

For issues of sexuality, morality and motherhood, see Elizabeth Domansky, 'Militarization and reproduction in World War I Germany', in G. Eley (ed.), *Society, Culture, and the State in Germany, 1870–1930* (Ann Arbor, MI: University of Michigan Press, 1996); Susan R. Grayzel, *Women's Identities at War: Gender, Motherhood, and Politics in Britain and France during the First World War* (Chapel Hill, NC: University of North Carolina Press, 1999); Philippa Levine, 'Battle colors: race, sex, and colonial soldiery in World War I', *JWH*, (1998), pp. 104–30, 9:4 and '"Walking the streets in a way no decent woman should": women police in World War I', *JMH*, 66 (1994), pp. 34–78; Annabelle Meltzer, 'Spectacles and sexualities: the "mise-en-scène" of the "Tirailleur Sénégalais" on the Western Front, 1914–1920', in B. Melman (ed.), *Borderlines: Genders and Identities in War and Peace* (New York: Routledge, 1998); and Regina M. Sweeney, *Singing Our Way to Victory: French Cultural Politics and Music during the Great War* (Middletown, CT: Wesleyan University Press, 2001).

For anti-militarism and war resistance, see: Harriet Hyman Alonso, *Peace as a Women's Issue: A History of the US Movement for World Peace and Women's Rights* (Syracuse, NY: Syracuse University Press, 1993); Jill Liddington, *The Long Road to Greenham: Feminism & Anti-Militarism in Britain since 1820* (London: Virago, 1989); Kathleen Kennedy, *Disloyal Mothers and Scurrilous Citizens: Women and Subversion during World War I* (Bloomington, IN: Indiana University Press, 1999); and Leila J. Rupp, *Worlds of Women: The Making of an International Women's Movement* (Princeton, NJ: Princeton University Press, 1997).

For the immediate aftermath of the war, see essays in Françoise Thébaud, *A History of Women: Toward a Cultural Identity in the Twentieth Century* (Cambridge, MA: Harvard University Press, 1994); Joy Damousi, *The Labour of Loss: Mourning, Memory and Wartime Bereavement in Australia* (Cambridge: Cambridge University Press, 1999); and Karin Hausen, 'The German nation's obligations to the heroes' widows of World War I', in M.R. Higonnet et al. (eds), *Behind the Lines: Gender and the Two World Wars* (New Haven, CT: Yale University Press, 1987).

For those researching individual nations, here are some good places to start. For Australia, Bruce Scates and Raelene Frances, *Women and the Great War* (Cambridge: Cambridge University Press, 1997) and essays in Joy Damousi and Marilyn Lake (eds), *Gender and War: Australians at War in the Twentieth Century* (Cambridge: Cambridge University Press, 1995); for Germany, Belinda Davis, *Home Fires Burning: Food, Politics and Everyday Life in World War I Berlin* and Ute Daniel, *The War from Within: German Working-class Women in the First World War* (Oxford: Berg, 1997); for Great Britain, Gail Braybon, *Women Workers and the First World War* (London: Croom Helm, 1981); Deborah Thom, *Nice Girls and Rude Girls: Women Workers in World War I* (London: I.B. Tauris, 1998); Angela

Woollacott, *On Her Their Lives Depend: Munitions Workers in the Great War* (Berkeley, CA: University of California Press, 1994), and Susan R. Grayzel, *Women's Identities at War: Gender, Motherhood, and Politics in Britain and France during the First World War* (Chapel Hill, NC: University of North Carolina Press, 1999) (for France as well); for France, also see Margaret H. Darrow, *French Women and the First World War: War Stories from the Homefront* (Providence, RI: Berg, 2000); for Russia, Barbara Alpern Engel, 'Not by bread alone: subsistence riots in Russia during World War I', *JMH*, 69:4 (1997), pp. 696–721; Jane McDermid and Anna Hillyar, *Midwives of the Revolution: Female Bolsheviks and Women Workers in 1917* (London: UCL Press, 1999) and Laurie Stoff, 'They fought for Russia: female soldiers of the First World War', in G.J. DeGroot and C. Peniston-Bird (eds), *A Soldier and a Woman: Sexual Integration in the Military* (Harlow: Pearson Education, 2000). For the United States, see Nancy K. Bristow, *Making Men Moral: Social Engineering during the Great War* (New York: New York University Press, 1996); Lettie Gavin, *American Women in World War I: They Also Served* (Niwot, CO: University Press of Colorado, 1997); Kathleen Kennedy, *Disloyal Mothers and Scurrilous Citizens: Women and Subversion during World War I* (Bloomington, IN: Indiana University Press, 1999); and Susan Zeiger, *In Uncle Sam's Service: Women Workers with the American Expeditionary Force, 1917–1919* (Ithaca, NY: Cornell University Press, 1999).

REFERENCES

Abraham, Richard. (1992) 'Maria L. Bochkareva and the Russian amazons of 1917', in Edmondson, Linda (ed.), *Women and Society in Russia and the Soviet Union*. Cambridge: Cambridge University Press.

Adamson, Walter L. (1999) 'The impact of World War I on Italian political culture', in Roshwald, Aviel and Richard Stites (eds), *European culture in the Great War: The Arts, Entertainment and Propaganda, 1914–1918*. Cambridge: Cambridge University Press.

Alberti, Johanna. (1989) *Beyond Suffrage: Feminists in War and Peace, 1914–28*. London: Macmillan.

Audoin-Rouzeau, Stéphane. (1995) *L'enfant de l'ennemi, 1914–1918*. Paris: Aubier.

Bard, Christine. (1995) *Les filles de Marianne: Histoire des féminismes, 1914–1940*. Paris: Fayard.

Becker, Annette. (1996) 'Life in an occupied zone: Lille, Roubaix, Tourcoing', in Cecil, Hugh and Peter Liddle (eds), *Facing Armageddon: The First World War Experienced*. London: Leo Cooper.

Beddoe, Deirdre. (1989) *Back to Home & Duty: Women between the Wars, 1918–1939*. London: Pandora.

Berkman, Joyce. (1990) 'Feminism, war, and peace politics: the case of World War I', in Elshtain, Jean Bethke and Sheila Tobias (eds), *Women, Militarism, and War: Essays in History, Politics, and Social Theory*. Savage, MD: Rowman & Littlefield.

Bessel, Richard. (1993) *Germany after the First World War*. Oxford: Clarendon Press, Oxford University Press.

Bessel, Richard. (1997) 'Mobilization and demobilization in Germany, 1916–1919', in Horne, John (ed.), *State, Society and Mobilization in Europe during the First World War*. Cambridge: Cambridge University Press.

Bland, Lucy. (1985) 'In the name of protection: the policing of women in the First World War', in Brophy, Julia and Carol Smart (eds), *Women in Law: Explorations in Law, Family and Sexuality*. London: Routledge Kegan Paul.

Bochkareva, Maria. (1919) *Yashka: My Life as Peasant, Officer and Exile*. New York: Frederick Stokes.

Bock, Gisela. (1994) 'Poverty and mothers' rights in the emerging welfare states', in Thébaud, Françoise (ed.), *A History of Women: Toward a Cultural Identity in the Twentieth Century*. Cambridge, MA: Harvard University Press.

Bordiugov, Genadii. (1996) 'The First World War and social deviance in Russia', in Cecil, Hugh and Peter Liddle (eds), *Facing Armageddon: The First World War Experienced*. London: Leo Cooper.

Braybon, Gail. (1981) *Women Workers in the First World War*. London: Croom Helm.

Brion, Hélène. (1918) *Déclaration lue au Premier Conseil de Guerre*. Epône: L'Avenir Social.

Bristow, Nancy K. (1996) *Making Men Moral: Social Engineering during the Great War*. New York: New York University Press.

Brittain, Vera. (1978) *Testament of Youth: An Autobiographical Study of the Years 1900–1925*. London: Virago (first published, 1933).

Brittain, Vera. (1981) *War Diary 1913–1917: Chronicle of Youth*. London: Victor Gollancz.

Bronner, Stephen Eric (ed.). (1993) *The Letters of Rosa Luxemburg: New Edition*. Atlantic Highlands, NJ: Humanities Press International.

Buckley, Suzann. (1977) 'The failure to resolve the problem of venereal disease among the troops in Britain during World War I', in Bond, Brian and Ian Hay (eds), *War and Society: A Yearbook of Military History*, Vol. 2. New York: Holmes and Meier.

Bucur, Maria. (2000) 'Between the mother of the wounded and the virgin of Jiu: Romanian women and the gender of heroism during the Great War', *JWH*, 12:2, pp. 30–56.

Bussey, Gertrude and Margaret Tims. (1980) *Pioneers for Peace: The Women's International League for Peace and Freedom 1915–1965* (reprint, 1965). London: WILPF British Section.

Cesarini, David. (1992) 'An alien concept? The continuity of anti-alienism in British society before 1940', *Immigrants & Minorities*, 11:3, pp. 25–52.

Chakravorty, Upendra Narayan. (1997) *Indian Nationalism and the First World War 1914–1918*. Calcutta: Progressive Publishers.

Christie, Nancy. (2000) *Engendering the State: Family, Work, and Welfare in Canada*. Toronto: University of Toronto Press.

Clements, Barbara Evans. (1994) *Daughters of Revolution: A History of Women in the USSR*. Arlington Heights, IL: Harlan Davidson.

Corbin, Alain. (1990) *Women for Hire: Prostitution and Sexuality in France after 1850*. Trans. Alan Sheridan. Cambridge, MA: Harvard University Press.

Cott, Nancy F. (1987) *The Grounding of Modern Feminism*. New Haven, CT: Yale University Press.

Crew, Jennifer. (1989) 'Women's wages in Britain and Australia during the First World War', *Labour History*, 57, pp. 27–43.

Culleton, Claire A. (1999) *Working-class Culture, Women, and Britain, 1914–1921*. New York: St Martin's Press.

Damousi, Joy. (1995) 'Socialist women and gendered space: anti-conscription and anti-war campaigns 1914–18', in Damousi, Joy and Marilyn Lake (eds), *Gender and War: Australians at War in the Twentieth Century*. Cambridge: Cambridge University Press.

Damousi, Joy. (1999) *The Labour of Loss: Mourning, Memory and Wartime Bereavement in Australia*. Cambridge: Cambridge University Press.

Daniel, Ute. (1988) 'Women's work in industry and family: Germany, 1914–18', in Wall, Richard and Jay Winter (eds), *The Upheaval of War: Family, Work and Welfare in Europe, 1914–1918*. Cambridge: Cambridge University Press.

Daniel, Ute. (1997) *The War From Within: German Working-class Women in the First World War*. Trans. Margaret Ries. Oxford: Berg.

Darrow, Margaret H. (1996) 'French volunteer nursing and the myth of war experience in World War I', *AHR*, 101:1, pp. 89–106.

Darrow, Margaret H. (2000) *French Women and the First World War: War Stories from the Homefront*. Providence, RI: Berg.

Davidson, Roger. (2000) *Dangerous Liaisons: A Social History of Venereal Disease in Twentieth-century Scotland*. Amsterdam and Atlanta, GA: Rodopi.

Davis, Belinda J. (2000) *Home Fires Burning: Food, Politics, and Everyday Life in World War I Berlin*. Chapel Hill, NC: University of North Carolina Press.

De Grazia, Victoria. (1994) 'How Mussolini ruled Italian women', in Thébaud, Françoise (ed.), *A History of Women*. Vol. V: *Toward a Cultural Identity in the Twentieth Century*. Cambridge, MA: Harvard University Press.

De Groot, Gerard J. (1996) *Blighty: British Society in the Era of the Great War*. Harlow: Addison Wesley Longman.

Dobson, Sean. (2001) *Authority and Upheaval in Leipzig, 1910–1920: The Story of a Relationship*. New York: Columbia University Press.

Donner, Henriette. (1997) 'Under the cross: why VADs performed the filthiest task in the dirtiest war: Red Cross women volunteers, 1914–1918'. *Journal of Social History*, 30:3 pp. 687–704.

Douglas, R.M. (1999) *Feminist Freikorps: The British Voluntary Women Police, 1914–1940*. Westport, CT: Praeger.

Downs, Laura Lee. (1992) 'Between Taylorism and *Dénatalité*: women welfare supervisors and the boundaries of difference in French metalworking factories, 1917–1930', in Helly, Dorothy O. and Susan M. Reverby (eds), *Gendered Domains: Rethinking Public and Private in Women's History*. Ithaca, NY: Cornell University Press.

Downs, Laura Lee. (1993) 'Women's strikes and the politics of popular egalitarianism in France, 1916–18', in Berlanstein, Leonard (ed.), *Rethinking Labor History: Essays on Discourse and Class Analysis*. Urbana, IL: University of Illinois Press.

Downs, Laura Lee. (1995) *Manufacturing Inequality: Gender Division in the French and British Metalworking Industries, 1914–1939*. Ithaca, NY: Cornell University Press.

Dubesset, Mathilde, Françoise Thébaud and Catherine Vincent. (1992) 'The female munition workers of the Seine', in Fridenson, Patrick (ed.), *The French Home Front 1914–1918* (English Edition). Oxford: Berg.

Early, Frances H. (1997) *World Without War: How US Feminists and Pacifists Resisted World War I*. Syracuse, NY: Syracuse, University Press.

Engel, Barbara Alpern. (1997) 'Not by bread alone: subsistence riots in Russia during World War I', *JMH*, 69:4, pp. 696–721.

Evans, Richard J. (1979) *The Feminists: Women's Emancipation Movements in Europe, America and Australasia 1840–1920*. London: Croom Helm.

Evans, Richard J. (1987) *Comrades and Sisters: Feminism, Socialism and Pacifism in Europe 1870–1945*. London: Croom Helm.

Feldman, Gerald D. (1966) *Army, Industry and Labor in Germany, 1914–1918*. Princeton, NJ: Princeton University Press.

Ferguson, Niall. (1999) *The Pity of War: Explaining World War I*. New York: Basic Books.

Floran, Mary [pseud. Mary Leclerq]. (1916) *L'Ennemi*. Paris: Calmann-Lévy.

Frevert, Ute. (1989) *Women in German History: From Bourgeois Emancipation to Sexual Liberation*. Trans. Stuart McKinnon-Evans. Oxford: Berg.

Gatrell, Peter. (1999) *A Whole Empire Walking: Refugees in Russia during World War I*. Bloomington, IN: Indiana University Press.

Gavin, Lettie. (1997) *American Women in World War I: They Also Served*. Niwot, CO: University Press of Colorado.

Gelblum, Amira. (1998) 'Ideological crossroads: feminism, pacifism, and socialism', in Melman, Billie (ed.), *Borderlines: Genders and Identities in War and Peace, 1870–1930*. New York: Routledge.

Gervereau, Laurent and Christophe Prochasson (eds). (1987) *Images de 1917*. Paris: BDIC.

Gilmartin, Christina Kelley. (1999) 'Introduction', to Lan, Hua R. and Vanessa L. Fong (eds), *Women in Republican China: A Sourcebook*. Armonk, NY: M.E. Sharpe.

Grayzel, Susan R. (1997a) 'Mothers, marraines, and prostitutes: morale and morality in First World War France', *IHR*, XIX:1, pp. 66–82.

Grayzel, Susan R. (1997b) '"The mothers of our soldiers' children": motherhood, immorality, and the war baby scandal, 1914–1918', in Nelson, Claudia and Ann Sumner Holmes (eds), *Maternal Instincts: Visions of Motherhood and Sexuality in Britain, 1875–1925*. Basingstoke: Macmillan.

Grayzel, Susan R. (1999) *Women's Identities at War: Gender, Motherhood, and Politics in Britain and France during the First World War*. Chapel Hill, NC: University of North Carolina Press.

Greenhut, Jeffrey. (1981) 'Race, sex, and war: the impact of race and sex on morale and health services for the Indian Corps on the Western Front, 1914', *Military Affairs*, pp. 71–4.

Greenwald, Maurine Weiner. (1980) *Women, War and Work: The Impact of World War I on Women Workers in the United States*. (Paperback, 1990). Ithaca, NY: Cornell University Press.

Griffiths, Gareth. (1991) *Women's Factory Work in World War I*. Stroud: Alan Sutton.

Grundlingh, Albert. (1987) 'The impact of the First World War on South African Blacks', in Page Melvin (ed.), *Africa and the First World War*. New York: St Martin's Press.

Gullace, Nicoletta F. (1997a) 'Sexual violence and family honor: British propaganda and international law during the First World War', *AHR*, 102:3, pp. 714–47.

Gullace, Nicoletta F. (1997b) 'White feathers and wounded men: female patriotism and the memory of the Great War', *JBS*, 36:2, pp. 178–206.

Gutzke, David W. (1994) 'Gender, class and public drinking in Britain during the First World War', *Social History*, 27:54, pp. 367–91.

Hane, Mikiso. (1988) *Reflections on the Way to the Gallows: Rebel Women in Prewar Japan*. Berkeley and Los Angeles, CA: University of California Press.

Harris, Ruth. (1993) 'The child of the barbarian: rape, race and nationalism in France during the First World War', *PP*, 141 (October), pp. 170–206.

Haste, Cate. (1992) *Rules of Desire: Sex in Britain, World War I to the Present*. London: Chatto & Windus.

Hause, Stephen, with Anne Kenney. (1984) *Women's Suffrage and Social Politics in the French Third Republic*. Princeton, NJ: Princeton University Press.

Hausen, Karin. (1987) 'The German nation's obligations to the heroes' widows of World War I', in Higonnet, Margaret R. et al. (eds), *Behind the Lines: Gender and the Two World Wars*. New Haven, CT: Yale University Press.

Hickel, K. Walter. (2001) 'War, region, and social welfare: federal aid to servicemen's dependents in the south, 1917–1921', *The Journal of American History*, 87:4, pp. 1362–91.

Higonnet, Margaret R. (ed.). (1999) *Lines of Fire: Women Writers of World War I*. Harmondsworth: Plume.

Holmes, Katie. (1995) 'Day mothers and night sisters: World War I nurses and sexuality', in Damousi, Joy and Marilyn Lake (eds), *Gender and War: Australians at War in the Twentieth Century*. Cambridge: Cambridge University Press.

Holton, Sandra Stanley. (1986) *Feminism and Democracy: Women's Suffrage and Reform Politics in Britain 1900–1918*. Cambridge: Cambridge University Press.

Hong, Young-Sun. (1996) 'World War I and the German welfare state: gender, religion, and the paradoxes of modernity', in Eley, Geoff (ed.), *Society, Culture, and the State in Germany, 1870–1930*. Ann Arbor, MI: University of Michigan Press.

Horne, John (ed.). (1997) *State, Society and Mobilization in Europe during the First World War*. Cambridge: Cambridge University Press.

Horne, John and Alan Kramer. (1994) 'German atrocities and Franco-German opinion, 1914: the evidence of German soldiers' diaries', *JMH*, 66 (March), pp. 1–33.

Huber, Michel. (1931) *La population de la France pendant la Guerre*. Paris: Presses Universitaires de France.

Hunton, Addie D. Waite and Kathryn M. Johnson. (1920) *Two Colored Women with the American Expeditionary Forces*. Brooklyn, NY: Brooklyn Eagle Press.

Huss, Marie-Monique. (1988) 'Pronatalism and the popular ideology of the child in wartime France: the evidence of the picture postcard', in Wall, Richard and Jay Winter (eds), *The Upheaval of War: Family, Work and Welfare in Europe, 1914–1918*. Cambridge: Cambridge University Press.

Hynes, Samuel. (1990) *A War Imagined: The First World War and English Culture*. (Paperback, 1992). New York: Collier.

Jackson, Alyson. (1996) 'Germany, the home front (2): blockade, government and revolution', in Cecil, Hugh and Peter Liddle (eds), *Facing Armageddon: The First World War Experienced*. London: Leo Cooper.

Jahn, Hubertus F. (1995) *Patriotic Culture in Russia during World War I*. Ithaca, NY: Cornell University Press.

Jeffery, Keith. (2000) *Ireland and the Great War*. Cambridge: Cambridge University Press.

Jelavich, Peter. (1999) 'German culture in the Great War', in Roshwald, Aviel and Richard Stites (eds), *European Culture in the Great War: The Arts, Entertainment and Propaganda, 1914–1918*. Cambridge: Cambridge University Press.

Jensen, Kimberly. (1998) 'Physicians and citizens: US medical women and military service in the First World War', in Cooter, Roger, Mark Harrison and Steve Sturdy (eds), *War, Medicine and Modernity*. Stroud: Alan Sutton.

Kaplan, Temma. (1982) 'Female consciousness and collective action: the case of Barcelona, 1910–1918', *Signs*, 7:3, pp. 545–66.

Kealey, Linda. (1998) *Enlisting Women for the Cause: Women, Labour, and the Left in Canada, 1890–1920*. Toronto: University of Toronto Press.

Keegan, John. (1994) *A History of Warfare*. New York: Vantage (English edition, 1993).

Kennedy, Kathleen. (1999) *Disloyal Mothers and Scurrilous Citizens: Women and Subversion during World War I*. Bloomington, IN: Indiana University Press.

Kent, Susan Kingsley. (1993) *Making Peace: The Reconstruction of Gender in Interwar Britain*. Princeton, NJ: Princeton University Press.

Kollwitz, Hans (ed.). (1988) *The Diary and Letters of Kaethe Kollwitz*. Trans. Richard and Clara Winston. Evanston, IL: Northwestern University Press.

Lagorio, Francesca. (1995) 'Italian widows of the First World War', in Coetzee, Frans and Marilyn Shevin-Coetzee (eds), *Authority, Identity, and the Social History of the Great War*. Providence, RI: Berghahn Books.

Leneman, Leah. (1994a) *In the Service of Life: The Story of Elsie Inglis and the Scottish Women's Hospitals*. Edinburgh: Mercat.

Leneman, Leah. (1994b) 'Medical women at war, 1914–1918', *Medical History*, 38, pp. 160–77.

Levine, Philippa. (1994) '"Walking the streets in a way no decent woman should": women police in World War I', *JMH*, 66, March, pp. 34–78.

Levine, Philippa. (1998) 'Battle colors: race, sex, and colonial soldiery in World War I', *JWH*, 9:4, pp. 104–30.

Liddington, Jill. (1989) *The Long Road to Greenham: Feminism & Anti-Militarism in Britain since 1820*. London: Virago.

Lomas, Janis. (1994) '"So I married again": letters from British widows of the First and Second World Wars', *History Workshop Journal*, 38, pp. 218–27.

Lunn, Joe. (1999) *Memoirs of the Maelstrom: A Senegalese Oral History of the First World War*. Portsmouth, NH: Heinemann.

Mann, Susan. (2000) 'Introduction', to *The War Diary of Clare Gass 1915–1918*. Montreal: McGill-Queen's University Press.

Marcus, Jane. (1989). 'Afterword: corpus/corps/corpse: writing the body in/at war', to Smith, Helen Zenna, *Not So Quiet … Stepdaughters of War*. (Reprint, 1930). New York: The Feminist Press.

Marwick, Arthur. (1977) *Women at War 1914–1918*. London: Croom Helm.

McDermid, Jane and Anna Hillyar. (1999) *Midwives of the Revolution: Female Bolsheviks and Women Workers in 1917*. London: UCL Press.

McPhail, Helen. (1999) *The Long Silence: Civilian Life under the German Occupation of Northern France, 1914–1918*. London: I.B. Tauris.

Meigs, Mark. (1997) *Optimism at Armageddon: Voices of American Participants in the First World War*. New York: New York University Press.

Melman, Billie. (1998) 'Re-Generation: nation and the construction of gender in peace and war – Palestine Jews, 1900–1918', in Melman, Billie (ed.), *Borderlines: Genders and Identities in War and Peace, 1870–1930*. New York: Routledge.

Melzer, Annabelle. (1998) 'Spectacles and sexualities: the "mise-en-scène" of the "Tirailleur Sénégalais" on the Western Front, 1914–1920', in Melman, Billie (ed.), *Borderlines: Genders and Identities in War and Peace, 1870–1930*. New York: Routledge.

Meyer, Alfred. (1991) 'The impact of World War I on Russian women's lives', in Clements, Barbara Evans, Barbara Alpern Engel and Christine D. Worobec (eds), *Russia's Women: Accommodation, Resistance, Transformation*. Berkeley and Los Angeles, CA: University of California Press.

Miller, Donald E. and Lorna Touryan Miller. (1993) *Survivors: An Oral History of the Armenian Genocide*. Berkeley and Los Angeles, CA: University of California Press.

Miller, May. (1930) *Stragglers in the dust*, in Perkins, Kathy A. (ed.). (1989), *Black Female Playwrights: An Anthology of Plays before 1950*. Bloomington, IN: Indiana University Press.

Mitchell, B.R. (1962) *Abstract of British Historical Statistics*. Cambridge: Cambridge University Press.

Moriarty, Catherine. (1997) 'Private grief and public remembrance: British First World War memorials', in Evans, Martin and Ken Lunn (eds), *War and Memory in the Twentieth Century*. Oxford: Berg.

Nagy, Margit. (1991) 'Middle-class working women during the interwar years', in Bernstein, Gail Lee (ed.), *Recreating Japanese Women, 1600–1945*. Berkeley and Los Angeles, CA: University of California Press.

Naidu, Sarojini. (1919) *Speeches and Writings of Sarojini Naidu*. (Second Edition). Madras: G.A. Natesan.

Nash, Mary. (1995) *Defying Male Civilization: Women in the Spanish Civil War*. Denver, CO: Arden.

Nelson, Keith L. (1970) 'The "Black Horror on the Rhine": race as a factor in post-World War I diplomacy', *JMH*, 42:4, pp. 606–27.

Ouditt, Sharon. (2000) *Women Writers of the First World War: An Annotated Bibliography*. London: Routledge.

Owens, Rosemary Cullen. (1997) 'Women and Pacifism in Ireland 1915–1932', in Valiulis, Maryann Gialanella and Mary O'Dowd (eds), *Women and Irish History*. Dublin: Wolfhound Press.

Page, Melvin E. (ed.). (1987) *Africa and the First World War*. New York: St Martin's Press.

Page, Melvin E. (2000) *The Chiwaya War: Malawians and the First World War*. Boulder, CO: Westview Press.

Paillard, Rémy. (1986) *Affiches 14–18*. Reims: Impr. Matôt-Braine.

Paret, Peter, Beth Irwin Lewis and Paul Paret. (1992) *Persuasive Images: Posters of War and Revolution from the Hoover Institution Archives*. Princeton, NJ: Princeton University Press.

Pati, Budheswar. (1996) *India and the First World War*. New Delhi: Atlantic Publishers.

Pedersen, Susan. (1993) *Family, Dependence and the Origins of the Welfare State: Britain and France, 1914–1945*. Cambridge: Cambridge University Press.

Petrone, Karen. (1998) 'Family, masculinity, and heroism in Russian war posters of the First World War', in Melman, Billie (ed.), *Borderlines: Genders and Identities in War and Peace, 1870–1930*. New York: Routledge.

Pugh, Martin. (1992) *Women and the Women's Movement in Britain 1914–1959*. Basingstoke: Macmillan.

Pugsley, Chris et al. (1996) *Scars on the Heart: Two Centuries of New Zealand at War*. Auckland: David Bateman.

Pyecroft, Susan. (1994) 'British working women and the First World War', *The Historian*, 56:4, pp. 699–710.

Rawls, Walton. (1988) *Wake Up, America! World War I and the American Poster*. New York: Abbeville.

Rivé, Philippe et al. (eds). (1991) *Monuments de mémoire: Les monuments aux morts de la Grande Guerre*. Paris: MPCIH.

Robert, Jean-Louis. (1988) 'Women and work in France during the First World War', in Wall, Richard and Jay Winter (eds), *The Upheaval of War: Family, Work and Welfare in Europe, 1914–1918*. Cambridge: Cambridge University Press.

Roberts, Barbara. (1985) '"Why do women do nothing to end the war?" Canadian feminist-pacifists and the Great War', CRIAW/ICREF Paper No. 13. Ottawa: CRIAW/CREF.

Roberts, Krisztina. (1997) 'Gender, class, and patriotism: women's paramilitary units in First World War Britain', *IHR*, XIX:1, pp. 52–65.

Roberts, Mary Louise. (1994) *Civilization Without Sexes: The Reconstruction of Gender in Postwar France*. Chicago, IL: University of Chicago Press.

Roshwald, Aviel. (1999) 'Jewish cultural identity in Eastern and Central Europe during the Great War', in Roshwald, Aviel and Richard Stites (eds), *European Culture in the Great War: The Arts, Entertainment, and Propaganda, 1914–1918*. Cambridge: Cambridge University Press.

Rouette, Susanne. (1997) 'Mothers and citizens: gender and social policy in Germany after the First World War', *Central European History*, 30:1, pp. 48–66.

Rozenblit, Marsha L. (1995) 'For fatherland and Jewish people: Jewish women in Austria during World War I', in Coetzee, Frans and Marilyn Shevin-Coetzee (eds), *Authority, Identity, and the Social History of the Great War*. Providence, RI: Berghahn Books.

Rupp, Leila J. (1997) *Worlds of Women: The Making of an International Women's Movement*. Princeton, NJ: Princeton University Press.

Sarafian, Ara. (1998) 'The archival trail: authentication of the treatment of Armenians in the Ottoman Empire, 1915–16', in Hovannisian, Richard G. (ed.), *Remembrance and Denial: The Case of the Armenian Genocide*. Detroit, MI: Wayne State University Press.

Sauerteig, Lutz D.H. (1998) 'Sex, medicine and morality during the First World War', in Cooter, Roger, Mark Harrison and Steve Sturdy (eds), *War, Medicine and Modernity*. Stroud: Alan Sutton.

Scates, Bruce and Raelene Frances. (1997) *Women and the Great War*. Cambridge: Cambridge University Press.

Schneider, Dorothy and Carl J. Schneider. (1991) *Into the Breach: American Women Overseas in World War I*. New York: Viking.

Schulte, Regina. (1997) 'The sick warrior's sister: nursing during the First World War' (trans. Pamela Selwyn), in Abrams, Lynn and Elizabeth Harvey (eds), *Gender Relations in German History: Power, Agency and Experience from the Sixteenth to the Twentieth Century*. Durham, NC: Duke University Press.

Shaw, Diana. (1996) 'The forgotten army of women: the overseas service of Queen Mary's Army Auxiliary Corps with the British Forces, 1917–1921', in Cecil, Hugh and Peter Liddle (eds), *Facing Armageddon: The First World War Experienced*. London: Leo Cooper.

Sherman, Daniel J. (1999) *The Construction of Memory in Interwar France*. Chicago, IL: University of Chicago Press.

Shute, Carmel. (1995) 'Heroines and heroes: sexual mythology in Australia 1914–18', in Damousi, Joy and Marilyn Lake (eds), *Gender and War: Australians at War in the Twentieth Century*. Cambridge: Cambridge University Press.

Sieder, Reinhard. (1988) 'Behind the lines: working-class family life in wartime Vienna', in Wall, Richard and Jay Winter (eds), *The Upheaval of War: Family, Work and Welfare in Europe, 1914–1918*. Cambridge: Cambridge University Press.

Smart, Judith. (1995) 'Feminists, food and the fair price: the cost-of-living demonstrations in Melbourne, August–September 1917', in Damousi, Joy and Marilyn Lake (eds), *Gender and War: Australians at War in the Twentieth Century*. Cambridge: Cambridge University Press.

Smith, Paul. (1996) *Feminism and the Third Republic: Women's Political and Civil Rights in France, 1918–1945*. Oxford: Clarendon Press.

Smyth, James J. (1992) 'Rents, peace, votes: working-class women and political activity in the First World War', in Breitenbach, Esther and Eleanor Gordon (eds), *Out of Bounds: Women in Scottish Society 1800–1945*. Edinburgh: Edinburgh University Press.

Sohn, Anne-Marie. (1994) 'Between the wars in France and England', in Thébaud, Françoise (ed.), *A History of Women*. Vol. V: *Toward a Cultural Identity in the Twentieth Century*. Cambridge, MA: Harvard University Press.

Sowerwine, Charles. (1982) *Sisters or Citizens? Women and Socialism in France since 1876*. Cambridge: Cambridge University Press.

Stites, Richard. (1990) *The Women's Liberation Movement in Russia: Feminism, Nihilism, and Bolshevism, 1860–1930*. (Reprint, 1978). Princeton NJ: Princeton University Press.

Stovall, Tyler. (1993) 'Colour-blind France? Colonial Workers during the First World War', *Race & Class*, 35:2, pp. 35–55.

Stovall, Tyler. (1996) *Paris Noir: African Americans in the City of Light*. Boston, MA: Houghton Mifflin.

Stovall, Tyler. (1998) 'The color line behind the lines: racial violence in France during the Great War', *AHR*, 103:3, pp. 737–69.

Summers, Anne. (1987) *Angels and Citizens: British Women as Military Nurses 1854–1914*. London: Routledge Kegan Paul.

Sweeney, Regina M. (2001) *Singing Our Way to Victory: French Cultural Politics and Music during the Great War*. Middletown, CT: Wesleyan University Press.

Talwar, Vir Bharat. (1990) 'Feminist consciousness in women's journals in Hindi: 1910–1920', in Sangari, Kumkum and Sudesh Vaid (eds), *Recasting Women: Essays in Indian Colonial History*. New Brunswick, NJ: Rutgers University Press.

Tate, Trudi. (1998) *Modernism, History and the First World War*. Manchester: Manchester University Press.

Thébaud, Françoise. (1986) *La femme au temps de la guerre de 14*. Paris: Stock.

Thébaud, Françoise. (1994) 'The Great War and the triumph of sexual division', in Thébaud, Françoise (ed.), *A History of Women in the West. Vol. V: Toward a Cultural Identity in the Twentieth Century*. (English Edition). Cambridge, MA: Harvard University Press.

Thom, Deborah. (1998) *Nice Girls and Rude Girls: Women Workers in World War I*. London: I.B. Tauris.

Tomassini, Luigi. (1991) 'Industrial Mobilization and the labour market in Italy during the First World War', *Social History*, 16:1, pp. 59–87.

Tomassini, Luigi. (1996) 'The home front in Italy', in Cecil, Hugh and Peter Liddle (eds), *Facing Armageddon: The First World War Experienced*. London: Leo Cooper.

Usborne, Cornelie. (1988) '"Pregnancy is the woman's active service". Pronatalism in Germany during the First World War', in Wall, Richard and Jay Winter (eds), *The Upheaval of War: Family, Work and Welfare in Europe, 1914–1918*. Cambridge: Cambridge University Press.

Vance, Jonathan F. (1997) *Death So Noble: Memory, Meaning, and the First World War*. Vancouver, BC: UBC Press.

Vellacott, Jo. (1987) 'Feminist consciousness and the First World War', in Pierson, Ruth Roach (ed.), *Women and Peace: Theoretical, Historical and Practical Perspectives*. London: Croom Helm.

Ward, Margaret. (1995) *Unmanageable revolutionaries: Women and Irish Nationalism*. (Reprint, 1989). London: Pluto Press.

Watson, Janet S.K. (1997) 'Khaki girls, VADs and Tommy's sisters: gender and class in First World War Britain', *IHR*, XIX:1, pp. 32–51.

Wheelwright, Julie. (1989) *Amazons and Military Maids: Women who Dressed as Men in Pursuit of Life, Liberty and Happiness*. London: Pandora.

Wheelwright, Julie. (1992) *The Fatal Lover: Mata Hari and the Myth of Women in Espionage*. London: Collins & Brown.

Wilson, Trevor. (1986) *The Myriad Faces of War: Britain and the Great War, 1914–1918*. Cambridge: Polity Press.

Wiltsher, Anne. (1985) *Most Dangerous Women: Feminist Peace Campaigners of the Great War*. London: Pandora.

Winter, Jay. (1995) *Sites of Memory, Sites of Mourning: The Great War in European Cultural History*. Cambridge: Cambridge University Press.

Wishnia, Judith. (1987) 'Feminism and pacifism: the French connection', in Pierson, Ruth Roach (ed.), *Women and Peace: Theoretical, Historical and Practical Perspectives*. London: Croom Helm.

Wood, Elizabeth A. (1997) *The Baba and the Comrade: Gender and Politics in Revolutionary Russia*. Bloomington, IN: Indiana University Press.

Woodeson, Alison. (1993) 'The first women police: a force for equality or infringement?', *Women's History Review*, 2:2, pp. 217–32.

Woollacott, Angela. (1993) 'Sisters and brothers in arms: family, class, and gendering in World War I Britain', in Cooke, Miriam and Angela Woollacott (eds), *Gendering War Talk*. Princeton, NJ: Princeton University Press.

Woollacott, Angela. (1994a) '"Khaki Fever" and its control: gender, class, age and sexual morality on the British homefront in the First World War', *JCH*, 29, pp. 325–47.

Woollacott, Angela. (1994b) *On Her Their Lives Depend: Munitions Workers in the Great War*. Berkeley and Los Angeles, CA: University of California Press.

Zeiger, Susan. (1999) *In Uncle Sam's Service: Women Workers with the American Expeditionary Force, 1917–1919*. Ithaca, NY: Cornell University Press.

INDEX

SEMINAR STUDIES IN HISTORY

General Editors: Clive Emsley & Gordon Martel

The series was founded by Patrick Richardson in 1966. Between 1980 and 1996 Roger Lockyer edited the series before handing over to Clive Emsley (Professor of History at the Open University) and Gordon Martel (Professor of International History at the University of Northern British Columbia, Canada and Senior Research Fellow at De Montfort University).

MEDIEVAL ENGLAND

The Pre-Reformation Church in England 1400–1530 (Second edition)
Christopher Harper-Bill   0 582 28989 0

Lancastrians and Yorkists: The Wars of the Roses
David R Cook   0 582 35384 X

Family and Kinship in England 1450–1800
Will Coster   0 582 35717 9

TUDOR ENGLAND

Henry VII (Third edition)
Roger Lockyer & Andrew Thrush   0 582 20912 9

Henry VIII (Second edition)
M D Palmer   0 582 35437 4

Tudor Rebellions (Fourth edition)
Anthony Fletcher & Diarmaid MacCulloch   0 582 28990 4

The Reign of Mary I (Second edition)
Robert Tittler   0 582 06107 5

Early Tudor Parliaments 1485–1558
Michael A R Graves   0 582 03497 3

The English Reformation 1530–1570
W J Sheils   0 582 35398 X

Elizabethan Parliaments 1559–1601 (Second edition)
Michael A R Graves   0 582 29196 8

England and Europe 1485–1603 (Second edition)
Susan Doran   0 582 28991 2

The Church of England 1570–1640
Andrew Foster   0 582 35574 5

STUART BRITAIN

Social Change and Continuity: England 1550–1750 (Second edition)
Barry Coward   0 582 29442 8

James I (Second edition)
S J Houston   0 582 20911 0

The English Civil War 1640–1649
Martyn Bennett   0 582 35392 0

Charles I, 1625–1640
Brian Quintrell   0 582 00354 7

The English Republic 1649–1660 (Second edition)
Toby Barnard   0 582 08003 7

Radical Puritans in England 1550–1660
R J Acheson   0 582 35515 X

The Restoration and the England of Charles II (Second edition)
John Miller   0 582 29223 9

The Glorious Revolution (Second edition)
John Miller   0 582 29222 0

EARLY MODERN EUROPE

The Renaissance (Second edition)
Alison Brown   0 582 30781 3

The Emperor Charles V
Martyn Rady   0 582 35475 7

French Renaissance Monarchy: Francis I and Henry II (Second edition)
Robert Knecht   0 582 28707 3

The Protestant Reformation in Europe
Andrew Johnston   0 582 07020 1

The French Wars of Religion 1559–1598 (Second edition)
Robert Knecht   0 582 28533 X

Phillip II
Geoffrey Woodward   0 582 07232 8

The Thirty Years' War
Peter Limm   0 582 35373 4

Louis XIV
Peter Campbell   0 582 01770 X

Spain in the Seventeenth Century
Graham Darby   0 582 07234 4

Peter the Great
William Marshall   0 582 00355 5

EUROPE 1789-1918

Britain and the French Revolution
Clive Emsley   0 582 36961 4

Revolution and Terror in France 1789–1795 (Second edition)
D G Wright   0 582 00379 2

Napoleon and Europe
D G Wright   0 582 35457 9

The Abolition of Serfdom in Russia, 1762–1907
David Moon   0 582 29486 X

Nineteenth-Century Russia: Opposition to Autocracy
Derek Offord   0 582 35767 5

The Constitutional Monarchy in France 1814–48
Pamela Pilbeam   0 582 31210 8

The 1848 Revolutions (Second edition)
Peter Jones   0 582 06106 7

The Italian Risorgimento
M Clark   0 582 00353 9

Bismarck & Germany 1862–1890 (Second edition)
D G Williamson   0 582 29321 9

Imperial Germany 1890–1918
Ian Porter, Ian Armour and Roger Lockyer   0 582 03496 5

The Dissolution of the Austro-Hungarian Empire 1867–1918 (Second edition)
John W Mason   0 582 29466 5

Second Empire and Commune: France 1848–1871 (Second edition)
William H C Smith   0 582 28705 7

France 1870–1914 (Second edition)
Robert Gildea   0 582 29221 2

The Scramble for Africa (Second edition)
M E Chamberlain   0 582 36881 2

Late Imperial Russia 1890–1917
John F Hutchinson   0 582 32721 0

The First World War
Stuart Robson   0 582 31556 5

Austria, Prussia and Germany, 1806–1871
John Breuilly   0 582 43739 3

EUROPE SINCE 1918

The Russian Revolution (Second edition)
Anthony Wood   0 582 35559 1

Lenin's Revolution: Russia, 1917–1921
David Marples   0 582 31917 X

Stalin and Stalinism (Second edition)
Martin McCauley   0 582 27658 6

The Weimar Republic (Second edition)
John Hiden   0 582 28706 5

The Inter-War Crisis 1919–1939
Richard Overy   0 582 35379 3

Fascism and the Right in Europe, 1919–1945
Martin Blinkhorn   0 582 07021 X

Spain's Civil War (Second edition)
Harry Browne   0 582 28988 2

The Third Reich (Third edition)
D G Williamson   0 582 20914 5

The Origins of the Second World War (Second edition)
R J Overy   0 582 29085 6

The Second World War in Europe
Paul MacKenzie   0 582 32692 3

The French at War, 1934–1944
Nicholas Atkin   0 582 36899 5

Anti-Semitism before the Holocaust
Albert S Lindemann   0 582 36964 9

The Holocaust: The Third Reich and the Jews
David Engel   0 582 32720 2

Germany from Defeat to Partition, 1945–1963
D G Williamson   0 582 29218 2

Britain and Europe since 1945
Alex May   0 582 30778 3

Eastern Europe 1945–1969: From Stalinism to Stagnation
Ben Fowkes   0 582 32693 1

Eastern Europe since 1970
Bülent Gökay   0 582 32858 6

The Khrushchev Era, 1953–1964
Martin McCauley   0 582 27776 0

NINETEENTH-CENTURY BRITAIN

Britain before the Reform Acts: Politics and Society 1815–1832
Eric J Evans   0 582 00265 6

Parliamentary Reform in Britain c. 1770–1918
Eric J Evans   0 582 29467 3

Democracy and Reform 1815–1885
D G Wright   0 582 31400 3